Factors Behind the Ukrainian Evangelical Missionary Surge from 1989 to 1999

Evangelical Missiological Society Monograph Series

Anthony Casey, Allen Yeh, Mark Kreitzer, and Edward L. Smither
SERIES EDITORS

———————————

A Project of the Evangelical Missiological Society
www.emsweb.org

Factors Behind the Ukrainian Evangelical Missionary Surge from 1989 to 1999

John Edward White

PICKWICK *Publications* • Eugene, Oregon

FACTORS BEHIND THE UKRAINIAN EVANGELICAL MISSIONARY SURGE FROM 1989 TO 1999

Evangelical Missiological Society Monograph Series 4

Copyright © 2020 John Edward White. All rights reserved. Except for brief quotations in critical publications or reviews, no part of this book may be reproduced in any manner without prior written permission from the publisher. Write: Permissions, Wipf and Stock Publishers, 199 W. 8th Ave., Suite 3, Eugene, OR 97401.

Pickwick Publications
An Imprint of Wipf and Stock Publishers
199 W. 8th Ave., Suite 3
Eugene, OR 97401

www.wipfandstock.com

PAPERBACK ISBN: 978-1-5326-6539-4
HARDCOVER ISBN: 978-1-5326-6540-0
EBOOK ISBN: 978-1-5326-6541-7

Cataloguing-in-Publication data:

Names: White, John Edward, author. | Fairbairn, Donald, foreword.

Title: Factors behind the Ukrainian evangelical missionary surge from 1989 to 1999 / John Edward White; foreword by Donald Fairbairn.

Description: Eugene, OR: Pickwick Publications, 2020 | Evangelical Missiological Society Monograph Series 4 | **Includes bibliographical references and index.**

Identifiers: ISBN 978-1-5326-6539-4 (paperback) | ISBN 978-1-5326-6540-0 (hardcover) | ISBN 978-1-5326-6541-7 (ebook)

Subjects: LCSH: Missions—Ukraine. | Religious awakening—Ukraine. | Ukraine—Religion.

Classification: BV2063 W55 2020 (print) | BV2063 (ebook)

Unless otherwise indicated, all Scripture quotations are from The ESV® Bible (The Holy Bible, English Standard Version®), copyright © 2001 by Crossway, a publishing ministry of Good News Publishers. Used by permission. All rights reserved.

Scripture taken from the New King James Version®. Copyright © 1982 by Thomas Nelson. Used by permission. All rights reserved.

Manufactured in the U.S.A.   03/11/20

Contents

List of Tables and Figures | viii
Foreword by Donald Fairbairn | ix
Acknowledgments | xiii

1. **Introduction** | 1
    Problem Statement   3
    Purpose Statement   3
    Research Questions   3
    Definitions   4
    Scope   5
    Limitations   6
    Significance Statement   6
    Direction for Research   7

2. **The Socio-Political Context of the Former Soviet Union** | 8
    Class and Social Networks in the Former Soviet Union   10
    Other Social Factors in the Former Soviet Union   13
    Politics, Religion, and Worldview in the Former Soviet Union   15
    Conclusions for the Socio-Political Context of the
    Former Soviet Union   20

3. **The Evangelical Church and Mission in the Former Soviet Union** | 21
    The State of the Evangelical Church Before Perestroika   21
    The State of the Evangelical Church During and After Perestroika   30
    The Ukrainian Missionary Surge From 1989 Onward   38
    Summary of Potential Factors Behind the Missionary Surge   57
    Directions for Further Research   58

4. Methods and Procedures | 59
Justification for the Research Paradigm 59
Data Collection Strategies and Procedures 63
Ethical Considerations 70
Data Analysis Strategy 73
Data Validation Strategy 78
Conclusion for Methods and Procedures 80

5. Results: The Story of the Ukrainian Evangelical Missionary Surge from 1989 to 1999 | 81
Preparation for the Surge in Soviet Times 82
Timing of the Surge 85
Source: Centers of Missionary Development 85
Vision 1: The Idea of Missions 100
Vision 2: God's Call and Answered Prayer 106
Motivation 1: Need and Opportunity for Missions 109
Motivation 2: Inspiration From Missionaries 117
Means 1: Tools for Ministry 124
Means 2: Missionary Structures 128
Means 3: Financial Support 142
Opportunity 1: Common Territory, Language, and Culture 152
Opportunity 2: Freedom for Missionary Work 153
Opportunity 3: God's Grace at Work 156
Comparison of Findings With the Literature Review 157
Conclusions 158

6. **Summary: A Model for the Ukrainian Evangelical Missionary Surge from 1989 to 1999** | 164
   Most Important Factors in the Missionary Surge   165
   Centers for Missionary Development   167
   Change: The Idea and Value of Missions   169
   Change: Motivation for Becoming a Missionary   174
   Communication and Facilitation Agents   178
   Context for Missions   184
   Comparison With Other Historical Missionary Surges   187
   Comparison With Other Contemporary Surges in Eastern and Central Europe   188
   Conclusion   189
   Recommendations for Further Research   190

Appendix A: The History of Missionary Surges | 193

Appendix B: Participant Information | 246

Appendix C: Comparison of Change Models with the Missionary Surge | 249

Bibliography | 255

Index | 271

List of Tables

1. Light of the Gospel Financial Spending Percentages by Department from 1989–92. | 57
2. Timeline of Key Events and People in the Ukrainian Evangelical Missionary Surge | 159
3. Key Factors Behind the Ukrainian Evangelical Missionary Surge | 161
A1. Examples of Missionary Surge Factors Within a Category Matrix | 240
B1. Participant Information | 246
C1. Comparison of Change Models With the Missionary Surge: Centers and Change (Rational Side) | 250
C2. Comparison of Change Models With the Missionary Surge: Change (Emotional Side) | 251
C3. Comparison of Change Models With the Missionary Surge: Communication and Facilitation Agents | 252
C4. Comparison of Change Models With the Missionary Surge: Context | 253

List of Figures

1. Literature map for the Ukrainian missionary surge of the 1990s showing the flow of literature related to the Ukrainian missionary surge, moving historically from top to bottom | 9
2. Map of Ukraine with key cities and oblasts marked. The borders internal to Ukraine show the different oblasts | 42
3. Map of the former Soviet Union with key cities and areas marked | 43
4. Model for the Ukrainian evangelical missionary surge from 1989 to 1999, showing the most important elements behind the surge. It portrays the flow of the missionary surge, from centers through communication agents to the change, through facilitation agents to the context | 190

Foreword

FOR CHRISTIANS IN THE Soviet Union and former Soviet Union, the late 1980s and early 1990s were a heady time, a period of unexpected openness to the gospel. Some people, both native Soviets and foreigners, had spent decades praying that Russia and the surrounding lands would return to the God of their fathers. Others were caught up in the enthusiasm of the moment, as the (officially) atheistic regime of the U.S.S.R. fell and a wave of missionary activity swept over the Russian steppes. I was in the second category. I had held no particular burden for the Soviet Union, and as late as the spring of 1989, I had scoffed at the idea that God would open Eastern Europe to the Gospel. But the Lord laughed at my skepticism, and by January 1990, I found myself, seemingly by accident, in Tbilisi, Georgia, in the vanguard of what would become a great western missionary push, what I call the "rush for Russia." After a year in Georgia, I began working directly with the indigenous missions society Light of the Gospel and teaching at what would later be called Donetsk Christian University. I had the privilege of knowing many of the people whom John White interviewed for this book, and I had a front-row seat for the surge in missionary activity that is his subject.

The rush for Russia may have been one of the most extraordinary missionary pushes in world Christian history, as countless western Christian agencies marshalled their donors, missionaries, and new recruits to put people on the ground in the newly independent countries of the entity that we then called the Commonwealth of Independent States. (That name ought to be a game-show question, for it is surely among the leaders in the running for political title that dropped from use the fastest!) Leading the way in the rush for Russia was the CoMission, a consortium of western agencies that sought to put short-term volunteers in schools throughout Russia to teach ethics and share the gospel. But for all the vast resources expended in this western push, and all the short-term good that was accomplished, the long-term results were very mixed, to say the least. Little lasting change came about in Russian society; there was certainly no significant uptick in Protestant Christianity in the realm. And while White is far too polite to say so, the infamous 1997 Russian law restricting religious freedom for Protestants was as much a response to the western rush for Russia as to anything else.

But alongside this massive western missionary push was another effort, much smaller, involving only a tiny fraction of the money, and receiving far less attention either inside or outside the former Soviet Union. This was the indigenous missionary movement that saw Soviets and former-Soviets seek to establish new missionary outreach across the vast sweep of Russia, especially in the far north, east, and northeast of Russia—what westerners call "Siberia." (To Russians, only the middle part of that vast region is properly Siberia. The rest has other names—Yakutia, the far East, Chukotka, Kamchatka, etc.) By their own admission, these indigenous missionaries knew little of missionary theory, had little formal education, never really had a grand plan or strategy, and seemed unlikely to be world changers. What they did have, though, was a confidence that the Lord had opened a door for them, that he had called them as missionaries, and that he would take care of them as they left home to serve him. At the center of this indigenous missionary surge were Ukrainians, particularly Baptists and Pentecostals. Ukraine had and has far more evangelicals than other parts of the former Soviet Union, and it was Ukrainians above all who led the surge. As it turned out, this indigenous movement arguably made more of an impact on Russian society than the massive and expensive western push. It was a modern-day David and Goliath story.

Now, more than three decades after the missionary surge began, we are long overdue for an academic analysis of the indigenous Ukrainian missionary surge, a work to complement the studies that have been made of the western rush for Russia. John White is in an outstanding position to offer such an analysis. He came to Ukraine after the surge had largely subsided and thus is able to look at it with the advantages of historical hindsight. At the same time, he has immersed himself thoroughly in Ukrainian culture and even married a Ukrainian, making him trustworthy enough that those he interviewed would speak candidly with him. And he has had the discipline to tell his story with focus, avoiding unnecessary complications such as constant comparisons between the Ukrainian and western missionary surges (a temptation to which I would surely have succumbed if I had been writing this book!).

The result is that a little-known but important story in modern missions has been told compellingly and, I think, accurately. But more than this, White has identified several crucially important factors that contributed to the (relative) success of the indigenous Ukrainian surge. For those of us who want to learn from the turbulent 1990s and the rush for Russia, there is much wisdom here that could be profitably applied to missions work in other regions as well. Those who take part in the next great missionary surge, or the one after that, would do well to heed the lessons of this book.

Donald Fairbairn

formerly professor at Donetsk Christian University
currently academic dean of the Charlotte (N.C.) campus,
Gordon-Conwell Theological Seminary

Acknowledgments

THERE ARE A NUMBER of people that I would like to thank for their contributions to this dissertation. First, I'd like to thank those who helped guide my research. Thanks to Dr. Hayward, for facilitating me and many others in Kyiv through the doctoral program. Thanks for all of the insight, flexibility, and support given along the way. Thanks to Drs. Steffen and Nehrbass for all of their constructive criticism to help me be both clear and complete.

Next, I'd like to thank all those who helped me in the process of researching and writing. Thanks to WorldVenture, Ivan Rusyn, and the Ukrainian Evangelical Theological Seminary for the support and time given to work on this project. Thanks so much to all my interview participants who shared their stories and guided me to others interested in helping. Thanks to Stella White and Yana Kryuchkova for transcribing many of my interviews that were done in Russian. Thanks to Gerry and Kathy Hawkins for their wonderful hospitality during my trips to California. And thanks to Ray Prigodich for doing the massive job of editing my dissertation two times and for providing needed perspective.

I'd also like to thank those who helped me get started on this study. Thanks to Scott Klingsmith and Taras Dyatlik for pointing out the need to research this topic long before I ever thought about starting a doctorate. Thanks to Jason Gupta and Mike Manna for helping me get into Biola's doctoral program and for all of the camaraderie along the way.

I'd really like to thank my family for all of the wonderful support and encouragement they've given me. Thanks to my parents for hosting us and helping us in times of research, recuperation, and war. Thanks to Eddie for dealing with Papa being busy with his doctorate your entire life—I hope you'll think it was worth it some day! Thanks so much, again, Stella, for giving me time to travel, to think, and to work and for loving me through it all.

And thanks to Jesus for His grace from the beginning until the end.

1

Introduction

THE EVANGELICAL CHURCH IN the Soviet Union suffered greatly under communism and focused mainly on survival, not mission. The laws of the land made evangelism extremely difficult and the propaganda against Christianity was very effective. Many of the leaders of the church turned inward under the pressures of persecution and infiltration by the KGB. The Soviet government officially showed tolerance while trying to destroy the church from the inside.[1]

Evangelical churches developed a "ghetto mentality," being unable to reach out to secularized people.[2] Many church leaders worried about taking new initiatives, fearing that they wouldn't work.[3] Some evangelical Christians even maintained that they should not "cast [their] pearls before swine" (Matt 7:6, NKJV) by preaching in markets, bus stops, and stores.[4] Not surprisingly, nearly all of the numerical growth churches experienced during the Communist period resulted from having large families.[5]

The coming of *glasnost* (openness) and the Fall of Communism led to freedom of thought and a huge interest in Christianity, which Michael Rowe described as an "evangelical explosion."[6] It was easy at first; anyone could just yell "Jesus loves you" or start playing a guitar and singing Christian songs to gather a crowd. People were eager to take any Christian literature available and attend Christian meetings.

Foreign missionaries came into the former Soviet Union like a flood. The Protestant missionary force grew from only a "handful of undeclared

---

1. Marsh, *Religion and State*, 65.
2. Pierson, *Dynamics of Christian Mission*, 331.
3. Melnychuk, "Istoriya i uroki," 221.
4. "Propoved' v narode," 14.
5. "Delayte uchenikami," 12.
6. Rowe, *Russian Resurrection*, 229–38.

missionaries" in 1986 to over 5,600 from 561 different ministries by 1997.⁷ In the meantime, national missionaries also were starting to work.

> In a country where there had been no missions and no charity work for sixty years, these new missionary groups saw enormous needs all around them. It was hard to know where to begin and so they tended to do something of everything: evangelistic meetings, prison visiting, Sunday schools, distribution of Christian literature, church planting, talks in schools, hospital visiting, distribution of relief.⁸

When this period of great spiritual interest waned toward the end of the 1990s, people began to analyze the successes and failures of the foreign mission effort. While there is a growing amount of literature regarding foreign missions in the former Soviet Union, very little analysis, especially in English, has been published on national mission efforts. Even volumes on the state of global mission focusing on non-Western missionaries tend to offer only a couple of pages about national missionaries in the former Soviet Union.⁹ Yet, there is reason to believe that these mission efforts, especially on the part of Ukrainian missionaries, were noteworthy.

As one travels around Yakutia, the largest region of Siberian Russia and about six times the size of Ukraine, one can hear the following joke: "Where do Ukrainians live?" The answer is "Around Yakutia and a few near Kyiv."¹⁰ In 2001, over 900 Ukrainians served as missionaries with over one-third of them working in Russia.¹¹ According to the director of missionary work for the Russian Union of Evangelical Christians-Baptists, Ruvim Voloshin,¹² the Ukrainian mission organization Light of the Gospel was considered one of the most active mission groups in all of Russia. Thus, Ukrainian missionaries in the 1990s had a substantial impact on Russia, in addition to other parts of the former Soviet Union.

---

7. Elliott and Corrado, "Protestant Missionary Presence," 335.

8. Rowe, *Russian Resurrection*, 248.

9. E.g., Lewis, *Christianity Reborn*; Pierson, *Dynamics of Christian Mission*; Pocock, *Changing Face of World Mission*.

10. Tupchik, "Poseshchenie Yakutii," 12.

11. Johnstone and Mandryk, *Operation World*, 6th ed., 645.

12. Voloshin, "Analiz razvitiya."

Problem Statement

In 2000, a conference, called, *Rus'-Mission (or Eastern Slavic Mission) in the 21st Century* was held in Moscow for ministers and missionaries from across the former Soviet Union. One of the goals of the conference was to analyze the missionary work of the 1990s. Taras Pristupa,[13] former Director of Missionary Work for Light of the Gospel and, at that time, president of the Ukrainian mission organization Hope to People, claimed that they were not able to do a deep, critical analysis of the 1990s. He explained that there was only one way to do such an analysis objectively, which was to invite an independent foreign expert group of Christian specialists for a spiritual audit and consultation.[14] Both Ukrainian and foreign mission leaders have expressed the need for such a study to be undertaken,[15] but it has still not been done.[16] Therefore, a deeper analysis is needed of this historical period, including an analysis of factors that contributed to the surge of Ukrainian mission involvement in the 1990s. The factors behind the Ukrainian missionary surge remain unclear.

Purpose Statement

The purpose of this grounded theory study is to discover and explain factors that contributed to the surge in the number of Ukrainian evangelical missionaries from 1989 to 1999 (see Scope section below for why these years were chosen). The study focuses on gathering data from mission organizations and churches in the former Soviet Union, especially from their key leaders and members as well as from mission and church documents.

Research Questions

This study's central question is, what factors contributed to the surge in numbers of Ukrainian evangelical missionaries during the period from 1989 to 1999? In order to determine which sub-questions would be the most helpful, I have conducted a separate study on the history of missionary surges, which can be found in Appendix A. That study revealed some categories of factors that have influenced missionary surges historically, which

13. Pristupa, "Prepyatstviya."
14. Pristupa, "Prepyatstviya."
15. Klingsmith, "Factors in the Rise," 393; Pristupa, "Prepyatstviya."
16. Taras N. Dyatlik and Sergei F. Rybikov, personal communication, December 30, 2011.

are depicted in table A1. These categories of factors form the basis of the following sub-questions:

1. Were there new sources of people available to become missionaries at that time? What kinds of people became missionaries during the surge?
2. What kinds of statements of vision influenced the surge?
3. What kinds of motivation influenced people to become missionaries?
4. What means were used to enable the surge (e.g., mission organizations, finances)?
5. What kinds of opportunities for missions contributed to the surge (e.g., worldview change, religious freedom, openness to hear about Christianity)?

These five typical categories of factors will be asked about during this study, but due to the open-ended nature of grounded theory research, factors that do not fit into these categories may also emerge from the data.

Definitions

For the purposes of this study, the following definitions will be used.

1. Missionary: The term missionary will refer to the commonly-accepted definition in the former Soviet Union. A missionary is a person sent to do ministry among unreached people with the goal of starting a new church.[17] This ministry is cross-cultural in some, but not all, cases.
2. Evangelical: Evangelical missionaries are those who hold to the four characteristics of historical evangelicalism as defined by David Bebbington: "*conversionism*, the belief that lives need to be changed; *activism*, the expression of the gospel in effort; *biblicism*, a particular regard for the Bible; and what may be called *crucicentrism*, a stress on the sacrifice of Christ on the cross."[18]
3. Conversionism: Conversionism is the belief that people need "to turn away from their sins in repentance and to Christ in faith."[19]
4. Activism: Activism is a desire for and an effort toward the conversion of others to Christian faith.[20] It is not necessarily limited to sharing the

---

17. Pristupa, "Kto mozhet byt' missionerom?," 2–4; Voloshin, "20 let spustya . . ."
18. Bebbington, *Evangelicalism in Modern Britain*, 3.
19. Bebbington, *Evangelicalism in Modern Britain*, 5.
20. Bebbington, *Evangelicalism in Modern Britain*, 10.

INTRODUCTION 5

gospel, but is sometimes expressed through philanthropy, or enforcing the "ethics of the gospel."[21]

5. Biblicism: Biblicism is the belief "that the Bible is inspired by God," and "that all spiritual truth is to be found in its pages."[22]

6. Crucicentrism: Crucicentrism is the belief that Christ's sacrifice on the cross is central to Christian faith since "Christ died as a substitute for sinful mankind," making God "the author of salvation."[23]

7. Oblast: An administrative division in Ukraine or Russia, roughly equivalent to *province* or *state*.

8. Siberia: The Asian territory of Russia that lies east of the Ural Mountains and stretches all the way to the Pacific Ocean, extending from Mongolia and China in the south to the Arctic Ocean in the north. It covers almost five million square miles and occupies one twelfth of the landmass of the entire earth.[24]

9. Fall of Communism: The period of time when communism ended in the former Soviet Union. The Soviet Union itself came to an official end on December 25, 1991, helping lead to the establishment of 15 separate, noncommunist countries. The Fall of Communism is considered to have begun on that date with the results being felt over the months and years that followed.

Scope

This study focuses on Ukrainians who served as missionaries during the period from 1989 to 1999. The year 1989 was chosen as a starting point since in 1988 the Soviet Union celebrated a Millennium of Christianity, leading to a new openness to religion in the years that followed.[25] There was no clear ending point of the missionary surge, although the mission work of one of the most active missionary organizations, Light of the Gospel, seemed to taper off by the end of the 1990s. So, this study will investigate missionary activity up until the end of 1999, a period of 11 years. For convenience, I will often use the phrase *Ukrainian missionaries in the 1990s*, but this phrase

21. Bebbington, *Evangelicalism in Modern Britain*, 12.
22. Bebbington, *Evangelicalism in Modern Britain*, 12–13.
23. Bebbington, *Evangelicalism in Modern Britain*, 14–15.
24. Thubron, *In Siberia*, 1, 4.
25. Forest, *Religion in the New Russia*, 6, 8; Sawatsky, "Protestantism in the USSR," in *Religious Policy*, 54.

will include 1989–99. This study does not explore the missionary work of Russian nationals or others who were not Ukrainian citizens during this period. It includes all types of Ukrainian citizens who became missionaries, not limited by ethnicity or first language.

Limitations

This study does not claim to examine all possible factors behind the surge in Ukrainian evangelical missionaries because the impetus of the Holy Spirit and the individual responses of Ukrainian evangelicals offer far too many variables to allow for such a claim. So, it is possible that some important factors could be missed. In addition, the factors that will be emphasized will largely depend on study participants' perceptions. Some participants may have a stake in the results of the study.

Significance Statement

Understanding factors contributing to the surge in Ukrainian missionaries in the 1990s will provide clarity and a means of analysis for those involved in the surge. Many have been frustrated by a lack of understanding of what happened during this period.[26] New understanding will help national mission organizations and church leaders to improve the state of missionary work in the former Soviet Union in such areas as recruitment, organization, leadership, and methodology. It will help foreign mission leaders who work in the former Soviet Union as well, especially those who partner with nationals.

Further, this study will provide useful material for those involved in mission education and training. The surge in Ukrainian missionaries in the 1990s can serve as an example and motivate other Ukrainians to go into mission work. It can help Ukrainian evangelicals to think of their country as a missionary sending country, not just a missionary receiving one. It can motivate national churches in other countries to send out missionaries, as well.

In addition, the results of this research will help fill the literature gap that exists regarding Ukrainian missionary work in the 1990s. They will help balance the big picture of mission in the former Soviet Union, adding to the literary corpus on foreign mission work. Finally, this study can serve as a foundation for future research of missionary surges from other parts of the world and missionary surges from Ukraine after 2000.

---

26. Pristupa, "Prepyatstviya."

Direction for Research

It seems clear that further research into the factors behind the Ukrainian evangelical missionary surge of the 1990s is both needed and would be valuable. Having now determined the purpose and scope of this research, I will next turn to a review of the literature. In chapter 2, I will look at the socio-political situation in the former Soviet Union both prior to and during the 1990s in order to better understand the context of the Ukrainian evangelical missionary surge.

2

The Socio-Political Context of the Former Soviet Union

IN CONSIDERING THE UKRAINIAN evangelical missionary surge in the 1990s, I first reviewed all the available literature, which enabled me to position my study within the overall existing literature.[1] I explored authors' viewpoints in the same way that I later learned from study participants.[2]

I started my literature review by investigating the history of missionary surges, and this research helped me to accumulate a list of potential factors for the Ukrainian missionary surge of the 1990s. That study is found in Appendix A. In this chapter, I will review the socio-political context of the former Soviet Union. Then, in chapter 3, I will study the state of the evangelical church and mission in the former Soviet Union, finally looking at what literature exists specifically on the Ukrainian missionary surge. The literature map in figure 1 below gives an outline of the path my literature review takes.

The socio-political context of the former Soviet Union is an undeniably broad topic, and one that cannot be covered in great detail here. The aspects that are relevant to this study are those that underwent change immediately before and after 1989, as these may have played a role in the Ukrainian missionary surge that occurred. Yale Richmond[3] gives a good overview of Russian culture (which was very similar to Ukrainian culture during the timeframe of our study) and Kent Hill[4] provides a good summary of the important changes that occurred up until the Fall of Communism in the Soviet Union in 1991.

---

1. Creswell, *Qualitative Inquiry*, 102–3.
2. Creswell, *Research Design*, 26.
3. Richmond, *From Nyet to Da*.
4. Hill, *Soviet Union on the Brink*.

THE SOCIO-POLITICAL CONTEXT OF THE FORMER SOVIET UNION

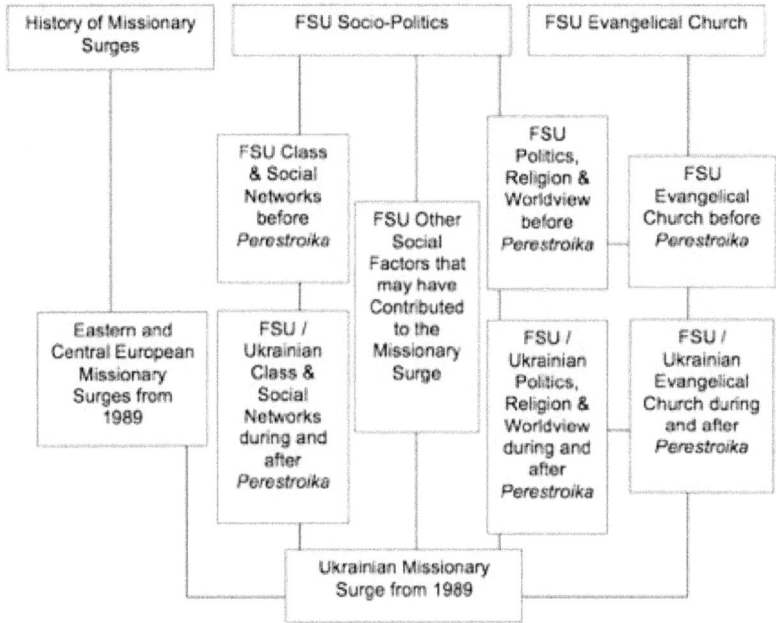

Figure 1. Literature map for the Ukrainian missionary surge of the 1990s showing the flow of literature related to the Ukrainian missionary surge, moving historically from top to bottom.

Note: FSU = Former Soviet Union.

The key changes that occurred in the late 1980s began with *perestroika* (restructuring), a government program initiated by Mikhail Gorbachev in 1987 to restructure and improve the economy.[5] An important part of these changes was *glasnost*, a policy first mentioned by Gorbachev in 1988 that allowed for more freedom of speech.[6] The process of *perestroika* and *glasnost* produced many effects, including allowing the celebration of a Millennium of Christianity in 1988 and subsequently permitting greater freedom of religion. The effects of *perestroika* and *glasnost* cannot neatly be divided into the period before 1989 and the period from 1989 onward. Instead, they had an accumulating effect from 1987 through 1991, when the Soviet Union fell. So, I will divide most of the material below into two periods: before *perestroika*, and then the period of *perestroika* and beyond.

---

5. Goldman, "Perestroika"; Petrov, "Construction, Reconstruction, Deconstruction," 184.

6. Petrov, "Construction, Reconstruction, Deconstruction," 193.

Several specific areas deserve investigation. First, I will explore how changes in class and social networks affected interest in Christianity and the potential for missionary work. Next, I will look at a few other social issues that may have influenced the missionary surge. Finally, I will discuss politics, religion, and worldview, which can each help us better understand the missionary surge.

Class and Social Networks in the Former Soviet Union

When the Soviet Union went through *perestroika* and eventually fell in 1991, evangelical Christians' position in society changed dramatically. I will briefly explore the changes that occurred in class structure and social networks in the former Soviet Union in the late 1980s and early 1990s and the effects upon people's interest in evangelical Christianity.

Class and Social Networks Under Communism Before *Perestroika*

The economy and social life of the Soviet Union was tightly controlled by the government.[7] Officially, the Soviet Union had a classless society, yet there was clearly some stratification.[8] The state-party was the highest class, with workers being the middle class, and peasants (farm workers) being the lower class.[9] The differences between these groups were not based on ownership of property since all property was socialized, but on access to goods and services.[10] Evangelical Christians were usually placed into the lowest part of the lowest class (peasants) due to their supposedly outmoded belief in God.[11]

Evangelicals' place in society

Anyone choosing to become an evangelical Christian faced both social and economic consequences. Evangelicals did not have access to higher education. They generally were allowed only low-paying, menial jobs.[12] Often

---

7. Christensen, "Perestroika and the Problem," 130; Field, "Soviet Society," 120.
8. Piirainen, "Survival Strategies," 102.
9. Matthews, *Class and Society*, 52; Mayer, "Collapse of Soviet Communism," 761.
10. Piirainen, "Survival Strategies," 104; Teckenberg, "Social Structure," 29.
11. Hill, *Soviet Union on the Brink*, 330.
12. Elliott and Richardson, "Growing Protestant Diversity," 201; Wanner, "Advocating New Moralities," 284.

evangelicals had difficulty finding housing or receiving permission to live in a new city.[13] These pressures led some "deeply believing Christians" to stop going to church.[14] Thus, the Soviet evangelical church was a church of the poor[15] and persecuted.

Johannes Reimer further described the perception of Soviet evangelicals as "third-class, old fashioned, often simply as stupid, unlearned people."[16] This perception separated them from the greater society and created a subculture that became used to being anti-social and feeling inferior. Ironically, Western Christians helped contribute to this inferiority complex by presenting Soviet evangelicals as weak, needing the West's help.[17]

Evangelical social networks

Social networks play a vital role in the process of conversion.[18] Since evangelicals were in the lower class, it was easiest for them and often quite effective to reach out to those closest to them socially: other simple workers.[19] Evangelicals also ministered to the marginalized in orphanages, retirement homes, hospitals, and prisons. They were known for their hard work and kindness, which brought them numerous converts.[20]

The evangelical community seemed to be a part of something more and better, removed from the general class structure.[21] Soviet evangelical churches had tight networks of mutual care and service that helped sustain the members amidst government persecution and discrimination. These networks involved financial, emotional, and spiritual support.[22] Thus, many who lacked support in Soviet society were attracted to evangelical churches, especially women who faced discrimination and a lack of social mobility.[23]

---

13. Walters, "Russian Orthodox Church," 143–44.
14. Lawrence, "Observations on Religion and Atheism," 582.
15. Sawatsky, *Soviet Evangelicals*, 355.
16. Reimer, "Mission in Post-Perestroika Russia," "Unprepared for the Task," para. 1.
17. Reimer, "Mission in Post-Perestroika Russia."
18. Richardson, "Active vs. Passive Convert," 170; Stark, *Triumph of Christianity*, 68.
19. Lawrence, "Observations on Religion and Atheism," 580.
20. Savinskii et al., "Istoriya YeKhB."
21. Coleman, "Conversion Narratives," 97.
22. Wanner, "Advocating New Moralities," 281.
23. Dunn and Dunn, "Religion as an Instrument," 477.

Class and Social Networks During *Perestroika* and the Fall of Communism

Perestroika led to a "severe structural and institutional crisis"[24] because new institutions that are needed in a democratic civil society were not established.[25] This crisis affected everything from public transportation to food supply to paying salaries to the wiping out of life savings.[26]

Changes in the class of evangelicals

After the Millennium of Christianity was celebrated in 1988 (described in greater detail later in this chapter), evangelicals were finally able to officially establish charitable organizations to do ministry. Evangelicals not only reached equal status with the rest of society, but in numerous cases they were given a special place in society. As the government failed, the charitable ministry of evangelicals was encouraged and even began to be depended upon to care for the needy in society, and especially for alcoholics and drug addicts who needed rehabilitation.[27] Thus, the role of evangelicals was reversed from being parasites in society[28] to being valuable members of it.

During this time of economic turmoil, evangelical Christianity also attracted people by providing financial opportunities. Evangelicals were also invited to help rebuild the economy, at least in part because of their connections to rich foreigners.[29] Humanitarian aid came from abroad, providing for many needy church members.[30] This kind of help was nothing new for the church, which in its first days provided for its members.[31] However, it is true that some people came to evangelical churches only for financial benefit.

---

24. Kerr and Robinson, "Hysteresis Effect," 837.
25. Motyl, "Structural Constraints," 435.
26. Heyns, "Emerging Inequalities," 179; Parker, "Assessing Perestroika," 266; Pelkmans, "Introduction: Post-Soviet Space," 2; Vihavainen, "Cultural and Moral Upheaval," 82.
27. Lyubashchenko, "Protestantism in Ukraine," 270; Wanner, "Missionaries of Faith and Culture," 749–50.
28. Fitzpatrick, "Social Parasites," 408.
29. Sawatsky, "After the Glasnost Revolution," 56.
30. Wanner, "Appeal of Evangelicalism," 256.
31. Stark, *Triumph of Christianity*, 113.

The new influences of evangelical social networks

Most Soviet citizens' social networks were closely tied to the workplace. When the economic turmoil of *perestroika* hit, many people lost their jobs and social status, and thus sought out new networks for support.[32] Many evangelical church-based communities offered both economic and social support during this period of crisis.[33] Having been marginalized for so long, evangelicals could sympathize with those who now found themselves at the margins of society. Plus, evangelicals could offer connections not just with a local group of believers, but with a worldwide church, and with a God beyond this world.[34] Therefore, many people were drawn to evangelical church communities.

Christianity tended to create new social networks and destroy old ones. When a person converted, she often told her family and friends, leading to more conversions through her social networks.[35] Yet, some societal connections might be broken because of conversion. Loyalty to Christ and fellow Christians took precedence over family and friends, who might decide to cut off their relationship.[36] Additionally, the evangelical faith was portable, since a Christian could travel to new places and integrate into different Christian communities.[37]

Finally, evangelical communities offered opportunities for an improved status. Evangelical churches offered many positions of responsibility, including deacon, preacher, and leader of various ministries. For those who had never achieved such status in the secular world, these positions were very fulfilling.[38] Thus, evangelical churches' social networks gave people the opportunity to play an important role.

Other Social Factors in the Former Soviet Union

There are a few other social factors that can help us understand the Ukrainian missionary surge of the 1990s. I will address each one as a whole, not separating out each factor specifically before and after 1989. Each of these

---

32. Pelkmans, "Introduction: Post-Soviet Space," 4–5; Wanner, "Appeal of Evangelicalism," 265.
33. Wanner, "Advocating New Moralities," 281–82.
34. Wanner, "Appeal of Evangelicalism," 255.
35. Stark, *Triumph of Christianity*, 68–69.
36. Wanner, "Appeal of Evangelicalism," 250.
37. Wanner, "Appeal of Evangelicalism," 255–56.
38. Wanner, "Appeal of Evangelicalism," 250, 267.

factors either provided an opportunity for missionaries to achieve success or the means for missionaries to operate.

The Communists' Unintentional Preparation for Christian Mission

Stephen Neill and Paul Hattaway made interesting arguments as to how the Roman Empire[39] and the Chinese Communist government,[40] respectively, helped prepare the way for the spread of Christianity by improving infrastructure, establishing one language, bringing peace, and reducing idolatry (in the case of China). Similarly, the Soviet Communist government helped prepare the way for Christian mission by standardizing the Russian language and requiring it in schools, massively improving literacy, establishing peace in conflicted areas like the Caucasus, reducing the power of the Orthodox Church, and drastically improving the means of transportation around the country.

Minority Nationalities' Interest in Christianity

Some minority groups, like the Nenets, felt a connection with the Soviet evangelical movement, since both were repressed by the government. When communism ended, these groups' shared experiences helped form a bridge for the Gospel, bringing many of the Nenets to Christianity.[41] Also, members of some minority groups, like some Kyrgyz, feared extreme Islam, and thus turned to Christianity.[42]

The Problem of Widespread Alcoholism

Alcoholism was a long-standing problem in Russia and the Soviet Union. Stephen White noted that "the consumption of all forms of alcoholic drink . . . increased eight times between 1940 and 1984."[43] As people gave up on Marxist ideology in the late 1980s, many were left empty and hopeless.

---

39. Neill, *History of Christian Missions*, 24–25.
40. Hattaway, *Back to Jerusalem*, 12.
41. Vallikivi, "Christianization of Words and Selves," 60.
42. Pelkmans, "Introduction: Post-Soviet Space," 145; Rybikov, "Missionerskoe sluzhenie."
43. White, *Russia Goes Dry*, 38.

Mass alcoholism was one of the results of this hopelessness.[44] One government leader drew a picture of the problem by asserting that if someone had to choose between a bottle of vodka today and 10,000 dollars tomorrow, the bottle would definitely have the advantage.[45] The state of society was tragic.

Politics, Religion, and Worldview in the Former Soviet Union

Russian Orthodoxy has been the predominant religion in the former Soviet Union for 1,000 years.[46] For most of that time, by law only foreigners could hold to other religions. Unlike in Western Europe, religion was a matter of birth, not of choice.[47] Most people believed that to be Russian is to be Orthodox. Then when communism came in 1917, atheism became the political standard, although many people still considered themselves to be Orthodox at some level.

Communist Ideology Before *Perestroika*

The Soviet Union developed a comprehensive ideology, of which, atheism was a key component. Tom Casier called communist ideology "not simply an ornament, but . . . a central pillar of power."[48] There were about eleven million people who served as "ideological activists," maintaining the system.[49]

Right and wrong were determined not by religion, but "on the basis of Soviet doctrine."[50] Many Soviet teachings were very similar to biblical ones, yet religious teaching was considered "a comfortable myth" and anti-scientific, while Soviet teaching was considered scientific, and therefore, true.[51] Even the term *spirituality* was changed in communist ideology to mean good values or a high level of culture. The whole system was based on the authority, truth, and good of communism.

---

44. Reimer, "Mission in Post-Perestroika Russia."
45. Sipko, "Sotsial'nyy portret rossiyanina."
46. Richmond, *From Nyet to Da*, 26.
47. Marsh, *Religion and the State*, 50.
48. Casier, "How Ideology Mattered to Soviet Politics," 35.
49. Remington, "CPSU Ideological Work," 155.
50. Durasoff, *Russian Protestants*, 205.
51. Fletcher, *Soviet Believers*, 155.

Government Propaganda Against the Evangelical Church

The Soviet government promoted an atheistic hegemony that was widespread and effective. Atheist propaganda could be found everywhere—in education, at places of work, and even in places of recreation.[52] The KGB made documentaries about Protestants to discredit them, even saying that "they offered human sacrifices."[53] The communists especially focused on converting young people to atheism from kindergarten on.[54] Outside of school, about 99% of all children participated in communist groups for various age levels: the Komsomol (Communist Youth League), the Pioneers, and the Young Octobrists.[55]

Yet, there was a softening in the harsh atheistic propaganda after Vladimir A. Kuroedov retired as chair of the Council of Religious Affairs in 1984. His successor, Konstantin Kharchev, publicly said that churches and religious belief were unlikely to disappear in the near future.[56]

Government Persecution of the Evangelical Church

After a period of greater rights and freedom for evangelicals from 1917 to 1929,[57] Soviet policy changed abruptly with the Law on Religious Associations (sometimes referred to as the Law on Cults). Philip Walters explained:

> According to this law, the only permitted activity for believers is to meet in a registered building for an act of worship. Everything else is either illegal or in fact discouraged by authorities: organizing meetings, libraries, educational activity for young people; evangelizing; unofficially printing and distributing religious literature; and raising money for welfare or charitable activity.[58]

This law effectively prohibited missionary work, forbidding pastors from preaching in other churches or calling people to repent. Many pastors and evangelists who disobeyed this law were put into prison.[59] It is estimated that about 22,000 evangelicals were sent to labor camps in

---

52. Walters, "Russian Orthodox Church," 144.
53. Heydt, *Candles Behind the Wall*, 83.
54. Sawatsky, *Soviet Evangelicals*, 297.
55. Heydt, *Candles Behind the Wall*, 95; Sawatsky, *Soviet Evangelicals*, 299.
56. Sawatsky, "Protestantism in the USSR," in *Protestantism and Politics*, 248.
57. Prokhanoff, *Autobiography*, 175–76.
58. Walters, "Religion in the Soviet Union," 3.
59. Znakevich, "Evangelism and Church Planting," 83.

Siberia.⁶⁰ When the government arrested pastors, the pastors' churches could then be closed, with the church buildings often being turned into movie theaters or museums.⁶¹

In cases where churches remained open, the government often made its own people the pastors. In any case, pastors had to report their attendance and new converts, often leading to pressure on these converts to deny their faith.⁶² The government also put pressure on churches not to include youth. Baptist church leader Jacob Zhidkov even taught that Christians should imitate Christ by being baptized only after the age of 30,⁶³ making one wonder where his loyalties lay.

Following a period of reduced persecution beginning around the time of the Second World War, Khrushchev launched another wave of persecution from 1959 to 1964, closing churches, imprisoning Christians, and promising to "show the last Christian on TV."⁶⁴ Although there was still some persecution of individual believers, state pressure on the evangelical churches slowly subsided from 1964 to 1985.⁶⁵

Changes and Problems in Ideology During *Perestroika* and Beyond

During the days of *perestroika*, the Communist Party's authority started slipping, as did communist values. Even though most people would have agreed that these values were good,⁶⁶ without belief in the Communist Party's authority, many people began to ignore those values. Organized crime began to flourish and cheating, lying, and stealing became commonplace.⁶⁷ Many Soviet people felt a growing "emptiness and meaningless of life, life without purpose."⁶⁸ So, "the spiritual vacuum . . . propelled people on the quest for new values, ideals and faith."⁶⁹

---

60. Rowe, *Russian Resurrection*, 93.
61. Latourette, *Expansion of Christianity*, 3:78–79; Sawatsky, *Soviet Evangelicals*, 47.
62. Znakevich, "Evangelism and Church Planting," 86–87.
63. Nikolskaya, *Russkiy protestantizm*.
64. Rowe, *Russian Resurrection*, 136–38.
65. Hill, *Soviet Union on the Brink*, 111.
66. Yurchak, *Everything Was Forever*, 8.
67. Wanner, "Advocating New Moralities," 279.
68. Cherevko, "Theology of Mission," 16.
69. Gruenwald, "Icon in Russian Art, Society and Culture," 162.

The Millennium Celebration in 1988 and New Openness to Christianity

By 1987, Gorbachev had released almost all political and religious prisoners, and negative propaganda against Christians was significantly reduced.[70] The evangelical movement would reach a new level of freedom in 1990 when the Law on Freedom of Conscience was passed, effectively ending the 1929 Law on Religious Associations.[71]

But before that event occurred, the key event that led to a significant change in freedom of religion and people's view of religion was the celebration of a Millennium of Christianity in 1988. In 988, Prince Vladimir had baptized the people of Kievan Rus' (the forerunner to Russia and the Soviet Union) into Orthodox Christianity, and even before Mikhail Gorbachev took power, the government had decided to commemorate this historic event.[72] Five weeks before it was supposed to begin, Gorbachev met with Orthodox Patriarch Pimen at the Kremlin. An official from the Council of Religious Affairs described the importance of the meeting in this way: "Until Gorbachev received the patriarch . . . it was B.C. Afterward it was A.D."[73]

The Millennium celebration was put on in a grand fashion.[74] The Kremlin and the Bolshoi Theater were opened to the celebration, and for a few short weeks, "it seemed as though the Communist Party had yielded primacy to Holy Russia, which was being reborn before the eyes of an astonished population."[75]

The effects of the Millennium celebration were many-fold. Bibles were allowed to be published and imported.[76] Protestants were able to invite foreign evangelists, including Billy Graham and Luis Palau.[77] Soviet evangelicals were able to do ministry freely.[78] As a result, huge numbers of people heard the Gospel and mass baptisms occurred frequently during the summers of 1989 and 1990.[79]

---

70. Bourdeaux, "Introduction," 7; Hill, *Soviet Union on the Brink*, 251, 255.
71. Hill, *Soviet Union on the Brink*, 262.
72. Hill, *Soviet Union on the Brink*, 258–59.
73. Forest, *Religion in the New Russia*, 6, 8.
74. Forest, *Religion in the New Russia*, 11.
75. Bourdeaux, "Glasnost and the Gospel," 114.
76. Sawatsky, "Protestantism in the USSR," in *Religious Policy*, 333.
77. Sawatsky, "Protestantism in the USSR," in *Religious Policy*, 334; Znakevich, "Evangelism and Church Planting," 108–9, 111.
78. Chaplin, "Church and Politics," 97.
79. Sawatsky, "Protestantism in the USSR," in *Religious Policy*, 334.

The Attraction of Evangelical Christianity as Communism Fell

As the Soviet Union fell, evangelical Christianity went from being marginalized to becoming a logical alternative to communism. If communist ideology claimed that there was no God and communism had now failed, it was reasonable to take a closer look at Christianity. It might have been more natural to look at historical Christianity in Russia, namely Orthodox Christianity, yet many were interested in the West that had overcome communism.

Pirrko Poysti described well some of the amazing changes that were occurring during *perestroika*:

> After the doors opened for Christian work in 1988, it was easy to gather a crowd of thousands to hear the gospel. You did not need extensive advertisement campaigns. People were hungry to hear the Word of God. Some came out of curiosity, but most were sincere in their desire to know more about God and the Bible, which for so many years had been a forbidden book.[80]

Probably some of these people had secretly become Christians earlier[81] and some were now finally repenting after having seen Christians' lives for years.[82]

Evangelical Christianity provided answers for many people's spiritual searching. People were attracted to evangelical Christianity as a new source of truth and certainty, replacing that which the Communist Party had offered. People were drawn to God as one who could guide them in times of hardship.[83] Some people desired really caring relationships, and evangelical Christianity proved not to be filled with the "superstitious lunatics" of Soviet propaganda, but to be a community of kindness and peace.[84] And yet probably the most important things for most people were the morals and values that evangelical Christianity offered. Since "society was floundering in an ideological vacuum,"[85] the idea of offering moral education in schools was introduced. This morality was something that could potentially fill the void left by the downfall of communism, which affected all of society,[86] but was particularly acute in schools.

---

80. Poysti, "Soul Winning," 6.
81. Sawatsky, "Protestantism in the USSR," in *Religious Policy*, 319.
82. Mikhail Dubovik, personal communication, April 4, 2011.
83. Wanner, "Advocating New Moralities," 279.
84. Wanner, "Advocating New Moralities," 280.
85. Solodnikov and Sokolov, "Teaching Our Kids," para. 4.
86. Kolodny et al., *Religion and the Churches*, 6.

Conclusions for the Socio-Political Context of the Former Soviet Union

Social and political forces certainly played a role in offering new opportunities for evangelicals and making their faith more attractive. Evangelicals were given a greater voice and evangelical social networks brought support, comfort, and status at a time when many people needed them, especially people from certain minority nationalities and those suffering from alcoholism. New freedoms, many coinciding with the Millennium celebration, and the period of crisis led people to search for truth and values to replace those lost with the end of communism. But were the Soviet evangelical churches ready to use these new opportunities for ministry and missions? I will turn to this question in the next chapter.

3

The Evangelical Church and Mission in the Former Soviet Union

I WILL NOW CONSIDER the state of the evangelical church in the former Soviet Union, including its readiness for and activity in missionary work. First, I will look at the evangelical church before *perestroika*. Then, I will turn to the state of the evangelical church during *perestroika* and the following years. Finally, I will look at the existing literature on the Ukrainian missionary surge from 1989 to 1999.

The State of the Evangelical Church Before *Perestroika*

The former Soviet Union has traditionally been a Christian land, with Eastern Orthodoxy becoming the official religion of Kievan Rus' in the year 988. Evangelical Christianity came to Russia in the eighteenth century, mainly through Protestant immigration from Western Europe.[1] Evangelicalism grew into a significant movement in the nineteenth century as a result of more intentional evangelical missionary work. However, evangelical churches were considered illegal until 1879[2] and were only granted full religious liberty by Tsar Nicholas II in 1905.[3] At that point, there were about 86,000 Baptists and 20,000 Evangelical Christians.[4]

With this new freedom,

---

1. Sawatsky, "Protestantism in the USSR," in *Protestantism and Politics*, 237.
2. Nikolskaya, *Russkiy protestantizm*, 24.
3. Rowe, *Russian Resurrection*, 45.
4. Sawatsky, *Soviet Evangelicals*, 27. At this point in time, Evangelical Christians had a denomination that was distinct from the Baptist denomination. Later, over the years 1944 and 1945, the two denominations would join together along with the Pentecostals to form the Union of Evangelical Christians-Baptists.

evangelicals were quick to capitalize on the new situation and organized systematic expansion. At a congress of the Evangelical Christians in 1910, [Ivan] Prokhanov set as a goal the organization of one congregation in each of 70 regions of the empire. From this one congregation five more were to be started.[5]

Yet, the Russian government and the Russian Orthodox Church continued to interfere with their work. There were cases of evangelical worship services and denominational congresses being banned, the Evangelical Christians' Bible School was shut down, and some pastors were even sent into exile.[6] Even so, the evangelical church grew, reaching a total membership of between 150,000 and 200,000 by the coming of communism in 1917.[7]

National missionary work began at this time. There was significant outreach among minority groups, and a national missionary society was founded in 1906. Due to financial difficulties, the missionary society was not able to continue its work for long, although local missionary societies furthered the ministry to some extent.[8]

Evangelical Church Growth and Decline Under Communism

During the initial years of communism, the evangelical church experienced the largest growth it had ever known up to that point. In fact, Walter Sawatsky called the period from 1917 to 1929 the "Growth Decade" of the evangelical church.[9] As mentioned earlier, the Soviet government granted evangelicals increased religious freedom since it believed that the Orthodox Church was a greater threat to the new communist government, and therefore, it hoped to draw people away from Orthodoxy by granting greater freedom to evangelicals.[10] In addition to many local ministries, Evangelical Christians sent over 600 missionaries across Russia by 1928.[11]

In 1929, evangelicals reached their peak at about 700,000 to 800,000 adult members[12] although some have claimed that the evangelical church

---

5. Sawatsky, *Soviet Evangelicals*, 36.
6. Rowe, *Russian Resurrection*, 61.
7. Rowe, *Russian Resurrection*, 91.
8. Karetnikova, "Missionary Movement in Russia," 69–70.
9. Sawatsky, *Soviet Evangelicals*, 38.
10. Latourette, *Expansion of Christianity*, 7:86; Sawatsky, *Soviet Evangelicals*, 37.
11. Prokhanoff, *Autobiography*, 153.
12. Dyck, "Revival as Church Restoration," 78; Nikolskaya, *Russkiy protestantizm*, 91.

had 10,000,000 attendees, including all children.[13] After going through many peaks and valleys in times of persecution and renewal, the evangelical church fell to about 400,000 adult members in 1989–90.[14]

Regardless of this overall loss in membership, Pankhurst noted a "shift toward evangelical Protestantism" and a "weakening of the Russian Orthodox Church."[15] Sawatsky noted that in the 1960s and 1970s the evangelical church had grown mainly in urban areas and new regions such as Siberia and Kazakhstan.[16] New evangelical youth were coming out of atheist families.[17]

It is also important to consider the reasons behind this church growth. Certainly one reason that the evangelical church experienced growth was that their members had large families.[18] Also, some atheists turned to Christ after being disillusioned by Marxism and materialism. Some became Christians after seeing the example of Christian families. Others were affected by hearing foreign radio broadcasts.[19] Despite hardships, the evangelical church survived, and at times, even grew.

Ongoing Evangelical Mission Work

Soviet evangelical churches were able to conduct some limited missionary work under communism, despite the persecution they faced. The Evangelical Christians-Baptists followed the motto "Every Baptist a missionary," and most of their success came from the efforts of laypeople.[20] Much evangelical mission work focused on the margins of society. Pentecostals, even more than Baptists, tended to gain converts from among the poor.[21] Baptists reached out to drug addicts and alcoholics.[22] Evangelicals ministered in orphanages, retirement homes, hospitals, and prisons.[23] Prior to 1988, these ministries were not large, but they would be expanded greatly in the years of freedom to come.

13. Rowe, *Russian Resurrection*, 91.
14. Hill, *Soviet Union on the Brink*, 94, 367.
15. Pankhurst, "Sacred and the Secular in the USSR," 187.
16. Sawatsky, *Soviet Evangelicals*, 420.
17. Sawatsky, "Protestantism in the USSR," in *Protestantism and Politics*, 255.
18. "Delayte uchenikami," 12.
19. Bourdeaux and Bourdeaux, *Ten Growing Soviet Churches*, 19.
20. Kolarz, *Religion in the Soviet Union*, 300–301.
21. Kolarz, *Religion in the Soviet Union*, 335.
22. Sinichkin, *Vsyo radi missii*, 210.
23. Savinskii et al., "Istoriya YeKhB."

Migration was tightly controlled under communism, so it was very difficult to travel to new places for missionary work. As it turned out, the government helped some evangelicals migrate by sending them to labor camps in remote areas where they could, in a sense, be missionaries.[24] Pentecostals were sometimes able to move as a group in order to evangelize new areas. In the Far East, through exile and deliberate migration, a Pentecostal church was formed, although it was also from this church that many emigrated out of the USSR in 1987 due to the brutality they experienced.[25] Thus, traditional missionary work was extremely difficult in Soviet times.

Nontraditional national missionary work

After 1929, church leaders could officially minister only within their own church buildings. So, evangelicals made the first week of the year (between New Year's Day and Orthodox Christmas) a special celebration, during which they would invite non-Christian friends and relatives to come hear special sermons and pray.[26] In other cases, evangelicals would try to get away from the watchful eye of the government by holding services out in the forest where they could preach freely.[27] Church services were the main focus of ministry in Soviet times.

No religious activity was allowed in public, so evangelicals used birthday parties, weddings, and funerals as opportunities to invite non-Christians and share the Gospel with them.[28] Sawatsky said that "attending funerals at gravesides . . . could best be described as an evangelistic rally."[29] Furthermore, evangelicals would use music to attract young people or to drown out government agitators who sometimes came and tried to thwart their evangelism.[30]

---

24. Kolarz, *Religion in the Soviet Union*, 320, 334.
25. Sawatsky, "Protestantism in the USSR," in *Protestantism and Politics*, 254–55.
26. Sawatsky, *Soviet Evangelicals*, 69–70.
27. Bourdeaux and Bourdeaux, *Ten Growing Soviet Churches*, 116, 119.
28. Cherevko, "Theology of Mission," 14.
29. Sawatsky, *Soviet Evangelicals*, 71.
30. Bourdeaux and Bourdeaux, *Ten Growing Soviet Churches*, 115; Sawatsky, "Protestantism in the USSR," in *Protestantism and Politics*, 255.

Foreign missionary work

During the Communist period, a few foreign Christian missions worked in the Soviet Union. The three longest-standing ones were Slaviska Missionen from Sweden, Light in the East from Germany, and the Slavic Gospel Association from the United States. Later, Brother Andrew's Open Doors, Joe Bass's Underground Evangelism, and Richard Wurmbrand's Jesus Christ to the Communist World started doing missionary work in the USSR as well.[31] All of these groups were limited in what they could do, but they did make some impact.

Radio ministry was used to evangelize through the barrier of the Iron Curtain, but its reach was limited since up until 1988 the Soviet Union invested more than one billion dollars per year to jam all Western radio programming. Despite these efforts, many Soviets were still able to listen by shortwave radio.[32] In any case, radio ministry appears to have been more effective at encouraging believers than in evangelizing unbelievers.

Resources for Evangelical Mission Work

Soviet evangelicals did not have many resources at their disposal. They named obtaining Bibles as their greatest need, followed by obtaining Christian literature.[33] Thus, it is important first to consider the access evangelicals had to these vital resources.

Bibles and Christian literature

Under communism, Soviet evangelicals had very little access to Bibles or opportunities for serious Bible study.[34] Many non-Christians were also interested in reading the Bible. This spiritual thirst was quite surprising considering the atheist indoctrination that all Soviet children received.[35] These facts point to the significant impact a greater supply of Bibles would have.

Bibles and New Testaments were very limited resources in the Soviet Union after the Law of Religious Associations was passed in 1929. After 10,000 incomplete Bibles and 25,000 New Testaments were printed in Kyiv

---

31. Sawatsky, *Soviet Evangelicals*, 394–96.
32. Hill, *Soviet Union on the Brink*, 202–3.
33. Sawatsky, "Protestantism in the USSR," in *Protestantism and Politics*, 56.
34. Sawatsky, *Soviet Evangelicals*, 471.
35. Deyneka and Deyneka, *Christians in the Shadow of the Kremlin*, 11–12.

in 1927, no Bibles were printed in the USSR until 1956.[36] So, in the 1950s and 1960s, many churches had to share a handful of Bibles, passing them between families and making more copies by hand.[37] This lack of Bibles coincided with severe persecutions under Stalin and Khrushchev.[38] Yet, Christians survived with what Bibles they had.

In 1968, the government allowed the Bible to be published again, but only in limited quantities until 1988.[39] Unofficially, in 1969 underground Christian publishers invented a printing machine to produce Bibles and Christian literature. In particular, *Bring Them the News about Christ* and *Revival That We Need* by Oswald Smith became favorites among Christian young people.[40]

By 1975, the majority of preachers had a New Testament, and the evangelical church's goal became to supply each Christian household with a Bible. Then, the goal became to provide each newly baptized believer with a Bible.[41] Foreign missionaries made great efforts to import Bibles and other Christian literature.[42] For example, from 1974 to 1984, the United Bible Societies provided the Union of Evangelical Christians-Baptists (the registered church) with 100,000 copies of Christian literature in Russian and German. This included printing the *Bratskii Vestnik (Fraternal Herald)*, an 80-page Christian journal.[43] However, only about 11% of the approximately 4.1 million Bibles and New Testaments that Soviet evangelicals received between 1945 and 1986 were legally imported or printed in the Soviet Union.[44] The rest of the copies were smuggled in by foreign missionaries.

Other resources

Evangelicals faced severe limitations in most resources. Religious groups had lost the right to own property in 1918, a fact that the government had used many times to stop their activities.[45] Unregistered churches had no official access to buildings, so they held their services in private residences,

36. Sawatsky, *Soviet Evangelicals*, 40.
37. Znakevich, "Evangelism and Church Planting," 84.
38. Latourette, *Expansion of Christianity*, vol. 7; Rowe, *Russian Resurrection*.
39. Rowe, *Russian Resurrection*.
40. Znakevich, "Evangelism and Church Planting," 93–94.
41. Sawatsky, "After the Glasnost Revolution," 54, 56.
42. Sawatsky, *Soviet Evangelicals*, 412.
43. Parsons, *Christianity Today in the USSR*, 66.
44. Hill, *Soviet Union on the Brink*, 270.
45. Bourdeaux, "Glasnost and the Gospel," 115.

in the forest, or in secret locations.[46] In March 1990, a new property law was passed, allowing religious groups to own buildings again.[47]

Financially, evangelicals were also seriously limited. Despite some increased in income in 1979, the Union of Evangelical Christians-Baptists struggled financially in the late 1980s due to a loss of membership combined with commitments to building projects and supporting evangelists.[48] Foreign missionaries offered some financial help,[49] but a serious deficit of resources remained.

Potential for New Missionaries

Despite all these difficulties, Soviet evangelical churches had great potential for sending out new missionaries. There was a resurgence of young people who were more ready than the older generation to be bold, not having experienced the times of harshest persecution under Stalin and Khrushchev. In addition, there were believers in underground churches who were used to standing against the government.

Growing activity of evangelical youth

In the 1970s and 1980s, many young people became active in evangelical churches. Even though the government officially reported just three percent of youth as interested in religion, many Westerners observed an increasing number of religious youth during this period.[50] As early as 1974, various public figures requested help with special ministries to youth and children, despite religious work with children being illegal.[51] In 1989, many youth were active in ministry in Evangelical Christian-Baptist churches, doing music ministry, preaching, serving as deacons, and engaging in pastoral ministry.[52] That generation of children was taught the importance of bringing the Gospel to others.[53] Reflecting back, Ruvim Voloshin noted that the most

---

46. Znakevich, "Evangelism and Church Planting," 84.
47. Bourdeaux, "Glasnost and the Gospel," 115.
48. Sawatsky, *Soviet Evangelicals*, 426–27; Sawatsky, "Protestantism in the USSR," in *Religious Policy*, 340–41.
49. Sawatsky, *Soviet Evangelicals*, 403.
50. Yelensky, "Religiosity in Ukraine," 214.
51. Sawatsky, "After the Glasnost Revolution," 56.
52. Savinskii et al., "Istoriya YeKhB."
53. Dyck, "Missiya yevangel'skikh tserkvey," 211–12.

active people in ministry during the 1990s were those who had repented and became Christians as young people during the 1970s and 1980s.[54]

The demographics of the increase of youth in the evangelical church are very interesting as well. The increase of religious youth was concentrated in larger cities, with a greater number of new male members than female ones and a greater number of those with at least a high school or trade school education.[55] With the long-standing deficit of men and educated members in Soviet evangelical churches, these trends certainly increased the potential of evangelicals to take steps forward. Since the Soviet Union had undergone "massive urbanization,"[56] the concentration of active Christian youth in cities was particularly strategic for future ministry.

Furthermore, certain people helped inspire the new generation of Christian youth. Many evangelical pastors had been imprisoned, and they became heroes to young people.[57] In addition, several traveling preachers gave a challenge:

> They visited churches, preached the Gospel, and encouraged and taught believers how to be faithful to God and successful witnesses of Christ. They paid special attention to Christian youth and taught them to obey the Word of God. They organized special seminars and trained pastors, youth leaders, and youth to spread the Gospel in an atheistic society. Young people attended the seminars for several reasons: they liked to be together, they liked to learn more about the practical life of a Christian, and they wanted to see those brave pastors and evangelists who had become their heroes.
>
> Those traveling evangelists taught believers that every church should be a missionary church, every family a missionary family, and every believer a missionary.[58]

Potential for mission from the underground church

During 1944 and 1945, the three largest Protestant denominations—the Evangelical Christians, the Baptists, and the Pentecostals—united to form

---

54. Voloshin, "Analiz razvitiya."

55. Sawatsky, "Protestantism in the USSR," in *Protestantism and Politics*, 255; Yelensky, "Religiosity in Ukraine," 214.

56. Pankhurst, "Sacred and the Secular in the USSR," 185.

57. Znakevich, "Evangelism and Church Planting," 94.

58. Znakevich, "Evangelism and Church Planting," 95.

the Union of Evangelical Christians-Baptists.[59] The Soviet government had some hand in this unification, which made the church easier to infiltrate and control.[60] Over time, the church fell more and more in line with the wishes of the government. After leaders made such statements as that the goal of church services was "not the attraction of new members but satisfaction of the spiritual needs of believers" and after they emphasized the importance of avoiding "harmful missionary tendencies," an "initiative group" decided to challenge the leadership in August 1961.[61] This group broke away to form an unregistered, underground union of Evangelical Christians-Baptists. The registered church would officially apologize for its "anti-evangelical instructions" in 1966, but the damage had already been done, and the underground church remained separate.[62]

The underground Evangelical Christian-Baptist Church immediately declared its first goal to be "the preaching of the Gospel."[63] They focused on evangelism and youth work and were creative when opportunities arose during *perestroika*, inviting the first foreign evangelists to the Soviet Union.[64] The unregistered church was definitely more active in evangelism than the registered church.[65] The underground church also had the advantage of having some good, intellectual leaders who stood out in stark contrast to the "fanatics portrayed by the Soviet press."[66]

There was also a group of underground Pentecostal churches that broke away from the registered Evangelical Christians-Baptists. Despite persecution, these Pentecostals were able to preach the Gospel and plant new churches in smaller towns and villages. They sent out small teams to evangelize on weekends and encouraged their people by sharing about their ministry experiences.[67] Thus, these underground Pentecostal churches were also ready for bigger opportunities of mission work.

---

59. The registered Union of Evangelical Christians-Baptists is commonly referred to as simply the Baptist Union. Unregistered and autonomous Baptist churches are not a part of this union. Pentecostals were part of the Baptist Union until 1989 when they left to form their own union.

60. Nikolskaya, *Russkiy protestantizm*; Rowe, *Russian Resurrection*.

61. Sawatsky, "Protestantism in the USSR," in *Protestantism and Politics*, 245.

62. Hill, *Soviet Union on the Brink*, 362.

63. Sawatsky, *Soviet Evangelicals*, 427.

64. Nikolskaya, *Russkiy protestantizm*, 275; Sawatsky, *Soviet Evangelicals*, 471; Sawatsky, "Protestantism in the USSR," in *Religious Policy*, 343.

65. Nikolskaya, *Russkiy protestantizm*, 165.

66. Pankhurst, "Sacred and the Secular in the USSR," 182.

67. Znakevich, "Evangelism and Church Planting," 104–5.

Potential for Missionary Work at the Beginning of Perestroika

The state of mission at the end of Soviet times was one of both potential and limitations. Soviet evangelical churches had some advantages: a strong faith, a growing and eager youth population, and an active underground church. Bibles and other Christian literature were becoming more available. Other resources were still limited. The picture of the Soviet evangelical churches at the end of the 1980s was a mixture of strengths and weaknesses. Very little missionary work was going on, but there was a clear desire for more from both inside and outside the Soviet Union.

The State of the Evangelical Church During and After *Perestroika*

As *perestroika* started to shake the foundations of the Soviet Union, the evangelical church was able to take new steps amidst increasing religious freedom and interest. Yet, the evangelical church was not entirely ready for this radical change, and so the church did not grow as it might have. In order to understand what happened and how it might have affected the Ukrainian missionary surge, I will first look at the growth and decline of the evangelical church in the former Soviet Union, then I will take a brief look at the impact of foreign missionary work, and finally I will turn to some of the problems that affected church growth and the potential for missionary work.

Evangelical Church Growth and Decline During *Perestroika* and After Communism

Perestroika and the Fall of Communism led huge numbers of people to show interest in the evangelical church.[68] Although there was some church growth, it was not nearly as much as some anticipated. Finding exact figures is difficult, given the massive changes going on and the establishment of many new churches across newly-established countries, often in newly-established denominations. Even the largest denomination of Soviet times, the Union of Evangelical Christians-Baptists, experienced a split as a large group of Pentecostal churches left to form their own union in 1989—a union which was shortly thereafter split again.[69] In any case, we will briefly

---

68. Glick, *Chto govoryat novoobrashchennye*, 5; Golovin, "Worldview," 1–2.
69. Glukhovskiy, *Kratkaya istoriya*, 356–57, 365–73.

look at the statistics that are available on evangelical churches from the two largest countries of the former Soviet Union: Russia and Ukraine.

According to *Operation World*, evangelicals in Russia grew from 831,000 in 1990 to 1,000,000 in 2000[70] whereas Ukraine's evangelical population actually shrank from 1,418,600 in 1990 to 1,358,000 in 2000.[71] It is likely that the 1990 figure in *Operation World* for Ukraine was too high, comparing the number of Evangelical Christians-Baptists with figures from Daniel Glick,[72] so it is possible that some church growth actually did take place. Another possibility is that the emigration of evangelicals offset much of the church growth that was happening. Regardless, the growth in both Russia and Ukraine was not that large considering the masses of people that showed interest in the evangelical church in the 1990s.

In order to try to see the dynamic of growth, I will look at the number of baptisms that occurred in Russia and Ukraine for the Union of Evangelical Christians-Baptists. In Russia, baptisms reached their peak in 1993 at 1,479 for the year, dropping to less than half that number in 1998.[73] In Ukraine, baptisms in the Union of Evangelical Christians-Baptists reached their peak in 1999 at 10,621, dropping to less than half that number by 2005.[74] However, the increase in baptisms in Ukraine was steady only through 1993 (reaching 9,798), after which there was an ebb and flow of baptisms up through 2001, after which the decrease was significant.[75] Looking at the number of religious communities, the highest growth occurred in 1989 (over 50%) while the lowest growth occurred in 1994 (1.8%).[76] Considering these statistics, it seems clear that church growth occurred primarily through 1993, after which the growth was not that significant.

Since missionary surges are sometimes connected with awakenings and revivals, it is interesting to consider whether an awakening occurred in Russia and Ukraine. According to these statistics above, there does not appear to be any such connection. Sergei Golovin actually called the "awakening" an "illusion."[77] Thus, although there was certainly a very interested mission field, the evangelical churches of Russia and Ukraine

70. Johnstone, *Operation World*, 5th ed., 467; Johnstone and Mandryk, *Operation World*, 6th ed., 540.
71. Johnstone, *Operation World*, 5th ed., 551; Johnstone and Mandryk, *Operation World*, 6th ed., 645.
72. Glick, *Chto govoryat novoobrashchennye*, 7.
73. Sipko, "Sotsial'nyy portret rossiyanina."
74. Glick, *Chto govoryat novoobrashchennye*, 7.
75. Glick, *Chto govoryat novoobrashchennye*, 7.
76. Kolodny et al., *Religion and the Churches*, 28–29.
77. Golovin, "Worldview," 2.

do not appear to have experienced significant church growth, with most growth that did occur coming by 1993.

Foreign Missionary Work in the Former Soviet Union

As mentioned in the introduction, the number of Protestant missionaries grew to over 5,600 from 561 different missionary organizations by 1997.[78] Many missionaries came with a sense of urgency, fearing the door for missionary work would soon close. Walter Sawatsky called this time the "frantic evangelism phase."[79] Thus, many of these missionaries evangelized without long-term strategies.

Yet, there were some good results from foreign missionary work. Those mission organizations that had previous experience in the Soviet Union were often strategic and effective in ministry. Peter Penner concluded that there were many positive results from foreign missionary work, including national leadership training through theological education, effective church ministry, mission, and evangelism.[80] After government limitations on what could be received through the mail were removed, "Very quickly the warehouses in the West containing Russian language literature were depleted."[81] The United Bible Societies, through various distributors, provided 850,000 Scriptures to the Soviet Union in 1989.[82] Thus, some good did come out of the large expansion in foreign missionary work.

Despite these good points, one big problem was that many foreign missionaries failed to establish healthy partnerships with national churches. Many did not work with national churches at all, thus creating "mission without ecclesiology."[83] Of course, national evangelical churches were also responsible for not taking more initiative with these new converts.[84] To another extreme, sometimes foreign missionaries worked with nationals but forced them to follow their rules strictly, ignoring cultural differences and individual gifts. This kind of control also often led to poor long-term results.[85] One additional difficulty came from the Russian Orthodox Church, which felt that its people were being stolen by the great wave of Western

---

78. Deyneka and Deyneka, "Evangelical Foreign Missionaries in Russia," 56–57.
79. Sawatsky, "Return of Mission," 99.
80. Penner, "Critical Evaluation," 145.
81. Sawatsky, "Protestantism in the USSR," in *Religious Policy*, 334.
82. Hill, *Soviet Union on the Brink*, 272.
83. Sawatsky, "Return of Mission," 107.
84. Sipko, "Sotsial'nyy portret rossiyanina."
85. Penner, "Critical Evaluation," 130–31.

missionaries. In response, the Russian Orthodox Church advocated new laws to restrict foreign missionaries.[86] So, there were quite mixed results from foreign missionaries over this period of time.

Problems That Affected Church Growth

As indicated above, the evangelical church did not grow in proportion either to the freedom it gained or to the massive interest shown by society. I will now explore several factors behind this lack of growth. The first two factors are related to the activity of those in the church and the latter three factors are related to changes occurring in society as a whole.

Separate evangelical church subculture

Although the evangelical church had prayed for revival for many years, it was not really ready for one. It was ready for Christ to return, for persecution or emigration, but not for influencing society.[87] Evangelicals had learned how to survive, but at the cost of forming a subculture isolated from the rest of society.

One reason that the evangelical church formed a subculture was that it lost some of its best leaders during the years of persecution.[88] This loss led in turn to the loss of a missionary spirit. Over time the church developed a distinct Christian language that non-Christians could not understand and a strict Christian uniform of lifestyle that non-Christians could not accept.[89] The answer to many critical questions about the church was "because it is done this way in our denomination."[90] Taras Pristupa made the bold assertion that the evangelical church had become man-centered instead of God-centered.[91] New leaders with a missionary spirit were needed.

Despite these obstacles, a few evangelicals without significant education or resources started sharing the Gospel. Many of these evangelists were rebuked by church leadership. Yet, because of these bold heroes of faith, non-Christians and new Christians began coming to evangelical churches

---

86. Deyneka and Deyneka, "Evangelical Foreign Missionaries in Russia," 57.
87. Sinichkin, *Vsyo radi missii*, 209.
88. Smirnov, "Missionerskaya strategiya."
89. Pristupa, "Prepyatstviya."
90. Puzynin, *Gospel Christians*, 212–13.
91. Pristupa, "Prepyatstviya."

in 1988.[92] Unfortunately, many of these newcomers could not find a place where they belonged. They did not find acceptance or fellowship.[93] So, many of them drifted away, saying that they had tried it but discovered that it was not for them.[94] The evangelical church clearly lacked readiness for the freedom that came after 1988. This fact makes the missionary surge that would follow even more surprising.

Emigration of evangelicals

As the Iron Curtain began to weaken, there were opportunities for Soviet citizens, including evangelicals, to emigrate. Many Baptists were able to leave the USSR between 1976 and 1980.[95] As communist ideology became more and more irrelevant, people began looking for ways out, many through emigration.[96] In 1988, 108,000 Soviet citizens emigrated, with 228,600 the following year.[97] The Soviet German community was swept with "a wave of emigration fever"[98] that led to huge numbers of Mennonites and Baptists leaving, causing a leadership drain on the churches. Potential leaders of a missionary movement were lost.

On the other hand, many of these emigrants were replaced. In considering the Tashkent church in Uzbekistan, Nalitov points out that starting in 1989, the church lost preachers, choir directors, singers, and long-standing church members. Yet, many new believers came into the church who became new preachers and singers.[99] Thus, at the very least, the loss of some church leaders opened the door for new leadership from the growing church youth population.

Difficulties due to low biblical literacy in society

In the 1990s in the former Soviet Union, the general interest in Christianity was real, but there was difficulty in helping non-Christians to

---

92. Smirnov, "Missionerskaya strategiya."
93. Golovin, "Worldview," 16–17.
94. Golovin, *Mirovozzrenie*, 59.
95. Nikolskaya, *Russkiy protestantizm*, 282.
96. Reimer, "Mission in Post-Perestroika Russia."
97. Hill, *Soviet Union on the Brink*, 324.
98. Sawatsky, "Return of Mission," 100.
99. Nalitov, "Yubiley Tashkenskoy tserkvi."

truly understand the nature of the Gospel.[100] Generations of people had grown up without Christianity, being constantly immersed in atheistic teaching.[101] The Soviet Union had become an "amnesiac society," having forgotten about its Christian roots.[102] Of course, some might dispute these statements,[103] but the level of biblical knowledge for most Soviet people was certainly quite low.

Without basic biblical literacy, the task of evangelism was difficult. As Sergei Golovin shared, "The good news does not make sense without comprehending the bad news."[104] Thus, interested non-Christians were open to learn, but they needed to be taught from the very beginning. Unfortunately, many Christians, whether national or foreign, were not aware of this need or were simply unwilling to go through the effort of long-term discipleship. So, much potential fruit was lost. Furthermore, a group of people was formed in the post-Soviet world who believed in Christianity but did not belong to a church. This tendency was strongest among young people.[105] This group also came about, at least to some extent, due to a lack of discipleship.

The resurgence of traditional Orthodoxy

Many people of the post-Soviet world during *perestroika* turned to evangelical Christianity because the Russian Orthodox Church was perceived to have compromised itself with the communist government. But in fact, many people wanted to return to Orthodoxy once it had restored itself from compromise.[106] Evangelical Christianity could not provide an historical national identity the way that Russian Orthodoxy did since it was not connected to the state or nationalism. Many people began to see evangelicals as a "cultural other."[107] So, Orthodoxy started drawing people back from evangelical Christianity on a popular level.

Many Russians desire a faith that is more mystical than that which characterizes evangelical Christianity.[108] Russian Orthodoxy provided a mysticism

---

100. Sawatsky, "Protestantism in the USSR," in *Protestantism and Politics*, 262.
101. Golovin, *Bibleyskaya strategiya blagovestiya*, 30–31.
102. Davie, "Europe," 80.
103. E.g., Wanner, *Communities of the Converted*, 7; Zuckerman, *Society without God*, 22.
104. Golovin, "Worldview," 53.
105. Lambert, "Trends in Religious Feeling," 111, 114.
106. Gruenwald, "Icon in Russian Art, Society and Culture," 176.
107. Wanner, *Communities of the Converted*, 14.
108. Murarka, "Religion in Russia Today," 2842.

and reverence that evangelical Christianity often did not.[109] Thus, people in the post-Soviet world sometimes did not feel comfortable in evangelical church worship, preferring a Russian Orthodox style of worship.

Russian Orthodoxy gained additional power through being declared a privileged religion by the Russian Parliament on September 19, 1997.[110] This new law made religious activity of non-privileged groups (i.e., evangelicals) more difficult, and thus, had a negative effect on evangelical churches and missionary work.

Economic and societal instability

In addition, many people turned away from evangelical Christianity because they were so focused on their own problems. They had a "present orientation."[111] How could they be expected to spend so much time in church services? Why should they worry about tomorrow if they weren't sure how to make it through today? Of course, some would go ahead and light a candle for prayer in an Orthodox Church to give them a chance for a better future. But that was about all the time and resources that they would spend on it.

Other people were so frustrated with the changes that had taken place that they longed for the values and stability of the Soviet Union. Yurchak referred to this as "post-Soviet nostalgia,"[112] as people remembered the "very real humane values, ethics, friendships, and creative possibilities that the reality of socialism afforded."[113] These people had a "past orientation."[114] They were often older people who had been treated with honor under communism (especially veterans) and had looked forward to a comfortable retirement. After the Fall of Communism, many of these people could barely make ends meet with their state pensions and they were often pushed aside by younger people. Evangelical Christianity could not restore their former positions in society.

---

109. Wanner, *Communities of the Converted*, 137.
110. Kartavenko, "Sluzhite Gospodu," 4.
111. Kearney, *World View*, 96.
112. Yurchak, *Everything Was Forever*, 8.
113. Yurchak, *Everything Was Forever*, 8.
114. Kearney, *World View*, 97.

The Lack of Ministry Opportunities at Home Led Some Into Missions

Yet, despite all of these problems that negatively affected church growth, one problem actually contributed to the Ukrainian evangelical missionary surge. Missionary work provided new ministry opportunities for several different groups of people. As previously noted, the number of young people, and especially young men, in churches grew significantly during the final years of communism, particularly in cities, leading them to look for ways to minister beyond their church walls.[115] Since most ministry in Ukrainian evangelical churches is given to males with seniority, young men often have to wait a long time before being entrusted with ministry leadership. Going into missions offered them an alternative.

Also, young women (and even children) were able to find opportunities for ministry on the mission field that they could not get in their home churches. In Light of the Gospel's *Information Bulletins*, interviews were published promoting the value of women and children (and families in general) on the mission field.[116] Having women and children on the mission field was common for Light of the Gospel, which proved to be an advantage for the mission since diversity in an organization is a competitive advantage in dealing with diverse people and unexpected circumstances.[117]

Thus, there were many new opportunities for men, women, and children on the mission field that did not exist in their home churches. Similar to the way that migration sometimes happens, there was both the pull factor (attractive new opportunities for ministry on the mission field) and the push factor (limited ministry opportunities at home).[118] So, there were both positive and negative ecclesial factors involved in the Ukrainian missionary surge of the 1990s.

Conclusions Regarding the State of the Evangelical Church

Thus, the evangelical church experienced some real growth in the 1990s, but it was unable to take advantage of all the opportunities it had gained

---

115. Sawatsky, "Protestantism in the USSR," in *Protestantism and Politics*, 255; Yelensky, "Religiosity in Ukraine," 214.

116. Malov, "Chto znachit byt' docher'yu missionera?!," 4–5; Malov, "Zhenshchina—propovednik, missioner?!," 2, 1998, 4–7; Malov, "Zhenshchina—propovednik, missioner?!," 3, 1998, 4–7.

117. Bolman and Deal, *Reframing Organizations*, 290–91.

118. Iosifides, *Qualitative Methods in Migration Studies*, 15.

from the greatest religious freedom it had ever known. Many factors were involved, including some of the leadership of the evangelical church either emigrating or being stuck in their own subculture. There were also societal factors that negatively affected evangelical church growth, including a lack of biblical literacy, a resurgence of Orthodoxy, and continued instability. In addition, much foreign missionary work was not focused on helping Ukrainian national churches and missions.

Yet, the potential for missions that existed at the beginning of *perestoika* did yield some fruit. The increase in the number of church youth and the lack of opportunity for them in many churches led them to consider missionary work. Where there was no church, both young men and women of faith were needed. Thus, in addition to taking advantage of many opportunities to evangelize within Ukraine, a growing number of Ukrainians looked to evangelize beyond their borders.

The Ukrainian Missionary Surge From 1989 Onward

Very little literature on the Ukrainian missionary surge in the 1990s exists. As mentioned earlier, not much was documented by those involved in the surge at the time. However, the limited documentation available in English, Russian, and Ukrainian will provide some foundation for further research through interviews.

Why Ukraine?

Ukraine is known as the Bible Belt of the former Soviet Union.[119] Although its population was three times smaller than that of Russia when the Soviet Union broke up in 1991, it still had significantly more evangelicals. Ukraine had the largest numbers of Baptists and Pentecostals, both registered and unregistered.[120] In addition, Ukraine became a center for theological education, evangelical publishing, and Sunday schools[121]—three factors that helped increase the number of potential missionaries.

Ukraine had a number of other advantages for missionary work as well. In the 1990s, nearly all Ukrainians could speak Russian fluently (about one-third spoke Russian as their first language), allowing them to

---

119. Pelkmans, "Introduction: Post-Soviet Space," 10.

120. Hill, *Soviet Union on the Brink*, 111; Wanner, "Advocating New Moralities," 274.

121. Wanner, *Communities of the Converted*, 1; Yelensky, "Religiosity in Ukraine," 214.

travel easily across the former Soviet Union.[122] Ukraine has a history of religious pluralism and has been the home of a large number of different ethnicities,[123] which has allowed evangelicalism to grow much more than in areas of the former Soviet Union where Russian Orthodoxy or Islam have been dominant.

Finally, it is interesting to note that it was the western side of Ukraine that had the largest numbers and greatest activity of evangelicals.[124] The western border of Ukraine had changed a number of times, so some evangelicals who used to live in Poland ended up living in the Soviet Union. This area was more exposed to the West and western religions than most of the rest of the Soviet Union. All these factors contributed to Ukraine becoming a missionary sending country.

Overview of Ukrainian Missions

The Millennium of Christianity celebration of 1988 was a turning point for evangelism and missionary work.[125] From 1989 to 1993, hundreds of mission organizations were founded in Ukraine. Some were quite small while others became large, successful entities, engaging in evangelistic and cross-cultural ministries.[126] Particularly in the area of cross-cultural missions, Ukrainians were much more active than their neighbors in Russia, having more than twice the number of evangelical missionaries.[127] Scott Klingsmith further observed that

> Ukraine has by far the largest and most active missionary force. Already by 1993, Ukrainian churches had sent more cross-cultural missionaries than the rest of the ECE [Eastern Central European] countries. They have sent missionaries to Turkey, the former Yugoslavia, Germany, and China, as well as to [other parts of] the former USSR.[128]

Numerous independent mission organizations were founded in Ukraine during this period. About 100 evangelical mission or charity organizations were at work by 1990, often working in connection with Bible schools and

122. Wanner, "Appeal of Evangelicalism," 258.
123. Wanner, *Communities of the Converted*, 13.
124. Sawatsky, "Protestantism in the USSR," in *Religious Policy*, 331.
125. Mokienko, "Modern Protestants in Ukraine," 315.
126. Johnstone, *Operation World*, 5th ed., 553.
127. Johnstone and Mandryk, *Operation World*, 6th ed., 543, 750.
128. Klingsmith, *Missions Beyond the Wall*, 54.

foreign mission societies.[129] Of course, not all of these mission organizations were significantly involved in sending out missionaries. Grigorii Komendant, then president of the Baptist Union in Moscow, cynically commented in 1991 that there were 314 missions working, of which, "14 of them are actually working; the other 300 are just collecting money."[130]

According to Torsten Löfstedt, Ukrainian and Belarusian Pentecostal churches sent out thousands of missionaries to Russia in the late eighties and early nineties.[131] Although this figure may be inflated by including many short-term missionaries, it is true that for one major Russian Pentecostal denomination (the Russian Church of Christians of Evangelical Faith), as of 2005, 42 of the 56 bishops were originally missionaries from Ukraine or Belarus.[132] In any case, the Ukrainian Pentecostal contribution to missions work in Russia has been significant.

Foreign Influences on Ukrainian Missions

As mentioned earlier, there was a great influx of foreign mission agencies following the Millennium celebration in 1988. Some foreigners helped support national missionaries and motivate the formation of national mission agencies. For example, the Assemblies of God of the US supported hundreds of Ukrainian missionaries as well as helping in the publishing and delivering of Bibles and in the establishment of various Ukrainian seminaries.[133] Not all of these foreign mission organizations were from the West, however. The Latvian Christian Mission helped inspire some Ukrainians to start mission work after having been attracted to the way the Latvians had "struck a balance between service and evangelism."[134] Interestingly, the Latvian mission was founded by Joseph Bondarenko, who was originally from Ukraine.[135]

After the celebration of a Millennium of Christianity in 1988, the second key event for the Ukrainian missionary surge was the Moscow Congress on Evangelization which took place in October 1990 sponsored by the Lausanne Committee for World Evangelization. Participants included 900 Soviets and 100 Westerners from various mission organizations.[136] The

129. Sawatsky, "Protestantism in the USSR," in *Religious Policy*, 344–45.
130. Sawatsky, "After the Glasnost Revolution," 59.
131. Löfstedt, "Pentecostal and Charismatic Denominations," 10.
132. Corrado, "Serving by Faith," 1.
133. Boyechko, *Neskorena tserkva*, 209–10.
134. Rowe, *Russian Resurrection*, 249.
135. Bondarenko, *KGB's Most Wanted*.
136. Rowe, *Russian Resurrection*, 257–58.

conference was a celebration of mission in which representatives from a broad spectrum of evangelical movements were able to learn from one another.[137] Exposure to the outside world, and especially to foreign churches and mission organizations, provided a new vision for the possibility of mission work.[138] This time was both motivating and enabling for Soviet missionaries, many of whom came from Ukraine.

In addition to providing vision and motivation, foreign sources helped financially support Ukrainian ministries. American and German sponsors particularly gave toward church planting and Christian broadcasting in Ukraine.[139] Some of these funds came with foreign values that negatively influenced Ukrainian missionary efforts.[140] But in any case, numerous churches, missions, seminaries, and publishing houses were established in the 1990s as a result of foreign financial support.[141]

Ukrainian National Church Support of Missions

Despite the problem of a separate evangelical church subculture having been created during Soviet times, there was some support for missionary work in Ukrainian national evangelical churches. Much of the initiative during the missionary surge was taken by parishioners instead of by traditional church leadership. The registered Union of Evangelical Christians-Baptists' leadership was particularly hesitant to support missionary work. However, in the autonomously registered and unregistered churches, the leadership was more supportive of initial mission efforts.[142] Both Baptists and Pentecostals sent out missionaries to unevangelized regions such as Siberia and Central Russia, and many of these young missionaries saw significant fruit from their work.[143]

Ukrainian National Mission Organizations

There is not a lot of documentation available about individual Ukrainian mission organizations. Most of what I have found is on the Baptist mission

---

137. Voloshin, "Analiz razvitiya."
138. Sawatsky, "Return of Mission," 101.
139. Wanner, "Advocating New Moralities," 274–75.
140. Wanner, "Missionaries of Faith and Culture," 742.
141. Lyubashchenko, "Protestantism in Ukraine," 267.
142. Hill, *Soviet Union on the Brink*, 302.
143. Znakevich, "Evangelism and Church Planting," 114–15.

Light of the Gospel, which I will address in more detail in the next section. I will include here what information I found on some other Ukrainian mission agencies. For the reader's convenience, I have included maps of Ukraine in figure 2 and the former Soviet Union in figure 3.

Figure 2. Map of Ukraine with key cities and oblasts marked. The borders internal to Ukraine show the different oblasts.

Note: Adapted from "English Map of Ukraine, without marked Oblasts," by Sven Teschke, 2004. Used under creative commons license.

In the early 1990s, Elliott and Richardson[144] reported on the work of three national mission groups, two of which were based in Ukraine (the third being the Latvian Christian Mission). These missions were Light of the Gospel, based in Rivne, with 50 full-time workers and 100 part-time workers and *Vozmozhnost'* (Possibility), based in Donetsk, with 13 full-time workers and 47 part-time workers.[145] In a later source, Vladimir Franchuk listed a number of Pentecostal mission organizations, including three that did mission work outside of Ukraine: Voice of Hope (based in Lutsk), Possibility (based in Mariupol—a city in the oblast of Donetsk, as noted above), and Good Samaritan (based in Rivne).[146] Franchuk also explained

---

144. Elliott and Richardson, "Growing Protestant Diversity."
145. Elliott and Richardson, "Growing Protestant Diversity," 198.
146. Franchuk, *Prosila Rossiya dozhdya*, 937–38.

that the mission Possibility was founded on December 9, 1989, and that he was chosen as its first president. Over its history, the mission has planted over 60 churches in the Russian regions of Udmurtia, Siberia, Sakhalin, and Kalmykia.[147] Since it was impossible to establish a legal missionary organization before 1988, Good Samaritan mission in Rivne started informally when Western Ukrainian Pentecostal churches sent Slavik Radchuk (from Rivne) and Sergei Sharapa (from Minsk) on a vision trip in the winter of 1985 to investigate the needs of the different people groups in Siberia, the far north of Russia, Central Asia, the Caucasus, Transcaucasia, and the Volga region. Following that trip, an evangelistic group was sent in the spring of 1985 to the village of Uyuk, near Kyzyl, the capital of the Tyva Republic in southern Siberia. In 1986, missionaries were sent to Irkutsk Oblast, Buryatia, and the Russian Far East.[148]

Figure 3. Map of the former Soviet Union with key cities and areas marked.

Note: Adapted from "Russia: Boundaries, Hydrography," by d-maps.com, 2016 (http:// http://www.d-maps.com/carte.php?num_car=4266&lang=en). Copyright 2016 by d-maps.com. Adapted with permission.

In 1989, the underground Good Samaritan mission began to function as the mission organization for the new Pentecostal Union of Churches of

---

147. Franchuk, *Probuzhdenie*, 638.
148. Boyechko, *Neskorena tserkva*, 269–70.

Christians of Evangelical Faith. Other regional branches of the mission were established in Lviv, Odessa, and Ivano-Frankivsk. The Rivne branch of Good Samaritan mission was officially registered in 1990, the first director of the mission being Slavik Radchuk.[149] Between 1993 and 2009, the mission held 16 three-month missionary schools, each training about 25 missionaries for work within Ukraine and abroad. As of 2010, a total of 450 missionaries have worked or are working for Good Samaritan mission, having planted 110 new Pentecostal churches.[150]

Voice of Hope mission was founded in 1990 by the Pentecostal Union of Churches of Christians of Evangelical Faith in the Volyn Oblast with Nikolai Sinyuk as its director. Voice of Hope was a consolidation of various mission groups, plus some individual missionaries. By the middle of 1992, Voice of Hope had sent missionaries to seven regions of Russia: Karelia, the Komi Republic, Tatarstan, Udmurtia, the Caucasus, and Siberia, including Yakutia. As of 2009, the mission continued to be active, having 338 missionaries working in Ukraine, Russia, and Central Europe.[151]

In 2001, Johnstone and Mandryk reported that the largest Ukrainian mission was Light of the Gospel with 350 cross-cultural workers. The mission Star of Bethlehem had 30 cross-cultural workers, YWAM (Youth with a Mission) had 12 cross-cultural workers, Christ is the Answer Crusades had 9 cross-cultural workers, and OM (Operation Mobilization) had 2 cross-cultural workers. "Various Ukrainian agencies" had another 350 cross-cultural missionaries. Regarding missions with "near cultural workers," YWAM had 41, Campus Crusade for Christ had 38, Christ is the Answer Crusades had 32, IFES (International Fellowship of Evangelical Students) had 16, Global Outreach Mission had 10, Light in the East had 9, and OM had 2.[152]

Thus, Light of the Gospel seems to have been the largest Ukrainian mission organization in the 1990s, although there were also a number of other significant mission organizations, especially Pentecostal ones. Franchuk estimated that, at its peak, there were about 300 Pentecostal Ukrainian missionaries working in Russia.[153] This is a much smaller estimate than Löfstedt[154] gave above, but it is certainly large enough that it should have appeared in *Operation World*'s statistics.[155] Perhaps these Pentecostal missions fell under

---

149. Boyechko, *Neskorena tserkva*, 272–74.
150. Boyechko, *Neskorena tserkva*, 277, 279.
151. Boyechko, *Neskorena tserkva*, 262–65.
152. Johnstone and Mandryk, *Operation World on CD ROM*, 6th ed.
153. Franchuk, *Prosila Rossiya dozhdya*, 922.
154. Löfstedt, "Pentecostal and Charismatic Denominations."
155. Johnstone and Mandryk, *Operation World on CD ROM*, 6th ed.

the various Ukrainian agencies category or perhaps they weren't reported at all. In any case, I will next examine the literature available on the Light of the Gospel mission organization and hope to find out more about Pentecostal missions through the interview process in this dissertation.

Light of the Gospel Mission

In turning to Light of the Gospel, I should first mention that I have a personal connection with the mission. Although I arrived in Ukraine after the mission disbanded, I worked at Donetsk Christian University, a school founded by Light of the Gospel. It was at that school that I was able to find Light of the Gospel's *Information Bulletins* that formed the majority of the following literature review.

Since these *Information Bulletins* were written with the goals of providing news and encouraging prayer and financial support for Light of the Gospel mission, they do not directly speak to my research question. However, they did provide some ideas of potential factors behind the missionary surge in addition to some potential people to talk to further about the surge.

The history of Light of the Gospel

I will next conduct a brief survey of the history of the missionary organization Light of the Gospel. This historical survey should allow us to see how this important Baptist missionary structure came about and developed, it being one of the facilitating factors behind the Ukrainian evangelical missionary surge of the 1990s.

THE BEGINNINGS OF LIGHT OF THE GOSPEL (1988–93)

At the time of *glasnost*, the lines between the registered and underground churches had already begun to blur as a number of churches came out of the underground church and registered autonomously (i.e., separately from the larger registered Baptist Union). A group from these autonomous Baptist churches began to cooperate with a group from the Baptist Union, and in the 1970s and 1980s these groups met together at youth meetings and conferences and worked together to obtain and distribute illegal Christian literature.[156]

---

156. Melnychuk, "Istoriya i uroki," 218.

A number of these Christians would regularly meet together for prayer, and it was out of these prayer meetings that a vision was formed to start a mission at the end of 1988. These Christians consulted with a lawyer and attempted to register their organization, and after some difficulty,[157] they were finally able to register the missionary organization Light of the Gospel on February 25, 1989.[158] The organization was directed by Sergei Tupchik[159] with Oleksii Melnychuk serving as deputy director.[160]

Changing from an Organization to an Association (1993–98)

By 1993, Light of the Gospel had grown significantly. From 13 people in 1989, the mission grew to 170 staff and missionaries who worked with another 300 volunteers. They had opened about 70 mission stations in Russia, Ukraine, Central Asia, and the Caucasus and had established four regional branches—in Yakutsk (the Eastern Branch, in Siberia), Kazan (Central Russia), Kharkiv (northeastern Ukraine) and Makiivka (the Donetsk Branch in southeastern Ukraine)—and soon would open a fifth in Moscow (Russia). Donetsk Bible College offered three different programs for potential missionaries and ministers, and the art exhibition ministry, *The Life of Jesus Christ and the Revelation*, had already helped plant several churches.[161]

Considering the state of the former Soviet Union at the time, Light of the Gospel was still seeing significant fruit as Oleksii Melnychuk observed that baptisms were happening everywhere.[162] Yet, Sergei Tupchik noted that the initial hunger for information about the Gospel had already been satisfied.[163] Thus, although the ministry of Light of the Gospel was still going well, there had been a decline in responsiveness to the Gospel.

On July 1, 1993, the missionary organization became an international association, with each of the branches becoming independent and working together voluntarily. The leadership felt that this new ministry structure was the most faithful to the original purposes and functions of the mission.

---

157. Melnychuk, "Istoriya i uroki," 219–21.
158. "Mezhdunarodnaya assotsiatsiya 'Svet Yevangeliya,'" 2.
159. Melnychuk, "Istoriya i uroki," 219.
160. Melnychuk, "Poydi i skazhi . . ." 4.
161. "Mezhdunarodnaya assotsiatsiya 'Svet Yevangeliya,'" 2–3.
162. Melnychuk, "Tret'ya konferentsiya," 4.
163. Tupchik, "Tret'ya konferentsiya," 46.

Giving could now be directed either to the Association or to any of the independent organizations.[164]

The new International Association "Light of the Gospel" took on a new director in Stanislav Kasprov,[165] with Sergei Tupchik becoming the chair of the board of trustees.[166] The new independent missions that were formed each took pieces of the original mission organization, in nearly every case focusing on a single geographical area or just one type of ministry. Thus, Evangelical Ministry took over the Kharkiv Branch.[167] The Good News mission took over the Kazan Branch.[168] The Donetsk/Makiivka Branch became Light of the Resurrection.[169] The Eastern Branch became Gospel to the East.[170] Light of the Gospel's Christian literature ministry became the Christian Charitable Publishing Foundation.[171] The Art Exhibition Ministry[172] and the Foundation for Theological Education (i.e., Donetsk Bible College[173]) became independent. Also, a new ministry based in Moscow, Pool of Bethesda—House of Mercy, joined the new International Association.[174] The only exception to the rule was the Missionary Brotherhood based in Rivne, Ukraine, which actually continued mission work in other parts of Ukraine, Russia, and Tajikistan.[175] These changes meant that Light of the Gospel would continue to send out and support Ukrainian missionaries, but would do so in a less unified way.

Over the period between 1993 and 1998, a few more structural changes took place. In January 1995, the Television and Radio Company Resurrection based in Makiivka, Ukraine, joined the Light of the Gospel Association.[176] Later, in 1996, the Christian Charitable Foundation Kindness, based in the Ternopil Oblast of Western Ukraine, joined Light of the Gospel.[177] Also in 1996, the mission Missionary Brotherhood changed its name to

164. "Mezhdunarodnaya assotsiatsiya 'Svet Yevangeliya,'" 3.
165. Kartavenko, "Zavtrashniy den' Assotsiatsii," 6.
166. Tupchik, "Mir vam," 3.
167. "Khristianskoe obshchestvo 'Evangel'skoe sluzhenie,'" 4–5.
168. "Khristianskoe obshchestvo 'Dobraya Vest','" 1, 1994, 6–7.
169. "Khristianskoe obshchestvo 'Svet Voskreseniya,'" 1, 1994, 8–10.
170. "Khristianskaya missiya 'Evangelie—Vostoku,'" 15.
171. "Khristianskiy blagotvoritel'nyy izdatel'skiy fond," 12–13.
172. "Vystavka 'Zhizn' Iisusa,'" 11.
173. "Fond teologicheskogo obrazovaniya," 14.
174. "Vifezda—dom miloserdiya," 15.
175. "Khristianskoe obshchestvo 'Missionerskoe Bratstvo,'" 2–3.
176. "Soobshcheniya," 1, 1995, 1.
177. "Khristianskiy blagotvoritel'nyy fond 'Dobrota,'" 50.

Hope to People.[178] Finally, in 1997, Stanislav Kasprov and Sergei Tupchik turned over their respective roles to new director Leonid Kartavenko and new board chair Oleksii Melnychuk.[179] It was under this new leadership that the office of Light of the Gospel was moved from Rivne to Kyiv, Ukraine, to improve communication.[180]

Disintegration

Light of the Gospel no longer exists today. At the end of the 1990s, the leadership decided that *disintegration* (to use Melnychuk's term[181]) of the Association was the best choice to allow for the independence of the various individual mission organizations.[182] Oleksii Melnychuk explained that Light of the Gospel had been like a launch vehicle for a rocket. Once it had fulfilled its mission, the launch vehicle was no longer needed. Light of the Gospel had launched local churches and denominations into missions by giving an example of what to do.[183]

Some factors behind the surge of missionaries through Light of the Gospel

On the basis of the documentation available, I tried to discern some potential factors that influenced the missionary work of Light of the Gospel mission. This data seemed to be best organized using the five categories of factors of missionary surges from the rows of table A1 in Appendix A (spiritual, socio-political, ecclesial, leadership, and financial).

Spiritual factors

Since Light of the Gospel's *Information Bulletins* were written with the intent to encourage Ukrainian church members both to support missionaries and potentially to go as missionaries, it is not surprising that spiritual ideas were emphasized. These spiritual ideas can be grouped as three potential factors that influenced the Ukrainian evangelical missionary surge.

178. "Mezhdunarodnaya obshchestvennaya blagotvoritel'naya khristianskaya organizatsiya," 3–4, 1996, 34.
179. Tupchik, "Mir vam," 3.
180. Kartavenko, "Zavtrashniy den' Assotsiatsii," 7.
181. Melnychuk, "Istoriya i uroki."
182. Melnychuk, "Istoriya i uroki," 224–25.
183. Melnychuk, "Istoriya i uroki," 225.

The centrality of Jesus Christ and prayer

The main symbol for Light of the Gospel was Jesus Christ. An advertisement for an evangelistic outreach in 1990 asserted that Jesus Christ is the answer for everyone's problems.[184] Jesus Christ's story was also told through Light of the Gospel's The Life of Jesus Christ art exhibition ministry, which was founded by Pyotr Kislyak and taken all over the Soviet Union.[185]

Light of the Gospel valued complete dependence on the Lord and prayer.[186] Oleksii Melnychuk shared how the first director of Light of the Gospel, Sergei Tupchik, loved to encourage them to pray more.[187] The mission dedicated every third Thursday to fasting and prayer and had 84 different groups of people praying for them as early as 1990.[188] Furthermore, they did not just pray for themselves and their own mission, but in the first *Information Bulletin*, the leadership of Light of the Gospel encouraged prayer for the whole world, including the Soviet Union, for the month of January 1990.[189]

The salvation of souls and the spread of the Gospel

As to a general vision for ministry, we can look to Light of the Gospel's first director, Sergei Tupchik, who said that the mission organization's biggest interest was the salvation of souls.[190] Light of the Gospel's culture had a missionary spirit.[191] Hundreds were called to preach the Gospel in Siberia, European Russia, the Far East, and the Far North. They did not think about their status or financial support, but were focused on one idea: to save even a few.

A later Light of the Gospel director, Leonid Kartavenko, shared a vision to go to remote villages in the most severe environments of Yakutia, Siberia. On December 20, 1998, a missionary expedition was planned to travel from Moscow to Chukotka, covering 20,000 kilometers (12,400 miles), including 7,000 kilometers (4,300 miles) where there were no roads.[192] This story both

---

184. "*Informatsionnyy byulleten*'," 1.
185. "Vystavka," 2, 1992, 19.
186. Tupchik, *Informatsionnyy byulleten'*, 2–3.
187. Melnychuk, "Istoriya i uroki," 219.
188. "Molitva," 16–17.
189. "Vsemirnyy molitvennyy plan," 4–6.
190. Tupchik, "Spaseny, chtoby spasat'," 5.
191. Menshov, "My propoveduem Khrista," 5–6.
192. Kartavenko, "... Budete mne svidetelyami," 2–3.

emphasizes the vision of Light of the Gospel and serves as a concrete expression of its desire to spread the Gospel to the "end of the earth" (Acts 1:8).

Following one's calling

Taras Pristupa, the first Director of Missionary Work, declared that missionaries are sent by God Himself. Each missionary needed to obey God's calling above what his or her pastor, church, or mission might say. Those in authority, he said, also need to be attentive to the voice of the Holy Spirit, in order to understand God's sending and how best to help missionaries fulfill their calling. He shared the story of Paul's suffering as an apostle, who said, "We are fools for Christ's sake" (1 Cor. 4:10), in order to encourage those who struggle on the mission field.[193]

Socio-political factors

The Ukrainian missionary surge benefited from a number of changes in the broader society that stemmed from the coming of *perestroika* and the Fall of Communism. Freedom for evangelicals to operate and needs in society each contributed to the missionary surge.

Light of the Gospel enjoyed tremendous freedom to share the Gospel. In addition to general freedom, sometimes missionaries were given special privileges in society that they had never had before. There were numerous cases of missionaries being asked to speak publically about their faith.[194] These were tremendous opportunities for both evangelism and for influencing key civic and educational leaders.

Furthermore, Light of the Gospel became a place where people interested in spiritual things could turn. In 1991, Light of the Gospel received 25,000 letters from interested people.[195] Its art exhibition showing the life of Christ had 20,000 visitors.[196] Missionaries were able to respond to these pleas to hear the Gospel.

---

193. Pristupa, "Kto mozhet byt' missionerom?," 2–3.
194. "Khristianskoe obshchestvo 'Svet Voskreseniya,'" 1, 1998, 6–7.
195. "Otdel pisem," 17.
196. "Zhizn' Iisusa Khrista," 20–21.

Ecclesial Factors

It was specifically out of youth and prayer meetings that the leaders of Light of the Gospel came, from both the registered and underground Evangelical Christian-Baptist churches.[197] Thus, there was a new source of potential missionaries in the Ukrainian evangelical churches which helped power the missionary surge.

Light of the Gospel was a new organization, but its leadership did not try to create a new denomination. They wished to work together with existing church denominations to plant new, independent churches. They focused more on results than rules and avoided creating controlling structures.[198] To give one example, Light of the Gospel worked effectively together with the Russian Baptist Union in the Far East of Russia (Primorsky Krai) and in Yakutia.[199]

Yet, Light of the Gospel was not always accepted by other churches and Christians. Sergei Tupchik felt the need to explain that it was not bad that new churches did not necessarily fit into older church denominations. God was doing something new—but that revival and new life constituted a return to the old Gospel, and was something that should be embraced by all.[200] Even so, conflicts developed as more traditional churches judged Light of the Gospel missionaries for creating a different church culture, with women wearing earrings and members singing songs in different ways.[201] These factors spurred Light of the Gospel on to establish new missionary work, separating them further from the older denominational churches.

Leadership Factors

Since the leadership of Light of the Gospel was prominent in the *Information Bulletins*, leadership style and development was another area that was often discussed. Light of the Gospel missionaries used significantly different leadership styles than those in traditional evangelical churches. These differences could certainly be additional potential factors that influenced the Ukrainian missionary surge of the 1990s.

---

197. Melnychuk, "Istoriya i uroki," 218.
198. Melnychuk, "Istoriya i uroki," 221–22.
199. Voloshin, "Analiz razvitiya."
200. Tupchik, "Staroe novoe," 2–3.
201. Melnychuk, "Istoriya i uroki," 223.

Leadership was able to adapt amidst three regime changes

Ukraine and the former Soviet Union underwent significant change through the 1990s, and the way that Ukrainian missionary leadership was able to adapt certainly impacted the missionary surge. Using Aaron Wildavsky's[202] understanding of regime changes, Ukraine moved from a *regime of slavery* to *anarchy* to *equity*. Light of the Gospel, in particular, was able to adapt to each of these changes.

First, Light of the Gospel took some simple steps in evangelistic ministry which stood in stark contrast to the pattern followed by many traditional evangelical churches. This new, active, and initiative-taking attitude signaled a move from a regime of slavery and passivity to a regime of anarchy, to use Wildavsky's[203] term, or *individualism*, to use Lingenfelter's[204] term. Many traditional churches could not make this transition, being stuck in a survival mentality.

In 1993, Light of the Gospel went through another important adaptation. The mission had grown to have hundreds of missionaries and the Soviet Union had broken up into multiple countries. So, the mission restructured to become an association of independent missionary organizations,[205] a good choice as the former Soviet Union changed from a regime of anarchy to equity.[206] Light of the Gospel was able to make this transition naturally since it had long had a spirit of equity, being open to listen to ideas from all of its members and expecting all members to be proactive. This culture helped keep people together even though the organizational structure was loose.[207]

Flexible structure with young leaders and empowered members

Light of the Gospel started with 13 people who had no special education, financial means, or significant influence. They simply did ministry out of their own limited experience and according to what the circumstances

---

202. Wildavsky, *Moses as Political Leader*.
203. Wildavsky, *Moses as Political Leader*.
204. Lingenfelter, *Transforming Culture*.
205. "Mezhdunarodnaya assotsiatsiya 'Svet Yevangeliya,'" 3.
206. Wildavsky, *Moses as Political Leader*.
207. Bolman and Deal, *Reframing Organizations*, 243.

allowed.[208] Oleksii Melnychuk explained that their work was at first spontaneous and that structure was added later.[209]

According to Light of the Gospel's first Director of Missionary Work, Taras Pristupa, the organization had no central plan. Each missionary was independent and could make decisions as appropriate for the culture he or she worked in. They did have some basic principles, such as sending a minimum of two missionaries to a new place, since working alone was often very difficult,[210] but otherwise they were very flexible in the turbulent environment of the days of *glasnost* and the Fall of Communism. This flexible structure might be characterized as an *adhocracy*, which is "a loose, flexible, self-renewing organic form tied together mostly through lateral means."[211]

Light of the Gospel empowered its followers, allowing any of its members to take initiative. Once, Pyotr Kislyak came forward and shared that he had used a few religious paintings to witness to some soldiers. He suggested making a whole set of paintings about the life of Jesus Christ and showing it all over the city. The leadership agreed to help,[212] and the showing of these paintings became a major evangelistic ministry used all over the former Soviet Union. Thus, Light of the Gospel was able both to empower individual missionaries on the field and to involve them in making decisions about the direction of the organization. These two keys[213] certainly contributed to the success of the mission.

Leadership development

For several reasons, leadership development had been a significant problem during the years of communism. In addition to the legal restrictions on education and persecution (especially on those in leadership), there was a tendency not to develop new leaders, since it was thought they might be a threat to the current ones. As one Light of the Gospel pastor said, the church leader is considered to be a *good king* who has full authority from God, does not need to train future kings, and does not need to be replaced unless he becomes a bad king.

Light of the Gospel was able to change this pattern, at least to some extent, by several means. First, the response to the Gospel was so great during

---

208. "Mezhdunarodnaya assotsiatsiya 'Svet Yevangeliya,'" 2.
209. Melnychuk, "Istoriya i uroki," 221.
210. Menshov, "My propoveduem Khrista," 6–8.
211. Bolman and Deal, *Reframing Organizations*, 79.
212. Melnychuk, "Istoriya i uroki," 221.
213. Kelley, *Power of Followership*, 125–26.

the years of *glasnost* and immediately after the Fall of Communism that there was a need for new leaders to take care of many new followers. These new opportunities to lead made a huge difference,[214] as many new leaders were trained on the job. In addition, those young potential leaders who were unable to develop at home (because of the good king situation) were often able to leave for the mission field and become leaders there.

Finally, Light of the Gospel made theological education and leadership training available to its people. As far back as 1981, Walter Sawatsky pointed out the need for training and theological education, saying that Soviet evangelicals needed "better-educated missionaries able to employ flexible approaches for a modern paganized society."[215] Light of the Gospel offered specialized seminars, trainings, and conferences and opened Donetsk Bible College to give more formal training to missionaries.[216]

More democratic and participatory leadership

In another change from the traditional, Light of the Gospel adopted some policies that Oleksii Melnychuk described as more Western.[217] For example, they decided to have open votes instead of secret ones when making decisions. They imposed term limits on their elected leaders. They decided to be as transparent as possible regarding finances. These changes were radical since under communism the churches had tried to limit any information that the authorities could obtain. According to Melnychuk, as a result of these changes Light of the Gospel experienced easier transitions between leaders and had less significant conflict over finances and trust issues between leaders than many other organizations had.[218]

Light of the Gospel was also very practical, simply removing someone from his or her position if a more effective worker was found. Traditionally, only accusation of sin was justification for a change.[219] When internal conflict occurred over theology, an open vote (with each missionary and staff person having an equal vote) was conducted to decide the future course of

---

214. Lingenfelter, *Leading Cross-Culturally*, 122.
215. Sawatsky, *Soviet Evangelicals*, 442.
216. "Bibleyskiy kolledzh," 29–30; "Soobshcheniya," 2, 1992, 6; Satsyuk, "Seminar: Prepodavateli obuchayutsya," 11–12; "Tret'ya konferentsiya," 2–3.
217. Melnychuk, "Istoriya i uroki," 223.
218. Melnychuk, "Istoriya i uroki," 223.
219. Melnychuk, "Istoriya i uroki," 223.

the mission.[220] This change from the good king mentality is a good example of true power being exhibited through participation in decisions.[221]

Influential partnerships

Light of the Gospel formed several international partnerships that helped promote the Ukrainian missionary surge. It often worked together with radio evangelist Earl Poysti and his ministry, Russian Christian Radio.[222] Various branches of the mission worked together with Andrei Bondarenko's Latvian Tent Mission, with the German mission Light in the East, with the American mission InterAct Ministries, and with South Korean churches.[223] The mission certainly benefitted from these partners, who were key constituents for the mission.[224]

FINANCIAL FACTORS

In an attempt to be more transparent, finances were often discussed in Light of the Gospel's *Information Bulletins*. Thus, I was able to find some helpful information about Light of the Gospel's financial priorities, which are potentially a window upon some of the factors behind their surge in missionary work.

Financial sources

Taras Pristupa shared that the most difficult aspects of Light of the Gospel's work were recruiting missionaries and having enough finances.[225] Considering this, it is interesting to note that the mission first decided to follow George Müller's model and present their financial needs to God only,[226]

---

220. "Vostochnoe otdelenie," 13.
221. Adams, *Theory of Social Power*, 5.
222. Tupchik, "O vashey pomoshchi," 30.
223. Brumbelow, "Evangelical Ministries in Siberia," 1–3; "Khristianskoe obshchestvo 'Dobraya Vest,'" 3–4, 1996, 11; "Mezhdunarodnaya obshchestvennaya blagotvoritel'naya khristianskaya organizatsiya," 3, 1998, 27; "Soobshcheniya," 3–4, 1996, 6; Tupchik, "Poseshchenie Yakutii," 3–4, 1996, 14–15.
224. Bolman and Deal, *Reframing Organizations*, 229.
225. Menshov, "My propoveduem Khrista," 9.
226. Tupchik, *Informatsionnyy byulleten'*, 2.

asking others only to pray for more missionaries.[227] The mission always seemed to be provided for in these early years, although the sources for most giving were not documented.

Later, the mission seems to have changed its policy, making direct requests for gifts to readers of the *Information Bulletin*.[228] This change reflected their desire to increase the involvement of current constituents and to seek new ones.[229] Furthermore, it pointed to the mission's need for specific resources for ministry. One of the most common requests of this period was for funds for church buildings, which were needed because of legal or social difficulties in finding places to meet.[230] Buildings had value both practically and symbolically. Since the traditional Orthodox Church had long associated large beautiful church buildings with true Christianity, buildings had symbolic value to evangelical churches as well.[231] As Bolman and Deal emphasized, symbolism can be vitally important in the "identity, beliefs, and values"[232] of organizations. Thus, evangelical churches needed church buildings in order to better identify themselves with true Christianity in the eyes of many people in the former Soviet Union.

Financial allocations

Looking through the financial reports given in the *Information Bulletins* from 1990 to 1993, we can analyze Light of the Gospel's allocation of funds, as displayed in table 1 below. After 1993, when Light of the Gospel changed from being an organization to an association, no more general financial reports were published in the *Information Bulletins*.

From table 1, it is clear that Light of the Gospel's first three focuses (missionary work, evangelism, and literature) remained their priority over this period, with the possible addition of education as a fourth priority by 1991, when Donetsk Bible College was opened.[233] Light of the Gospel kept its administrative costs relatively low and did not consider children's ministry or humanitarian aid to be high priorities, although some Westerners gave humanitarian aid directly, which is not taken into account in these figures.[234]

---

227. Tupchik, "Spaseny, chtoby spasat'," 5.
228. E.g., "Khristianskoe obshchestvo 'Dobraya Vest'," 4, 1995, 11.
229. Bolman and Deal, *Reframing Organizations*, 229.
230. "Khristianskoe obshchestvo 'Evangel'skoe sluzhenie'," 4.
231. White, "Growth Amidst Persecution," 140.
232. Bolman and Deal, *Reframing Organizations*, 195.
233. Melnychuk, "Missionerskaya shkola," 13.
234. "Otdel blagotvoritel'nosti," 18.

Thus, a missionary focus on reaching adults was clear during this time period, although the focus later seems to have shifted to children in light of information included in *Information Bulletins* from 1997 and 1998.[235]

Summary of Potential Factors Behind the Missionary Surge

It is rather surprising to note how many negative factors in the state of the evangelical church existed during the Ukrainian evangelical missionary surge, including the emigration of key leadership and an inwardly focused church subculture. Yet, a growing evangelical youth population that was limited in ministry by many in church leadership could find an outlet for its energy through missionary work. Bibles and Christian literature were finally available as tools for missionaries. Thus, it appears that these positive factors overcame the negative ones.

Table 1. Light of the Gospel Financial Spending Percentages by Department from 1989–92[236]

Department	1989 (10 mos.)	1990	1991	1992
Missionary Work	31.7%	22.9%	26%	30.1%
Evangelism	27.1%	5.0%	18%	25.4%
Literature/Publishing	29.5%	10.9%	16%	10.0%
Education	1.0%	1.4%	22.5%	18.0%
Humanitarian Aid	6.2%	2.4%	1.4%	7.3%
Administration	3.0%	4.9%	8.7%	3.4%
Correspondence	0%	3.1%	2.8%	3.1%
Children's Work	0.3%	2.7%	1.2%	2.7%
Equipment and Buildings	0%	45.2%	0%	0%
Other	1.2%	1.5%	3.4%	0%

Clearly, the categories of spiritual and leadership factors seemed to be important based on my literature review of Light of the Gospel mission.

---

235. E.g., Ivanilov, "Khristianskiy lager," 8–9; Vishnyakova, "Priyut Dobrogo Pastyra," 9–10.

236. Based on "Finansovyy otchet," 1–2, 1990, 22; "Finansovyy otchet," 1, 1991, 35; "Raspredelenie sredstv," 1, 1992, 22; "Raspredelenie sredstv," 1, 1993, 34.

However, it is hard to judge which of the individual factors were the most important. In any case, spiritual and leadership factors are certainly categories of factors to keep in mind during the interviewing process.

Directions for Further Research

Upon completion of my literature review, it became clear that I needed to discover more about the Ukrainian evangelical missionary surge from key leaders of Light of the Gospel, including Sergei Tupchik, Oleksii Melnychuk, Leonid Kartavenko, and Taras Pristupa. One area that deserved further exploration was the area of finances. Where did the finances for Light of the Gospel come from? Was the Ukrainian missionary surge connected to an increase in financial giving, either local or foreign? Very little documentation was available on this issue.

In addition, key leaders from outside Light of the Gospel needed to be interviewed. Baptist Union leadership in both Ukraine and Russia could give additional perspective on the Light of the Gospel movement as well as lend insight into other Baptist mission work. Pentecostal church and mission leaders such as Vladimir Franchuk of Possibility mission, Slavik Radchuk of Good Samaritan mission, and Nikolai Sinyuk of Voice of Hope mission could also each provide helpful perspectives from different groups involved in the Ukrainian evangelical missionary surge of the 1990s.

Certainly, the Ukrainian missionary surge deserved more study. As Scott Klingsmith wrote after completing his research on East-Central European missionary sending movements,

> The missions situation in the Ukraine should be explored in more depth. It has some features which distinguish is (sic) somewhat from the ECE countries farther west. It was not a major missionary-receiving country, due to isolation during Communism, although there are a large number of missionaries there now. It has now become a major missionary-sending country. The mission Light of the Gospel itself is probably worth a full-scale study.[237]

In order to study the Ukrainian evangelical missionary surge effectively, I need to consider which methods and procedures would be the most appropriate and helpful in producing useful data. Therefore, I will now move to a discussion of how best to conduct research into factors behind the missionary surge.

237. Klingsmith, *Missions Beyond the Wall*, 195.

4

Methods and Procedures

THIS RESEARCH PROJECT USED a number of methods and procedures in accordance with the practices of qualitative research. The methods that I have chosen are tools that I believe will be the most helpful in producing a theory well-grounded in the data collected. In order to help the reader understand these methods and procedures more clearly, I will first explain the research paradigm, then the data collection strategy, ethical considerations, data analysis strategy, and finally, the data validation strategy.

Justification for the Research Paradigm

Before considering data collection, analysis, and validation strategies, I would like to explain the reasoning behind the approach chosen to research the surge in Ukrainian evangelical missionaries in the 1990s. As is true for any researcher, I have my own worldview and biases that affect how I conduct research on this issue.

Philosophical Worldview: Critical Realism

Defining my own worldview and how it affects the research does not come easily. I find myself drawn, on the one hand, to the postpositive worldview because I believe that objective reality exists and that there are real causes and effects in the world.[1] Yet, on the other hand, I am also drawn to the social constructivist worldview in that I believe that people hold subjective views of reality that are multiple, and that a researcher needs to "rely as much as possible on the participants' views of the situation being studied."[2]

---

1. Creswell, *Research Design*, 6–7.
2. Creswell, *Research Design*, 8.

I find a balance between these two positions in Paul Hiebert's[3] description of critical realism. According to Hiebert, objective reality does exist, yet human beings are limited in their ability to understand and interpret it. Objective reality is "subjectively known and appropriated in human lives."[4] I agree with Strauss and Corbin's assertion that only God can tell people the "real nature of reality."[5] Thus, similar to Richard Starcher's[6] position, my worldview is functionally constructivist (relying on subjective human perspectives) while still believing in an objective reality (that is known completely only by God). I admit that I will be unable to determine this objective reality fully through my research, but my aim is to understand it better, constructing a model that best reflects the views of those involved in the Ukrainian evangelical missionary surge of the 1990s.

Personal Identity and Potential Bias: Evangelical Christian and Missionary in Ukraine

I am an evangelical Christian who considers the Ukrainian missionary surge in the 1990s to be a good thing. I am personally interested in understanding factors behind this surge in the hope that this information might be useful in helping to produce further missionary surges in Ukraine and other parts of the world. Therefore, I may be biased to look for factors that could be repeated in the future.

Because I work as a missionary in Ukraine, I personally know some of the participants involved in the missionary surge of the 1990s. This fact should help me in gaining the trust of some of the interview participants, yet it might bias the way that I ask questions and interpret the data, based upon my previous relationships with them.

Research Paradigm: Qualitative Research

For this study, I have chosen to use qualitative methods, which John Creswell has defined as "a means for exploring and understanding the meaning individuals or groups ascribe to a social or human problem."[7] Qualitative research makes the most sense for the study since the nature of my research

---

3. Hiebert, *Missiological Implications*.
4. Hiebert, *Missiological Implications*, 74.
5. Strauss and Corbin, *Basics of Qualitative Research*, 4.
6. Starcher, "Qualitative Research."
7. Creswell, *Research Design*, 4.

is exploratory.[8] There is not a great amount of literature on the topic, which means that the study cannot be wholly historical and literature-based.

First, I conducted a significant literature review in order to learn more about the Ukrainian missionary surge. The data that I discovered was analyzed according to its context, with the understanding that the data was given from someone's particular point of view with a certain amount of bias.[9] After my literature review, I next gathered data through interviews of participants in the missionary surge. The advantage that I had from this method of gathering data was that I could question participants about their responses, something I could not do through literature review.[10] Thus, I was able to be much more flexible in collecting data through qualitative research,[11] including existing literature,[12] but not being limited by it.

I did not propose a hypothesis to be tested, as is traditionally done in quantitative research.[13] Instead, I followed the approach of emergence, in which theories emerge from the data collected.[14] Furthermore, I did not study something that has measurable variables, as is the case in quantitative research.[15] Factors that contributed to the surge in the number of Ukrainian evangelical missionaries in the 1990s were explored through learning the perceptions of the missionary surge participants. These perceptions are naturally subjective and cannot be quantified. My goal was to build general themes inductively and interpret meaning out of the participants' perceptions. This idea is at the heart of qualitative research.[16]

Strategy of Inquiry: Grounded Theory

The specific strategy of qualitative research that I used was grounded theory, following Kathy Charmaz's definition as "systematic, yet flexible guidelines for collecting and analyzing qualitative data to construct theories 'grounded' in the data themselves."[17] I chose this strategy because I wanted to derive a theory regarding the process of the Ukrainian evangelical missionary surge

8. Creswell, *Research Design*, 26.
9. Charmaz, *Constructing Grounded Theory*, 39; Henige, *Historical Evidence*, 12.
10. Henige, *Historical Evidence*, 241.
11. Freeman et al., "Standards of Evidence," 25.
12. Ambert et al., "Understanding and Evaluating Qualitative Research," 880.
13. Creswell, *Research Design*, 16.
14. Strauss and Corbin, *Basics of Qualitative Research*, 34.
15. Creswell, *Research Design*, 4.
16. Creswell, *Research Design*, 4.
17. Charmaz, *Constructing Grounded Theory*, 2.

based on the views of the participants in the surge.[18] Thus, I determined a theory (factors contributing to the surge) grounded in the data that I collected (interviews and documentation of participants).

Considering alternative strategies for qualitative research, grounded theory seemed to be the best because my study was focused upon the decision process of a specific group of people. It was not focused on an entire cultural group or a small group of individuals (for which ethnography or narrative research might be appropriate). The study was not trying to determine the essence of the experience of the Ukrainian missionary surge (for which phenomenological research would be best). This study could conceivably have been done as a case study, considering the bounded time period (1990s) and activity (Ukrainian evangelicals becoming missionaries) involved. Yet, some question whether case study is a methodology at all or simply a choice of the subject to be studied.[19] Regardless, case studies can use a number of different methods for data collection, and it made sense to use the strategy of grounded theory for data collection, considering the process and group of people being studied.[20]

Grounded theory follows the strategy of keeping data collection, data analysis, and eventual theory in close connection.[21] As in Charmaz's definition above, this method is very flexible, allowing the researcher to move back and forth between collecting and analyzing data before reaching a final theory. Grounded theory uses analytic codes and memo writing to produce concrete categories from the data and identify direction for further research. Sampling does not attempt to represent the population, but is done intentionally for constructing a theory.[22] I liken this method to detective work, in which the researcher does not need to ask every participant the same questions, but instead the researcher asks certain questions of certain people based on the analysis done thus far in order to reach a conclusion firmly supported by the data collected and recorded in the detective's notebook.

This strategy was appropriate for the study because it allowed me to do interviews of missionary surge participants, analyze the interview data, and then, based on this analysis, conduct more effective subsequent interviews by asking questions that the data suggested were important. The participants that I interviewed were scattered over a wide area, so it was important to

---

18. Creswell, *Research Design*, 13.
19. Creswell, *Qualitative Inquiry*, 73.
20. Creswell, *Research Design*, 13.
21. Strauss and Corbin, *Basics of Qualitative Research*, 12.
22. Charmaz, *Constructing Grounded Theory*, 5.

obtain good data in order to minimize the amount of travel needed and the number of times necessary to ask participants follow up questions.

Data Collection Strategies and Procedures

In order to build a strong grounded theory, I needed to collect rich data, which is data that can "reveal participants' views, feelings, intentions, and actions as well as the contexts and structures of their lives."[23] My strategy for collecting this data followed a modified version of Creswell's data collection circle, which is "a series of interrelated activities aimed at gathering good information to answer emerging research questions."[24] Creswell's idea that data collection is done in a circle, in which the researcher can move back and forth freely is very useful for flexible grounded theory research. Instead of starting my description of data collection by locating a site or individual as Creswell does, I began with the question of what sources of data will provide the richest information. Then, I moved to the question of site and followed Creswell's data collection circle further.

Data Sources

I wanted to use the best data sources available. Qualitative research usually includes multiple data sources in order to produce more accurate data that can be validated across sources.[25] I was told by Ukrainian church and mission leaders that very little written material exists on the missionary surge, so I knew that my focus would be on collecting data through interviews with participants in and observers of that surge.

Site

The Ukrainian evangelical missionary surge of the 1990s spread from Ukraine all across the former Soviet Union, so both documentation and the participants involved spread across this territory as well. This dispersion of data across multiple sites is typical for a grounded theory study.[26] Multiple locations were chosen in key areas where mission organization headquarters have been located (in the cities of Rivne, Kyiv, Lviv, and

23. Charmaz, *Constructing Grounded Theory*, 14.
24. Creswell, *Qualitative Inquiry*, 118.
25. Creswell, *Research Design*, 91.
26. Creswell, *Qualitative Inquiry*, 122.

Donetsk, Ukraine, as well as Moscow, Russia) and missionary activity has been conducted (many cities across Russia).

Access Strategy

In the former Soviet Union, access to both documentation and individuals generally comes through personal connections.[27] There is not a reliable database with access to all the libraries in Ukraine or Russia, let alone one with access to church, mission organization, or seminary collections. In order to find the information I was searching for, I needed to personally contact participants in the missionary surge and get their help in both accessing documents and finding people to interview.

Furthermore, it was vitally important to gain the trust of potential study participants in order to obtain rich data. Having worked in Ukraine as a missionary since 2000, I have built a level of trust with a number of church, mission, and seminary leaders that I believe helped me both in interviewing them, as well as in gaining their recommendation to meet and interview other key participants. Certain participants in the missionary surge were gatekeepers who were able to open the door to many additional data sources, including other participants and documentation.[28] It was vitally important to gain these gatekeepers' trust.

In addition, the issue of language is important in gaining access to data. I have gained a good level of competency in Russian, and being able to speak with participants in their first language seemed to increase their level of openness and trust, as well as understanding.[29] However, I do not speak the Ukrainian language, so this may have been a negative factor in speaking with Ukrainians who prefer to converse in Ukrainian (in each case they spoke with me in Russian). Finally, there were also some participants who preferred to speak with me in English, so I deferred to their preference, even if English was their second language.

As a missionary in Ukraine (married to a Russian-speaking Ukrainian), I am part outsider and part insider. Through my knowledge of Russian and the relationships I have built over the years, I believe that I am considered part insider and trustworthy, and thus able to form a research partnership with participants I am interviewing. Yet, being a foreigner and part outsider, I believe that I have had a platform from which to ask questions and learn, so that participants are interested in teaching me about

27. Richmond, *From Nyet to Da*, 110.
28. Creswell, *Qualitative Inquiry*, 125.
29. Richmond, *From Nyet to Da*, 130.

their understandings of factors behind the Ukrainian evangelical missionary surge in the 1990s. Therefore, I believe that being part outsider and part insider was very positive and allowed me to obtain good data.[30]

Finally, as is the case in grounded theory studies, I needed to receive permission to conduct interviews from participants in the study.[31] Having participants give written permission would have produced some amount of suspicion and put participants on their guard due to a history of persecution by the government and forced confessions of evangelical Christians. Therefore, I received permission from the Protection of Human Rights in Research Committee (PHRRC) to use oral consent from participants, which I believe eliminated some of their suspicions.

Theoretical Sampling

After conducting some initial interviews based on an examination of the available documentation, I analyzed the resulting data in order to produce some initial concepts and categories.[32] First, I realized that there were some significant differences between Baptist and Pentecostal participants, so I needed to make sure to get a reasonable number of participants from each group and during coding I would need, in certain cases, to separate their codes in order to better compare the groups. Secondly, although I wanted to keep my codes very specific in the initial coding stage, I realized that I would need some more general categories of codes both to focus my interview questions and to organize my data. So, I came up with some initial categories like the age of participants, books that motivated them, their financial support, their origin, the school that influenced them, whether a revival occurred, and the timing of the surge (i.e., the years of the surge). I also decided to add the category *Important Factor* when a participant emphasized a point as being particularly important, in order to differentiate it from other codes.

From there, I followed the strategy of theoretical sampling, which is gathering data "driven by concepts derived from the evolving theory . . . that will maximize opportunities to discover variations among concepts and to densify categories in terms of their properties and dimensions."[33] Thus, I attempted to interview those people who could give me information that would enable me to build upon the theories I had developed through the

30. Weiss, *Learning from Strangers*, 137–38.
31. Creswell, *Qualitative Inquiry*, 125.
32. Charmaz, *Constructing Grounded Theory*, 100.
33. Strauss and Corbin, *Basics of Qualitative Research*, 201.

data analysis (which continued to occur simultaneously with data collection). Theoretical sampling involved studying documents, as well, searching for information that could help develop theories.[34] It is also important to note that I did not just attempt to corroborate what I already thought to be true, but I attempted to investigate the range of the concepts that I was discovering, something known as "variational sampling."[35] This helped me more fully develop my theory.

Practically speaking, I used the idea of *snowball* or *chain* sampling, in which I aimed to interview those people who have the most information, or the richest data.[36] These people were usually mission organization and church leaders who could see the big picture of what was happening during the missionary surge. I identified these people both through researching the available documentation as well as by asking for recommendations from those I interviewed. Thus, a chain was formed between my participants and my documentation, as one connects to the next, and so on. One drawback of this model is that participants may be influenced by their relationships to the people who referred them to me.[37] Therefore, I needed to be careful in the way that I talked about how I connected to new participants. Also, it was very important to build a good rapport with participants so that they could feel a partnership with me in the research. This rapport offered them more freedom to speak than if they had been focused on their connection to the people who recommended them to me.

Number of Participants

The number of participants in the study depended upon the quality of the data collected as well as the need to interview a reasonably broad representation from the different kinds of people involved in the Ukrainian missionary surge. Regarding the quality of data, I analyzed the data as it was collected and developed concepts and categories to explore until a theory emerged. The goal of my qualitative research was to reach a point at which each of my categories was saturated, or in other words, at which "no new or relevant data seem[ed] to emerge regarding a category."[38]

---

34. Charmaz, *Constructing Grounded Theory*, 107.
35. Strauss and Corbin, *Basics of Qualitative Research*, 210.
36. Creswell, *Qualitative Inquiry*, 127.
37. Weiss, *Learning from Strangers*, 34.
38. Strauss and Corbin, *Basics of Qualitative Research*, 212.

For a grounded theory study, usually 20 to 30 participants are needed for saturation.[39] In order to achieve a reasonably broad representation of the Ukrainian evangelical missionary surge, I believed that I needed to conduct interviews with a minimum of 10 Baptists, 10 Pentecostals, 5 women, and 5 knowledgeable non-Ukrainians to provide some outside perspective. Of course, these categories overlap one another, but a minimum of 25–30 interviews seemed reasonable.

As I followed the snowball of people to interview, the goodwill of my participants led to more and more suggestions of potential participants. My first contacts were with Light of the Gospel leaders and missionaries, and I felt that I reached a point of saturation with them at about 12 interviews. However, I believed that I needed to interview at least three Baptists outside of Light of the Gospel in order to be fair in representing Baptists.

I had guessed that it might be difficult to find women to interview regarding the missionary surge, but it turned out to be even more difficult than I expected. I believe that this was due, at least in part, to the cultural tendency for men and women to be somewhat isolated from one another,[40] with people often talking in depth only to those of the same gender. For example, in one case I was told about a husband and wife who were both missionaries in Siberia as singles before getting married. I tried calling the wife, but the husband called me back, giving me an interview—the wife was busy. I did eventually conduct five interviews with women.

My last difficulty was connected to interviewing Pentecostals involved in the missionary surge. I ended up with 40 interviews as I was able to connect with key Pentecostal mission leaders only as my chain of interviews approached that number. By the time I interviewed my 40th participant, I felt that I had clearly reached a point of saturation since the last participant confirmed my main conclusions despite being quite detached from nearly all of the other participants. Although the total number of interviews was larger than I initially expected, it should allow me to apply my conclusions more broadly than if I had just focused on Light of the Gospel or on Baptist missions.[41]

Data Recording

As much as possible, I recorded face-to-face interviews on a digital recorder, which allowed me to focus on participants more than if I had needed to take

39. Creswell, *Qualitative Inquiry*, 126.
40. Ennis et al., *Introduction to the Russian Soul*, 17.
41. Charmaz, *Constructing Grounded Theory*, 114.

copious notes.[42] I generally interviewed participants in whatever place was most comfortable for them: in their homes or offices.[43] Due to the distances involved and the political conflict between Russia and Ukraine that began in 2014, it was necessary to conduct many of my interviews through Skype, in some cases using Skype-to-Skype, and in others using Skype to call a local telephone. I was able to record all of these conversations using the free application, the MP3 Skype Recorder. All of my interviews were conducted in either the Russian or English language, as preferred by the participant.

I used an interview protocol to guide my conversations with participants. This was not a strict series of questions, but a set of guidelines to help me organize how I would ask questions and a reminder of important areas to cover. I asked open-ended questions that gave participants a great deal of flexibility in how to answer, allowing them to express the issues that they felt were most important. I memorized the main details of the protocol so that I could maximize eye contact with participants and focus on them and their answers.[44]

In conducting interviews, I asked a number of different kinds of open-ended questions. These included sensitizing questions, which helped me get a better feel for what happened; theoretical questions, which helped me to better understand important concepts that were emerging; and guiding questions, which helped provide direction for the research.[45] I attempted to make my questions as neutral as possible in order to limit my influence on the participants and maximize their ability to express their own opinions.[46]

Although I had these many types of questions at my disposal, my goal was to focus on listening instead of questioning. I wanted to make my participants feel as comfortable as possible and to ask questions that would enable them to respond at length, "reexperiencing feelings in the described incident."[47] I tried to look for *markers*, which are "passing reference[s] made by a respondent to an important event or feeling state."[48] Sometimes asking about these markers led the conversation in an unexpected direction, but if a participant really wanted to talk about an event or feeling that she or he was not asked about, this new direction sometimes led to very rich data that could not have been obtained otherwise. Since I followed a functionally

---

42. Weiss, *Learning from Strangers*, 54.
43. Weiss, *Learning from Strangers*, 58.
44. Creswell, *Qualitative Inquiry*, 135.
45. Strauss and Corbin, *Basics of Qualitative Research*, 77–78.
46. Charmaz, *Constructing Grounded Theory*, 27.
47. Charmaz, *Constructing Grounded Theory*, 30.
48. Weiss, *Learning from Strangers*, 77.

constructivist approach to research, my goal was to understand the way participants saw the Ukrainian evangelical missionary surge, discovering their own terms, assumptions, and meanings.[49]

Field Issues

In an attempt to foresee and prevent potential problems, I did some limited data collection as a pilot project in order to evaluate the interview process and set better expectations regarding the process of data collection.[50] I conducted three face-to-face interviews with my digital recorder and three distance interviews through Skype. All of these interviews produced good data, although recordings of interviews conducted through Skype were of poorer quality than face-to-face interviews for which I used a digital recorder.

As I continued to conduct interviews, I found that I did have occasional difficulties in producing a quality recording through Skype, especially in the few cases where I had to call from Skype to a telephone. In these cases, too, I was not able to see my participant, and that did not make the connection as close on a personal level. In addition, I found that interviews were less productive if the participant was not informed ahead of time about the interview, which occurred only when I was unable to make e-mail contact before actually calling. In such cases, doing a follow-up interview produced better data. So, despite these various difficulties, my interviews produced a large amount of useful data.

In fact, I faced the problem of having too much data rather than too little. Participants were often eager to share their thoughts and give me numerous additional people to contact. I therefore had to address the difficulty of needing to limit my number of sources in order to get a fair representation across different groups of people while seeking saturation of the data. Thus, I had to make some hard decisions not to include certain potential participants.

Data Storage

I stored data on my personal computer, scanning printed documents, typing up notes, and transferring digital recordings. These digital recordings were all transcribed within the program NVivo. Considering the large amount of information that I collected, it was vital to use a database like NVivo to

---

49. Charmaz, *Constructing Grounded Theory*, 32.
50. Creswell, *Qualitative Inquiry*, 138–41.

organize it.⁵¹ I stored backups of my data and dissertation on my office computer as well as on an external hard drive. All paper documents were stored in my home.

Ethical Considerations

In pursuing this study, it was vitally important for me to act with integrity and to protect the research participants from any possible harm involved in the research.⁵² Integrity is important for any member of the academic community, and all the more so for me as a Christian who attempts to follow Jesus Christ's high standards. Furthermore, I chose this research topic because I believed it would benefit the participants in the Ukrainian evangelical missionary surge of the 1990s. I believed this issue was meaningful not just to me, but to all those involved in the surge, and thus, it was worth researching.⁵³

Protecting the Safety and Rights of Participants

In accordance with the ethical standards at Biola University, I submitted a proposal to the PHRRC, outlining my research procedures and explaining how I planned to protect the safety and rights of research participants. This study involved a *minimal risk* for participants, following the PHRRC definition that it "includes no deception of participants: no sensitive, culturally taboo, or socially controversial material or responses by participants. Also the research procedure is unlikely to impact or change the participants' physical, social, psychological, or spiritual status."⁵⁴

Ethical issues in data collection

As I collected data, I contacted key members of the Ukrainian evangelical missionary surge both in order to interview them and to get referrals from them to talk to others who might help me. They acted as gatekeepers who gave me greater authority to talk to others.⁵⁵ Furthermore, as I collected my first data through a pilot project, I looked for any potential difficulties in

51. Creswell, *Qualitative Inquiry*, 142.
52. Creswell, *Research Design*, 87.
53. Creswell, *Research Design*, 88.
54. Biola University, "PHRRC Part II Application Form."
55. Creswell, *Research Design*, 90.

establishing trust or respect or if any marginalization might occur through my study.[56] No such problems arose.

The interviewing process offered participants maximum freedom. I offered to meet them at a time and place most convenient for them, or communicate remotely, if that was the only alternative. I was as transparent as possible in explaining the research and goals to participants and in order to avoid any type of deception.[57] I asked for verbal consent from all participants and explained that participants did not have to answer any questions they felt uncomfortable with and that they could end the interview at any time. Any information given by participants off the record was not used.

The missionary surge was considered positive by most of the research participants, and it was thus easy and even enjoyable to discuss. However, I did realize that the surge had come to an end, and thus, there might be some painful memories associated with that for some participants. In addition, the political climate in Ukraine and Russia became unexpectedly heated in 2014, so I tried to avoid talking about any issues that might relate to current politics. Thus, I tried to be sensitive regarding these issues and to be as neutral as possible in any questions regarding them. My role as a foreigner and outsider may have helped me in appearing relatively neutral.[58]

Ethical issues in data analysis and storage

As I analyzed the data, I used aliases and pseudonyms to protect my participants' identities and their locations. I shared the data only with my dissertation advisor, as deemed necessary. I kept my data stored on a password protected computer and all of my notes locked up in my home. It was important to make sure that the data I collected and analyzed was not misused by others.[59]

Ethical issues in writing and disseminating research

It is fundamental to qualitative research to respect the confidentiality of all participants. I needed to be careful when writing up the research to minimize the possibility of readers identifying any of my participants.[60]

56. Creswell, *Research Design*, 88.
57. Creswell, *Qualitative Inquiry*, 242.
58. Weiss, *Learning from Strangers*, 138.
59. Creswell, *Research Design*, 91.
60. Weiss, *Learning from Strangers*, 131.

There was an exception to this rule in the case when I recounted historical events from the words of one participant. I received permission from this participant to use his real name in this context, which seemed appropriate considering the historical nature of the material. A list of pseudonyms with basic information about each one is given in Appendix B. All names used in this dissertation that are not in this list are actual names as referred to by other people or used by permission.

In addition, I needed to give serious consideration to possible repercussions from the publication of my research. I did not want my study to lead to any group involved taking advantage of another. I gave a copy of parts of my work to some of the research participants in order to get feedback regarding both accuracy and audience reaction before final publication.[61]

In writing up my research, I strived to avoid biased language, using language that is acceptable to those I was writing about and not making offensive or broad stereotypical statements.[62] Getting feedback from some of my participants who read parts of the paper before publication has hopefully helped eliminate problems in this area.

Benefits for Participants

As Weiss explained, participants are quite unlikely to be harmed through research interviews and may, in fact, benefit in multiple ways.[63] I agree with Creswell's idea of reciprocity, that researchers should strive to give back some kind of benefit to research participants.[64]

Therefore, I first gave participants the benefit of having their story told. Many people are encouraged just by having someone listen to them, and by publishing my research, I can multiply the number of listeners. Furthermore, the Ukrainian evangelical missionary surge was quite an accomplishment considering that it came on the heels of 70 years of government oppression of the church. Publishing information on the surge may motivate new people to get involved in mission work, which would be an additional encouragement to research participants (most of whom were or are involved in mission work), as they see a further effect from their testimonies.

Additionally, many participants in the missionary surge wanted to understand better what happened in the 1990s. This desire was expressed by Taras Pristupa at the Rus'-Mission in the 21st Century Conference in 2000

61. Creswell, *Research Design*, 92.
62. Creswell, *Research Design*, 92.
63. Weiss, *Learning from Strangers*, 130.
64. Creswell, *Qualitative Inquiry*, 44.

when he asserted the great need to analyze what had happened during the previous decade. My research has shed light on some of the factors behind the surge. Such information could be used by research participants who are mission leaders to help further the cause of mission work in the former Soviet Union today, which would indeed be a significant benefit.

Data Analysis Strategy

Since I collected data in two languages, Russian and English, I had to decide what common language to use in my data analysis. I chose to use English for my analysis since the final write-up would be in English. In cases where I needed to quote a Russian language source, I made the translation from Russian into English myself.

As mentioned earlier, grounded theory research closely connects data collection and data analysis. Data analysis includes coding and memo writing procedures that will be described in detail below. The codes and memos produced from preliminary data analysis provide clues as to the direction of further data collection, which is also known as theoretical sampling. Thus, collecting good data helped me to produce better codes and memos, and conversely, writing better codes and memos helped me understand what kinds of data I needed to obtain. John Creswell described this process as a "data analysis spiral"[65] in which the researcher constantly goes back and forth between collecting and analyzing data. This data analysis spiral involves constant reflection that produces conclusions tying together the data, codes, and memos in a satisfying way.[66]

This strategy helped me produce theories grounded in the data as opposed to verifying theories based on preconceived ideas.[67] Although this methodology is somewhat subjective (e.g., proposing codes to describe the data, writing memos that conjecture what the data means), all of the theories that I produced had to be connected to the data. Thus, this method provided me with a flexible way to collect and analyze data that drove me toward theories that explain all of the data.

---

65. Creswell, *Qualitative Inquiry*, 150.
66. Creswell, *Research Design*, 184.
67. Strauss and Corbin, *Basics of Qualitative Research*, 12.

Data Management

To begin using the data analysis spiral, I needed to use a good system of data management.[68] I decided to use the computer program NVivo both to store data and to analyze it through coding procedures. This program allowed me to retrieve data easily, to categorize it in codes, and to manipulate these categories in order to develop theories grounded in the data.

Coding Procedures

Different researchers have proposed various ways to conduct coding in a grounded theory study. There are certainly multiple ways to arrive at a well-grounded theory, but I prefer to use the main categories that Kathy Charmaz[69] presents: initial, focused, and theoretical coding. Charmaz[70] also notes the idea of axial coding, as proposed by Strauss and Corbin,[71] in which the researcher attempts to determine the axes or categories around which data revolve as an intermediate step before theoretical coding. I did not use the structure of axial coding in my analysis, but followed a more flexible model, as suggested by Charmaz.[72] In any case, it was useful to consider multiple methods of coding because different methods may provide helpful ideas as to how to analyze various kinds of data.

Initial coding

The purpose of initial coding was to give simple analytic codes that expressed the meaning behind the data. Codes might range from actions to basic concepts, but the key at this stage in coding was not to try to make far-reaching statements or formulate overarching principles, but to stick close to the plain meaning of the data. Therefore, I analyzed most data line by line and certain data word by word.[73] Some data produced multiple codes that expressed a range of possible meanings.[74] It was also useful to look over the big picture as the coding proceeded, considering how new data differed from the previous

---

68. Creswell, *Qualitative Inquiry*, 150.
69. Charmaz, *Constructing Grounded Theory*.
70. Charmaz, *Constructing Grounded Theory*.
71. Strauss and Corbin, *Basics of Qualitative Research*.
72. Charmaz, *Constructing Grounded Theory*, 61.
73. Charmaz, *Constructing Grounded Theory*, 47–50.
74. Strauss and Corbin, *Basics of Qualitative Research*, 109.

data analyzed,[75] but my goal was to produce all possible initial codes from the data and not to draw any conclusions at this point.

Initial coding was generally done quickly and spontaneously.[76] I followed the principle that it is better to produce too many codes and delete some later than to miss a code that might prove important. There is a great deal of flexibility in coding, but it was often helpful to use the specific terms that participants used, which are called "in vivo codes."[77] In many cases, these were translations of the original quote. The goal is to understand the feelings and opinions of those involved in the Ukrainian evangelical missionary surge of the 1990s, so I tried as much as possible to use their terminology to describe what happened.

Furthermore, having produced a set of initial codes, I then looked for gaps in the data that needed to be addressed.[78] Moving back to data collection on the data analysis spiral, I then directed my interviews and theoretical sampling toward filling these gaps of data. At the end of the day, my goal was to produce a great number of initial codes because I didn't know which codes would prove the most valuable.

Focused coding

My second step was focused coding, in which I took the initial codes I had written and analyzed them more carefully. It was at this point that I eliminated unneeded codes and consolidated the initial codes into fewer and more conceptual categories or focused codes. Here, my goal was to find the most important codes that had the greatest explanatory power. Some of the ideas of axial coding were useful at this point, in which my goal was to reassemble the data that was fractured during initial coding along axes or broader categories. I tried to start answering why questions during this step.[79]

The process of producing focused codes is not linear.[80] I continued to move back and forth on the data analysis spiral, and thus, new data obtained sometimes changed the way that I focused my codes. Furthermore, as I focused my codes into broader concepts, questions sometimes arose that the data didn't answer. These questions motivated me to return to data collection in order to find answers and develop my concepts further. This process

75. Strauss and Corbin, *Basics of Qualitative Research*, 120.
76. Charmaz, *Constructing Grounded Theory*, 48.
77. Charmaz, *Constructing Grounded Theory*, 55.
78. Charmaz, *Constructing Grounded Theory*, 50.
79. Strauss and Corbin, *Basics of Qualitative Research*, 427.
80. Charmaz, *Constructing Grounded Theory*, 58.

was fluid, as I continued to collect and analyze data, producing more and better-developed focused codes. My goal was to reach a point of saturation for each of my focused codes, in which no new information emerged during data collection or coding.[81] When saturation occurred for all of my codes, I was ready to move on to the last step of coding.

Theoretical coding

After producing a group of focused codes, I needed to form this information into theoretical codes.[82] The idea was to discover central categories that had the power to analyze the missionary surge. Then, I tried to write a storyline through integrating these categories.[83] This analytic narrative attempted to explain some of the factors behind the Ukrainian evangelical missionary surge of the 1990s.

The goal was to produce a theory with *density*, which was both precise in its description and broad in its explanatory power. A theory should be drawn from data that is varied—not just from one data source. Thus, at points where I lacked one of these characteristics in building a theory, I needed to return to data collection in order to obtain the data needed in order to build my theory's explanatory power.[84] Therefore, the ability to move back and forth along the data analysis spiral was vital from the beginning to the very end of coding.

I sometimes looked to other sources as well in order to refine my theoretical codes and narrative. Memos helped in this process, serving as a record of my ideas throughout the research process.[85] I also occasionally looked at the existing literature for centralizing ideas, but the literature often wasn't that helpful since I was working with data that produced many previously unpublished ideas.[86]

---

81. Strauss and Corbin, *Basics of Qualitative Research*, 136.
82. Charmaz, *Constructing Grounded Theory*, 63.
83. Strauss and Corbin, *Basics of Qualitative Research*, 146–48.
84. Strauss and Corbin, *Basics of Qualitative Research*, 158.
85. Strauss and Corbin, *Basics of Qualitative Research*, 153.
86. Strauss and Corbin, *Basics of Qualitative Research*, 155.

Memo Writing Procedures

Memos are "informal analytic notes"[87] that I wrote throughout the process of data analysis. Memos were connected to data sources, codes, and theories.[88] Writing memos gave me the freedom to jot down ideas about how data might be related, possible directions for forming a theory, and questions to follow up with later.[89] Thus, I was able simultaneously to keep the research close to the data through coding and make conjectures through memos about what the research was showing and where I should go next. Working in these two ways at once was more efficient than just doing coding.[90]

Similar to initial coding, initial memo writing was rather simple and even poorly expressed.[91] Memos were written spontaneously and creatively, not as a matter of function.[92] The point was to record all of my significant initial thoughts, even if they were proven wrong or needed to be rewritten later. Yet, in contrast to initial codes, my memos expressed concepts, not just descriptions. Memos are an attempt to build theory out of data.[93] Therefore, memos helped me to slowly develop my ideas and theories regarding factors behind the missionary surge.

It was important to write a memo after each period of data analysis. I did not necessarily need to write a lot, but it was useful to record my impressions at each step for future reference.[94] Looking through these memos helped me keep track of where the process was going. I used memos to point out data gaps that needed to be filled (leading me around the data analysis spiral yet again) and to ask questions and propose conclusions regarding my codes and categories.[95] Some of my memos were useful as text to be included in the writing up of my dissertation later.

---

87. Charmaz, *Constructing Grounded Theory*, 72.
88. Strauss and Corbin, *Basics of Qualitative Research*, 218.
89. Charmaz, *Constructing Grounded Theory*, 72.
90. Charmaz, *Constructing Grounded Theory*, 72.
91. Strauss and Corbin, *Basics of Qualitative Research*, 219.
92. Charmaz, *Constructing Grounded Theory*, 80.
93. Strauss and Corbin, *Basics of Qualitative Research*, 223.
94. Strauss and Corbin, *Basics of Qualitative Research*, 220.
95. Charmaz, *Constructing Grounded Theory*, 82.

Data Validation Strategy

Qualitative research does not strive for verification of results as quantitative research does. While I cannot call my results "verified knowledge,"[96] I can offer a strategy to show that my results do provide a "plausible account"[97] of what is happening. I do this by providing validation of the process used to obtain results. In other words, qualitative research strives for understanding: does what was done make sense? Some authors call this *trustworthiness* or *credibility*, but I will keep to Creswell's use of the term *validation*.[98]

Thus, data validation strategy is part of the process of my research. The reader can judge the soundness of my methods and results by evaluating the success of my validation.[99] John Creswell[100] suggests eight main strategies, of which I have included four. It was important to use multiple data validation strategies in order to show that my results are, indeed, accurate.[101] I employed the following validation strategies: crystallization; member checking; rich, thick description; and an audit trail.

Crystallization

First, I attempted to confirm the analysis of the data by drawing information from multiple data sources. Each of my theories could not be based on one data source alone. By obtaining multiple perspectives from different participants, I was able both to check the validity of my conclusions and to get a fuller (richer) description of the Ukrainian evangelical missionary surge. This process is called *triangulation* by Creswell,[102] but I prefer the term *crystallization* because the number of data sources used might be more than three.

Member Checking

Further, I checked the accuracy of my findings with participants in the study. I took parts of my finished work (conclusions from the data, not the

---

96. Charmaz, *Constructing Grounded Theory*, 132.
97. Charmaz, *Constructing Grounded Theory*, 132.
98. Creswell, *Qualitative Inquiry*, 201, 207.
99. Strauss and Corbin, *Basics of Qualitative Research*, 268.
100. Creswell, *Research Design*.
101. Creswell, *Research Design*, 191.
102. Creswell, *Qualitative Inquiry*, 208.

data itself) to various participants who could give their opinions on my findings.[103] It was important to choose participants who were more aware of the big picture of the Ukrainian evangelical missionary surge of the 1990s and to check with both Baptist and Pentecostal participants. It was desirable to find participants who could read English, but since that was not possible in each case, I had part of the research translated into Russian so that they could evaluate it.

Rich, Thick Description

In order to better convey my results, I strove to vividly describe participants' perceptions of what happened during the Ukrainian evangelical missionary surge of the 1990s. The more details and depth I could offer my readers, the better they could understand the basis for my findings.[104] These details included how I generated my concepts from the data and how these concepts are interrelated.[105] I used narrative as much as possible to describe these results from the research. Rich, thick descriptions also help provide a framework for transferring aspects of the study.[106] Therefore, I have tried to express both my findings and their significance for further application through rich details and an analytic narrative.[107]

Audit Trail

I have established an audit trail so that an external auditor could review my entire project.[108] Such an auditor would have no connection to my study, and thus, could objectively give her or his assessment of the work.[109] My audit trail includes all of my transcripts, coding, and memos, kept both in NVivo and on an external hard drive.

---

103. Creswell, *Research Design*, 191.
104. Creswell, *Research Design*, 191.
105. Strauss and Corbin, *Basics of Qualitative Research*, 270.
106. Creswell, *Research Design*, 200.
107. Strauss and Corbin, *Basics of Qualitative Research*, 272.
108. Creswell, *Research Design*, 192.
109. Creswell, *Qualitative Inquiry*, 209.

Conclusion for Methods and Procedures

The methods and procedures I have used provide a strategy for scholarly inquiry within the accepted bounds of qualitative research.[110] Therefore, I am confident that this methodology has produced a useful analysis of several important factors behind the Ukrainian evangelical missionary surge of the 1990s. After conducting my study using the methodology described above, I produced results that will be explained and analyzed in the next chapter.

---

110. Creswell, *Research Design*.

5

Results: The Story of the Ukrainian Evangelical Missionary Surge from 1989 to 1999

As a result of conducting 40 interviews with missionaries and church and mission leaders (including both Ukrainians and non-Ukrainians), I have identified some factors that highly influenced the Ukrainian evangelical missionary surge of the 1990s (see Appendix B for information about the participants). I conducted non-structured, open-ended interviews, using the grid of factors given in Appendix A (table A1) as a guide. While I followed the rows of the grid in doing my literature review of Light of the Gospel in chapter 3 (spiritual, socio-political, ecclesial, leadership, and financial factors), I think that my research results are better organized by the columns of the grid (source, vision, motivation, means, opportunity), which also correspond with my five research sub-questions. Quite frankly, the results of my research indicated that the ecclesial, leadership, and financial row factors were less important, or less explanatory, than I had originally guessed they would be.

Therefore, I have decided to explain the data in the following manner. First, in this chapter I will attempt to retell the story of the Ukrainian evangelical missionary surge, following my research sub-questions and using the factors that participants noted. Then, in chapter 6 I will attempt to apply what I have learned by constructing a model using the most important factors that emerged in order to help predict or influence future missionary surges.

In the course of my research, I noticed that Baptist and Pentecostal groups tended to work in isolation from one another. Often, the factors that led them to the mission field were identical, but in some cases there were differences. Of course, both groups had their own centers of missionary development and their own missionary structures, but there were some other areas that differed as well. So, I will make note of important differences between the Baptist and Pentecostal churches' involvement in the missionary surge.

In the historical section that follows, Preparation for the Surge in Soviet Times, as well as in sections where specific people are mentioned as having been influential (e.g., leaders of missionary organizations), real names are used. All of these names were shared by multiple participants and/or written sources with one exception, when one person told his own story and gave me permission to use his real name. Other than these cases, pseudonyms are used to protect the identities of the participants.

Preparation for the Surge in Soviet Times

Before getting into key factors that I found were behind the Ukrainian missionary surge, it's important to recall some of the events that happened in Soviet times that influenced and led to a number of these factors. As mentioned in my literature review above, the Millennium celebration in 1988 was the key event that led to greater freedom for Soviet evangelicals and it really marks the starting point for the Ukrainian evangelical missionary surge. However, I found through the course of my research a number of other, smaller events that also played a role in preparing evangelicals for the coming missionary surge. The Pentecostal churches' preparation for the surge seemed to begin the earliest, so I will first outline key events for the Pentecostal churches, and then turn to the Baptist churches' preparation.

Key Events for the Pentecostal Churches in Soviet Times

As he recounted in an interview during this study, in 1960, Vasily Boyechko was a young Ukrainian man who had just finished his service in the Soviet army in the Ural Mountains, having been discharged due to illness. He felt God's call to travel from the Urals east to Vladivostok, and he was able to visit small fellowships of evangelical Christians along the way in Western and Eastern Siberia, in Transbaikal, along the Mongolian border, and in the Far East. He was struck by the tremendous needs of evangelical churches—many struggling to survive, many without any men at all. This trip was the first look by a Ukrainian Pentecostal at the many needy people groups of Eastern Russia.

In 1969, Boyechko was invited to Czechoslovakia to represent the Soviet Union in a conference called "The Youth of Czechoslovakia for Christ."

It was the first missions conference held in the town of Olomouc, not far from Prague. It was a dangerous time since the Soviet army had occupied Czechoslovakia in 1968, so Boyechko was told not to speak openly in Russian, lest he risk arrest.

The conference was organized by Richard Wurmbrand, the Romanian pastor who had founded the Christian mission Jesus Christ to the Communist World,[1] now known as Voice of the Martyrs. At the conference, Boyechko met missionaries from about eight different countries, and after the conference, he started working with various missionaries, especially with those from Slavic Christian Mission (a.k.a., Slaviska Missionen, or Light for the Peoples, as it's known today) from Sweden and Finland. Through these connections as well as with the help of Christian brothers in Czechoslovakia, Christian literature and underground printing presses started making their way into the Soviet Union. Together, Boyechko and the brothers from Western Europe organized the unofficial mission called Good Samaritan. In 1972, Boyechko wrote the first charter for Good Samaritan as an underground mission with the goals of defending prisoners of faith and their families and preparing people to do missionary work in the Soviet Union.

At that time, Pentecostals started working together with Slavic Christian Mission from Sweden to gather information about the unreached peoples groups of the Soviet Union. The Swedish group gave them information that out of 104 people groups, 56 lived in the dark, with no Gospel witness whatsoever. In 1984, over 80 Pentecostal leaders from the western Soviet Union, Transcaucasia, Central Asia, and other parts of Russia gathered for an underground meeting in Rivne, Ukraine. Slavic Christian Mission had provided a map of the Soviet Union with all of the unreached people groups marked. At the meeting, participants committed not just to pray for these people groups but to find a way to reach them.

They agreed to send two "spies" to do further research about the unreached people groups. They sent Ukrainian Slavik Radchuk and Belarusian Sergei Sharapa to travel across Siberia and visit Central Asia, the Volga region, and the Caucasus as well. After hearing these two men's report, they decided to send out a missionary team in 1985 to Uyuk, in the Tyva Republic, and then in 1986 some long-term missionaries to Siberia and the Russian Far East, as outlined above.[2] So, the Pentecostal churches were already involved in sending missionaries and in reaching unreached people groups prior to the Millennium celebration in 1988.

1. Sawatsky, *Soviet Evangelicals*, 396.
2. Boyechko, *Neskorena tserkva*, 269–70.

Key Events for the Baptist Churches in Soviet Times

Baptist participation in the Ukrainian evangelical missionary surge seemed to be prepared for by a number of individuals starting missionary work on their own, many of whom would eventually join Light of the Gospel mission once it was established. Some of the first examples of independent Baptist missionaries in the late eighties were Pavel Timchenko and Sergei Popov (who were both Russians) in Yakutsk and Mikhail Trubchik (from Belarus) in Birobidzhan, in the Jewish Autonomous Oblast of the Russian Far East. In addition to these missionaries, in 1987 and 1988 Moldovans and Ukrainians established a mission in Chita, Siberia[3] that remained separate from Light of the Gospel. All of these missionaries helped inspire further mission work.

Baptist participants did not mention as many key events as Pentecostals did. They mentioned a number of smaller events, mostly without specific dates, including youth gatherings and training sessions. However, the one event that stood out was the launching of the Baptist mission Light of the Gospel on Christmas Day—January 7, 1989—in Zdolbuniv, Ukraine, a small city just outside of Rivne.

There wasn't a large meeting, but it included young Baptist leaders Oleksii Melnychuk, Taras Pristupa, and Sergei Tupchik. In addition, there were a few Baptist leaders who were a generation older than the first group, including Franz Antonovich Shumeiko. It was the first time that these men had openly shared their desire to do new kinds of ministry during *perestroika* and the first time that they heard the word *mission*. The younger leaders discussed their thoughts about mission with very basic ideas about what to do, including preaching and evangelizing, distributing Christian literature, and preaching on the radio.

The next day, January 8, the younger leaders turned to the older generation and asked their opinion about what to do. After having listened carefully, Franz Shumeiko revealed that he had been thinking almost the same thing that they had. They felt that this was a sign that the Lord was blessing their desire to do missions. Stepan recalled that Shumeiko then added words that the younger leaders would take to heart in their future ministry: "If you don't plant new churches, in a few years you will be forgotten."

A number of Baptist leaders also pointed to the Lausanne conferences in Manila (Philippines) in 1989 and in Moscow in 1990 as being influential. Only four Pentecostals were invited to the conference in Manila, and they were not embraced and helped by Western Pentecostals in the way that Western Baptists helped the Soviet Baptists. A larger number of Soviet

---

3. Voloshin, "Sviditel'stvo Ruvima Voloshina."

THE STORY OF THE UKRAINIAN EVANGELICAL MISSIONARY SURGE   85

Pentecostals were involved in the Moscow meeting, but again no serious networking happened with Western Pentecostals. Therefore, although Pentecostals participated, the Lausanne conferences did not have a significant impact on Pentecostal missions, as Damian recalled.

In contrast, the Lausanne conferences emboldened Ukrainian Baptists to think about missions, encouraging them through God's Word and the example of missionaries from around the world. Baptist leaders made key contacts (both within the Soviet Union and with foreign mission organizations and missionaries) and were given some evangelistic tools for doing missions, including a projector and the Jesus Film. Thus, the stage was set for the Ukrainian evangelical missionary surge.

Timing of the Surge

One more issue that needed to be addressed with interview participants was if the years I chose for my research really reflected the timing of the Ukrainian evangelical missionary surge. I based my choice, 1989–99, on when the Baptist mission Light of the Gospel was founded, not being entirely sure what a good end date for that mission was or when other mission organizations and missionaries were the most active.

In discussing the timing of the missionary surge with Baptists, most agreed with these dates. A few people said that the surge continued to some extent until 2004, and a couple of people thought that the biggest part of the wave was from 1989 to 1995, but overall, the dates 1989–99 seemed reasonable. Pentecostals also generally agreed with the 1989–99 timeframe, with a few pointing out that the biggest part of the Pentecostal wave was from 1991 to 1995. Despite the fact that the first Pentecostal missionaries were sent out in 1985 and 1986, the main Pentecostal missionary surge matched the timing of the surge of Baptists quite well. As one American missionary named Tamara who worked in a number of cities in Russia in the mid-nineties said, "I swear there were Ukrainians everywhere."

Source: Centers of Missionary Development

My first research sub-question addressed the issue of where missionaries came from. What kinds of people became missionaries? In other words, what was the source of new missionaries? As I continued my research, I was struck by the fact that missionaries seemed to develop in groups. They came out of certain places, often within certain age ranges. Something was happening such that centers of missionary development were forming. There were some general factors true of most Ukrainian evangelical missionaries as well as some specific places and characteristics that seemed to produce either Baptist or Pentecostal missionaries in separate, though often parallel, centers. I will first explore some of the general factors and then move to specific centers of Baptist and Pentecostal missions.

Spiritual Source: No Obvious Awakening, but the Preparation of a Certain Few

In the history of missions, often a revival or awakening precedes a missionary movement.[4] Awakenings produce many new, enthusiastic Christians, creating a new source from which missionaries may come. Therefore, I was interested to learn if participants in the Ukrainian evangelical missionary surge of the 1990s felt that a revival or awakening was one of the influences behind the surge.

Surprisingly, most participants said that there was not a significant revival or awakening in evangelical churches prior to the missionary surge. People were praying for revival and seeking revival, but overall they didn't see anything all that dramatic. There was an awakening at the Oleviste Church in Talinn, Estonia, in the 1970s and 1980s which affected some Ukrainians, mainly Pentecostals and charismatics, but it is difficult to connect this awakening to many of the people involved in the Ukrainian missionary surge. The only connection I found was to Slavik Radchuk, who visited the revival as a teenager, and there he was touched by the Holy Spirit and given the gift to be an evangelist.[5] As will be explained in more detail below, Radchuk became one of the initiators of the Ukrainian Pentecostal missionary surge.

Instead of talking about revival or awakening, some participants in the missionary surge talked about a small but important amount of church growth, especially among youth, which happened in the 1970s and 1980s. Some referred to this process as being not very visible; it was more internal within the churches. As one Ukrainian missionary named Timofey said,

> There was a small internal awakening of youth at the end of the seventies and beginning of the eighties. The church was being persecuted, was being pressured, but among the youth of different churches at that time there was a spiritual movement. Many

---

4. Fiedler, *Faith Missions*, 13; Johnstone, *Future of the Global Church*, 132; Lovelace, *Dynamics of Spiritual Life*, 21–22.

5. Kraeuter, *Great Soviet Awakening*.

experienced a renewal in their relationship with the Lord. And many of these later became the missionary workers of the 1990s.

It seemed that God was preparing a small but specific group of people, giving them, as Bogdan shared, an "internal drive" for missions in the future. This group included both Baptists and Pentecostals, especially from the underground or autonomously registered churches. In fact, there were inter-church youth meetings during the last years of communism, which helped develop and unite young, mission-minded church leaders.

The preparation for missions that these young people received took place on an individual basis, and was not something in which the church, at least in most cases, intentionally participated. Damian explained:

> Individual people were not prepared because they were mentored or taught in churches, because that kind of thing didn't happen. In churches they always said that people should preach the Gospel and that was the good side of church. But in churches, at least during the Soviet period, they never taught about missions in the sense of leaving your city, traveling 1,000 kilometers to go to some wild mountain or taiga or forest or Siberia and start a new church by yourself. Individual people understood this.... The Holy Spirit led them and each family or individual received a personal revelation from the Lord.

One Russian observer named Yulian said of the Ukrainian evangelical missionary surge that instead of an awakening leading to missions, "it was the opposite; missions led to awakening in the church." During the period of *perestroika*, many church leaders feared doing evangelism and missions, thinking that the period of freedom was actually a trap set by the government, similar to what had happened under Nikita Khrushchev. It took the boldness and success of evangelists and missionaries to show many in the church that the times really had changed.

So, it makes sense that more participants referred to an awakening or revival taking place during the period of 1989–99 rather than during the period which preceded it. Thus, I must conclude that awakening or revival was not a significant factor or source of missionaries for the Ukrainian evangelical missionary surge of the 1990s. Instead, God seemed to prepare certain individuals, especially among younger church leaders, for future missionary work.

Ecclesial Source: Looking for Opportunities for Ministry

As was suggested by some of the literature, most Ukrainian churches were not intentionally preparing people for missions (there were some exceptions which will be mentioned later), but instead, many Ukrainians went into missions because they couldn't get involved in the kind of ministry that they wanted to in their home churches. For example, young people often weren't allowed to lead ministries; leadership positions were reserved for those with more experience. Single women were also limited in ministry opportunities in their home churches. Yet, on the mission field, there were new opportunities available to all, including single women and young men.

Furthermore, as freedom for ministry grew during *perestroika*, a number of Ukrainians wanted to engage in more evangelistic ministries, but many in the church feared the repercussions either from the government or from letting sinners into their churches. Ukrainian missionary Daniel said,

> I gathered 5,000 people on the street and preached, and the whole church was against me. What were we doing? No one needs this. I simply understood that I needed either to open a new church—but that would be a church split, wouldn't it? That's not right. I really didn't want to cause a church split. So, when the idea of moving somewhere else came up, it seemed like it was from God.

Since many in Ukraine weren't ready to engage in evangelistic ministries or plant new churches nearby, those with a heart for ministry and missions were pushed out to the mission field.

Home Source: The Role of Families in Preparing Missionaries

In a number of cases, families played an important role in preparing people for the mission field. Many future missionaries grew up watching their parents minister to others. Some of their parents or other relatives even went to prison for their faith, and some died there. One participant named Yevgeny told how his mother brought him and his brother to their grandfather to be blessed as they went out as missionaries.

> He looked at us and cried, saying, "You are the happiest people on the earth! If God gave me the chance to live my life over, I would dedicate my life to preaching the Gospel." My grandfather said this despite having been put in prison for two years. He went to prison for preaching the Gospel. In other words, he was saying, "I would continue to do it."

In addition, a number of participants in the Ukrainian evangelical missionary surge went to the mission field together with other relatives. Some went to minister together—brothers and sisters with their whole families. Others went to different places led by the same missionary spirit. One missionary named Milana said,

> Then, at the same time, one of my brothers, one brother left for Yakutia to plant a church. Then, one brother left for the Volga region. Therefore, we all had this kind of attitude, this calling that we needed to go somewhere. And so we left for Primorsky Krai, for the city of Vladivostok, my sister and I.

Thus, a number of missionaries came from families in which they learned about the importance of ministry and were willing to go in support of their family and missions.

Ukrainian Source: What Made Ukrainians Ready to Be Missionaries?

As mentioned above, Ukraine had more evangelical churches and more evangelical Christians than Russia. Ukraine accounted for more than half the membership of the Soviet Baptist Union (which included Pentecostals at the time). Thus, it makes sense that it could provide more missionaries. Yet, there were other important factors besides advantages in numbers.

Bogdan pointed out that evangelical Christianity and the desire for missions were able to grow more on the periphery, away from the center of control in Moscow, in places like Ukraine and Siberia. For example, according to Radislav, Ukrainians had a tendency to believe the Bible more, having been less influenced by communist propaganda than Russians. Shawn gave the following example from his ministry:

> Bar none, whenever we would teach, and we just taught mostly from the Bible, when we would talk about something, you know from the Russians we got, well the Belarusians we got "maybe." From the Russians we got "no." And from the Ukrainians, "Well, the Bible says it, why not?"

Furthermore, Western Ukraine had an additional advantage. Since it had become part of the Soviet Union only in 1939, people there tended to be "more active" and "self-sufficient" in following God, according to Rostislav.

What else made Ukrainian evangelical missionaries stand out? The most obvious characteristic was that they were young. Typically, participants in the missionary surge were between 20 and 35 years old with most being under 30. Some were married and some were single. In general, young people had less holding them back. They had fewer family responsibilities and often didn't own their own homes in Ukraine.

In addition, the younger generation embraced the idea of missions more than older church leaders. Older church leadership was too used to being underground and preaching within the church; younger church leaders were ready to preach beyond the walls of church to non-Christians and to try something new. Scott described many of these young people as being "pent up," waiting for the chance to do ministry. Shawn described Ukrainians as having a "mission spirit," just wanting "to get out and go do something." Future Ukrainian missionaries were typically very active in ministry in their home churches (at least as active as they were allowed to be), but most had not yet been ordained and were not in major positions of leadership. Thus, many young Ukrainians were ready and willing to take initiative and leadership on the mission field.

Another interesting factor is that many Ukrainians had a tendency to be entrepreneurial, being willing to take initiative independently. Filipp shared that Ukrainian pastors were more willing to take initiative and stand up against the authorities (a very important question in the late eighties) than Russian pastors were. As an example of the differences, Filipp compared Ukrainians and Russians at the market:

> I can go to the market anywhere in Ukraine and ask how much a chicken costs there. For example, ten hryvnia at this place. I go to another place and it's nine hryvnia. Somebody else offers to sell for seven hryvnia, and that's okay. Everyone's there and selling at their own price. In Russia, you'll never find a situation like that. You go to the market in Russia. At the market it seems like you're selling your own product, but everyone asks each other, what price are you selling for? Ten? And everyone says, ten. Everyone will give the same price. That is the desire to settle for the same thing that everyone else is doing and not do something to stand out.

Furthermore, Ukrainians often were also more adaptable than others, which made them more successful on the mission field. For example, Shawn shared about some training in which he was involved:

> We're trying to teach about small groups, going deep into the Word, learning it, doing inductive Bible study methods, and these kinds of things. And we began to see that they got it very quickly. Russians would always say, oh that's bad, we can't do

that. That's too hard. It's going to cost money. And the Ukrainian guys always said, well just buy some cookies and tea, it's not expensive. Invite them over for cookies and tea and study the Bible. So, again, they adopted things quicker. And we're talking about peoples that are very similar in terms of backgrounds. But for some reason, the Ukrainians picked it up faster.

Being adaptable, Ukrainians were better able to serve others, according to Gerhard. Roman shared that "we did not consider ourselves part of the Ukrainian or Belarusian church. And that helped us to create a Russian church."

One reason for these differences was that Ukraine, especially Western Ukraine, had less "strict vertical authority" than other parts of the Soviet Union, which tended to be more "tsar-centered," according to Mikhail. This difference allowed young people in Ukrainian churches to be more independent and to develop more. Russian church leader Tristan additionally pointed out that Ukraine had more independent-minded churches and leaders in the form of the autonomous church movement, from which most of the leaders of the mission Light of the Gospel came. Thus, a Bible-believing, independent, and entrepreneurial spirit characterized young Ukrainians on the mission field.

Baptist Centers of Missionary Development

In addition to the general characteristics of Ukrainian evangelical missionaries that I've described above, I also identified some particular places or centers that developed either Baptist or Pentecostal missionaries. In the case of Baptists, I found a broader representation of missionaries from all across Ukraine, including a few from Kyiv, Odessa, Kharkiv, and Lugansk. However, there were certain places and organizations that attracted and/or generated much greater numbers of missionaries. These centers served to consolidate and motivate missionaries for the field. In most cases, this motivation was traditional, although it might be fairer to say that in the case of the Donetsk Oblast, as Kevin characterized the situation, missionaries were more "driven out" than sent out. I will now turn to each of these centers.

Western Ukrainian Baptist churches

One of the reasons why Western Ukraine became a very important center for Baptist missionaries was its history. As Vincent explained, Western

Ukraine's history meant that it was a center of growth for several different Christian denominations:

> A large section of the Ukraine only became part of the Soviet Union after World War II. So, that meant they already had considerable experience in church life and were growing. That's not just unique to the Evangelical Christian-Baptists. That's also true for the Orthodox. And there's a reason why . . . the Uniate Church, Greco-Catholics of Western Ukraine with their headquarters in Lviv did so well and really had very able people to start running a university when they opened that up more formally in 1990 or 91.

By Western Ukraine, I mean all of the Ukrainian oblasts west of the Kyiv Oblast. In particular, the cities of Rivne, Chernivtsi, and Vinnytsia were mentioned multiple times as places from which missionaries came. Oleg, being from Russia and having served in ministry in Eastern Ukraine, estimated that about 70% of the missionaries came from Western Ukraine.

Western Ukraine has a history of missionary work which had been "longer on the mind" of people there than in Eastern Ukraine, according to Bogdan. Thus, pastors and church leaders in Western Ukraine encouraged young people to think about missions. So, it is not surprising that the first leaders of Light of the Gospel came out of autonomous Baptist churches within a 300-kilometer (186-mile) radius of Rivne, including Western Ukraine, Western Belarus, and as far east as Kyiv, as Stepan shared.

The Donetsk Oblast Baptist Union

Perhaps the most unexpected Baptist center of missionary development was in the Baptist Union of the Donetsk Oblast. There was a large number of young people in the region. For example, in Mikhail's church, "we had 100 young people and almost 500 older people. There were no middle-aged people at all." Young Christian leaders wanted to do more ministry, but the oblast leadership of the Baptist Union refused to let them. All youth meetings had to be approved by the leadership, according to Mikhail. During one Ukrainian youth rally, the Donetsk youth were forbidden to stay for one last meeting. Filipp, who was a youth leader at the time, decided to go anyway. "And that was the last time I was invited to go to a youth rally. In other words, I was in 'the doghouse.'"

Yet, Donetsk youth longed to get more involved in ministry. American missionary Kevin shared a story about one church leader from the Donetsk Oblast:

> There were apocryphal stories of how when the power lines, high tension power lines, were being brought through his neighborhood, apparently he had pretty good up chains, maybe because he was a KGB reporter. And the high tension power lines were being draped through neighborhoods over people's houses, and they didn't like that, but the government says, "Who are you?" When it came to his house, the power lines zig zag so as not to go over this . . . [church leader's] house. And, that zig zagging of power lines around his house . . . correlates to young ministers seeing that if I want to serve the Lord, the only place that I can be given anything is if I go into mission.

Eventually, the Donetsk youth interested in ministry found out about Light of the Gospel and decided to join them, according to Filipp. Mikhail estimated that over 100 people left the Donetsk Oblast to become missionaries.

Thus, Baptists had significant centers of missionary development in Western Ukraine and the Donetsk Oblast. Many of these Baptists then would be further developed in the related organizations, Light of the Gospel and Donetsk Christian University, which I will discuss next.

Light of the Gospel mission organization

The prominent Baptist mission organization, Light of the Gospel, was headquartered in Rivne, and this organization proved to be another center for attracting future missionaries from throughout Ukraine. It brought together people from the Baptist Union, from the autonomous Baptists, and from unregistered Baptist churches. Stepan shared that many seekers as well as missionaries connected with Light of the Gospel since both groups sought Christian literature and Light of the Gospel was one of the main centers of distribution of Christian literature for the Soviet Union.

Light of the Gospel became the main mission organization for Baptists as many mission-minded people decided to partner with them. On the one hand, as Stepan shared, some people already doing missions decided to join the organization. On the other hand, some mission-minded people decided to join Light of the Gospel instead of starting their own organization. As Filipp shared, "We said that the most important thing was that if we worked with them, we wouldn't have to create our own structure. For us, the most important thing was doing ministry." And so, Light of the Gospel grew as both an attractor and sender of missionaries.

One way that Light of the Gospel gathered, encouraged, and directed potential missionaries was through their missionary conferences. The mission held its first conference in Rivne in 1990 with a "holiday-like atmosphere" and good speakers like Franz Shumeiko according to Stepan. Then, a second conference was held in Kyiv in 1991. Yulian particularly remembered one of the conference speakers:

> Johannes Reimer gave a talk on missions, and I still remember when he said, "What is the biggest blind spot, the neediest place in the world for missions and evangelism?" And he gave some statistics regarding the number of Christians in this place—I'm not sure. Uzbekistan. How could that be? Yes, the neediest place was Uzbekistan. You, that is, we, in Russia, Russian speakers need to go there! In other words, there were these challenges, given certain factors and information about needs. It was a challenge to some people and caused them to think. What can I do?

More conferences followed, both on a mission-wide and local level.

The conferences were not just inspirational, but also practical. At conferences, young people could find out where they could go and how Light of the Gospel could help them get there. They would learn about the cultures of people who needed to hear the Gospel, according to Oksana. And, as Philemon succinctly put it, "It's the connection with the right people, you know?"

Donetsk Christian University

Light of the Gospel began to work together with Earl Poysti, the radio preacher, and through Poysti, Sergei Tupchik was able to visit America. One of Tupchik's stops was at Denver Seminary, where he shared the needs that Light of the Gospel had for training. Out of that meeting, Light of the Gospel invited Denver Seminary Professor Ray Prigodich to come and teach a basic course on missions in Vorzel, outside of Kyiv, for its missionaries in August 1989. Another training session was held in July 1990, according to Samuel.

Light of the Gospel realized that they needed to set up a missionary training school and asked Denver Seminary to help by providing teachers, as Samuel shared. After reaching an agreement with Denver Seminary, Light of the Gospel was able to establish a Bible college in Eastern Ukraine in August of 1991. Originally called Light of the Gospel Bible College and then Donetsk Bible College, it later took on the name of Donetsk Christian University (DCU). Light of the Gospel was able to buy land in Donetsk from striking coal miners in order to build a school, as Nancy shared. This school, although far away from Light of the Gospel's headquarters, became another center for missionary development. It was meant to prepare young Ukrainians to serve with Light of the Gospel on the mission field. As Vincent shared, the school was "part of a way of doing mission."

Many came to the school already planning to become missionaries. As Gennady shared, he didn't decide to study at DCU merely in order to gain knowledge; he was hoping his studies would be "a bridge to future ministry." Oksana explained that the school helped give students a vision of how to work as missionaries and where to go. Teachers, often Americans, inspired students by telling about mission work all over the world, according to Milana. Plus, simply the gathering of so many missions-minded people served to increase the interest in missions further.

Some went to DCU not yet knowing what they wanted to do. Many of these soon became interested in missions as well. As Nancy shared, the school had an ethos of missions:

> The idea was that you come to DCU and this will enable you to do missions somewhere. All right? So everybody, everybody had some ideas about going somewhere. . . . But I think the idea was that this is just what we do. I mean it was so, it was so obvious that . . . this didn't have to be discussed. I mean this was just, this was the program. This is what we're doing.

When younger students like Sophia met DCU students who had already been on the mission field, or when they had the chance to meet working missionaries that DCU would invite, it really got them excited and was a "big push" for them to become missionaries as well.

Many DCU students eventually left for the mission field. In the first two years of the school, perhaps 80% of the graduates of the one-year program would leave for the mission field, according to Stepan, although this percentage decreased in later years. By 1994, the school moved away from a primary focus on missions to include other subjects, such as theology, Samuel explained. The school then also offered longer programs as well, up to three and later four years of study. Numerous DCU students still became interested in missions, especially as missionaries and missionary recruiters would regularly visit the school, as Nancy shared. Thus, DCU was a strong source of missionaries in the early 1990s and remained a source through the rest of the 1990s.

Pentecostal Centers of Missionary Development

In the case of the Ukrainian Pentecostal churches, I found more of a connection between Western Pentecostal churches and the Pentecostal mission organizations Good Samaritan and Voice of Hope than I did between Western Baptist churches and the Light of the Gospel mission. As explained above, both of these Pentecostal mission organizations came out of the initiative of Western Pentecostal churches. Therefore, I will first consider the Western Ukrainian center of Pentecostal missionary development, out of which came both the Good Samaritan and Voice of Hope missions. After looking at this largest center of missionary development, I will then look at two smaller but still noteworthy centers for missionary development in the Russian-speaking parts of Ukraine: Donetsk Oblast Pentecostal churches and the Odessa Missionary School. Finally, I will discuss the one significant center for Ukrainian evangelical missionary development that was located outside of Ukraine: Jelgava Bible School, in Latvia.

Western Ukrainian Pentecostal churches

I should first note that Western Ukrainian Pentecostal churches (from the Union of Churches of Christians of Evangelical Faith) came out of a movement led by German missionary Gustav Schmidt, as David explained. Like the Western Ukrainian Baptists, they were also greater in number and vitality than churches of their denomination in other parts of Ukraine. And not surprisingly, most of the Pentecostal missionaries came from Western Ukraine.

Rostislav described the Western Ukrainian churches as being "strong and unified," with a large contingent of youth who met together, supporting the idea of missions. This unity for missions, especially with support from church leadership, seemed stronger than what the Baptists had, especially as missions seemed to be preached from the pulpit more often. The first missionary team sent out unofficially by the Western Ukrainian Pentecostals through Good Samaritan mission in 1985 inspired others to think about missions, according to David. And then when freedom finally came, Rostislav said that it was as if "the whole energy of the church poured forth from within.... Those who had been in prison understood what missionary work was. They preached about it. They inspired the youth."

"I think that it was something supernatural, like in the Book of Acts, when the Holy Spirit came, especially on youth. Very young brothers and sisters left for everywhere that it was possible to go," said Rostislav. For example, David had wanted to go to the mission field at age 17 but was called into the army instead. In this heavy involvement of youth, there was a similarity to the Baptists. So in conclusion, the Western Ukrainian Pentecostals had a good overall combination of support from church leadership and large numbers of youth working together for missions.

Donetsk Oblast Pentecostal churches

Although it was not nearly as large a center for missions as Western Ukraine, Donetsk Oblast Pentecostal churches produced a number of missionaries who worked with the Pentecostal mission Possibility. Like-minded evangelicals (mostly Donetsk Pentecostals, although some were from the Lugansk Oblast and there were a few Baptists) gathered together to promote missions. Since official church leadership was unable to come to an agreement to do missions, these like-minded evangelicals formed the mission Possibility, according to Damian. Despite the fact that the Donetsk Oblast did not have the large Pentecostal churches that Western Ukraine did, they still produced a number of missionaries, generally more mature people with families, as Damian shared. Furthermore, David noted that even though Donetsk did not send out a very large number of missionaries, it still sent significantly more missionaries that made an impact in Russia than did most of the rest of Ukraine, not including Western Ukraine.

Odessa Missionary School

In addition to the Donetsk Oblast, the one other predominantly Russian-speaking center that developed Pentecostal missionaries was in Odessa at the missionary school founded by Pyotr Serdichenko in 1990. As the school found sponsors who would pay seven to ten dollars per month, it was able to bring in students for 30 to 40 days of study. The school offered a very practical education, as Rodion described:

> We gave them field studies by having them preach in our churches and study the structure of the church.... We taught them practical evangelism, homiletics.... We talked about the laws in the countries where they were going—where Muslims were, [we taught] about the Koran and the different branches of Islam.... In a short period of time we gave them what we could.

Then, graduates were sent to work in various parts of the former Soviet Union, with a concentration of graduates in the predominantly Muslim region of Tatarstan. Graduates would receive missionary support for about two years, and then they were on their own. So, although Odessa Missionary School did not produce a large number of graduates, it still made a significant impact on the Ukrainian evangelical missionary surge of the 1990s, as Damian and Rodion shared.

Jelgava Bible School in Latvia

One more important center for Pentecostal missions was located outside of Ukraine, in Jelgava, Latvia. It was called Jelgava Bible School or Christ for All Nations. The school was founded by Steve Bradcovich and the American organization, Calvary International, now known as Go to Nations. Bradcovich served as the pastor and leader of the school, while Linus LeFever was the school's director. The school operated from January 26, 1991, until 1993, when it moved to Moscow, Daniel shared.

Denis explained that freedom came first to Latvia, so they were able to start Jelgava Bible School quickly. David also described a movement of Christians in the Baltics, especially centered in Riga, Latvia. Many Ukrainians moved there to earn money, but the Spirit of God was at work, and those people who sought God were gathered together.

The leadership of the Jelgava Bible School sent out a recruitment letter to all the leaders of Pentecostal churches, David explained. Young Christians with a thirst for doing more for God told one another about the school, and after the first session of the school, students were encouraged to invite all their friends to come join them, Daniel shared. About 140 students made up the first class, David recalled. And thus, Jelgava Bible School was able to start guiding young Christians into missions. As Yevgeny explained: "Already at that time there was the 'Jelgava Movement,' mainly a missionary movement, which was like a skeleton that started its work. From the [various] countries of the CIS it gathered people, although a greater number were from Ukraine."

The school trained students for four months, giving them a vision to plant new churches. The goal the first year was to plant 20 churches in cities of over one million people, Daniel shared. The teachers were American missionaries and there was a feeling of freedom from tradition. David believed that this freedom created a good atmosphere for learning. The school was not very theological but focused more on challenging students to go into missions. They encouraged students to pray about missionary work, and the Lord would put certain Russian cities on students' hearts, Roman explained.

David described the moment during his studies at which he was led into becoming a missionary:

> In one class, a man of God really challenged us. He said, "How long do you want to live on this earth? Seventy years? Eighty?" And we said that 80 years would probably be better. And he said that in the Bible there is the idea of tithing. "Do you think that this is only about money? It's not about money. It's 10% of your life, your heart, your time." And he said, "Good. And if the Lord asks you for eight years or seven years of your life to do nothing, but just to serve Him? Earning money—that's not worthwhile. Not living for yourself. Not doing things to serve yourself—just serving Him. Of course, we serve and minister our whole lives, but will we give seven or eight years to serve only Him?" And then he was silent and said, "Good. Can I ask for something? Good—if not seven or eight years, would anyone give one year to go and serve on a mission field where no one has ever served before? Just to be a missionary to other people with God's love."

Jelgava Bible School had students from very different backgrounds, but they were all similarly motivated to do missions. Daniel shared his impressions:

> I felt sorry for the many people who had only been believers for a few months who came to Bible school and then really wanted to go as missionaries. I had been a believer from childhood and I felt ashamed—if they wanted to go, how could I be afraid? I understood that they wouldn't be successful, even if they had become really optimistic: "We will take the whole country for Christ! There will be an awakening everywhere!" I only knew a little, but I understood that it would be difficult, yes? Nevertheless, I gathered myself and went. Straight from Bible school, not going home, I bought tickets and left. I had never been in the city before. I didn't know anyone there. I just bought tickets by faith.

David estimated that from 1991 to 1993 about 25 to 30 missionary teams were sent out to Russia from Jelgava Bible School from three graduating classes, and then the school was closed. Out of those missionary teams, some became leaders of the Pentecostal Church in Russia, like Eduard Grabovenko (the head Bishop for the Russian Church of Christians of Evangelical Faith), but many were not successful and went home—perhaps around half, David again estimated.

Jelgava Bible School was very successful for a short period of time in gathering young Ukrainians and sending them out as missionaries, although many of them did not stay on the mission field for long. David concluded that there were two main reasons for the school's success. First, they received some of the best young people from Pentecostal churches—children of believers, and in some cases, children of church leaders. Second, as will be explained further below, the graduates ended up receiving very little to no financial support. This lack of support forced Jelgava Bible School graduates to be men and women of faith who were supported and blessed by God in their missionary work. In any case, David shared that "it was a unique moment when God gathered together leaders."

Vision 1: The Idea of Missions

As I was doing interviews with numerous participants in the Ukrainian evangelical missionary surge of the 1990s, very few participants brought up the idea of vision, but I often heard the Russian word for enthusiasm used. I thought that the word had a similar meaning to that of the English word, and it can have that meaning. But I heard the word so often that I eventually realized that there must be something more to the idea than just positive emotions about an interest. I finally realized that under communism, the word *enthusiast* referred to people who volunteered to engage in some good activity for the sake of a particular idea or cause. Thus, by saying that they went to the mission field due to enthusiasm, participants meant that they became missionaries because they believed in the idea or cause of missions. Doing missions was considered a worthwhile, valuable activity—even if many doing it had no experience or training in how to do it or sought to gain anything out of it. They were amateurs seeking to volunteer their time for the good of God's kingdom.

Before moving on to the enthusiasts themselves, it is worth noting that this enthusiasm for missions was especially promoted by a couple of people with Slavic roots living in the West. The first was Earl Poysti, a radio preacher who was mentioned a number of times by a wide variety of participants across different denominations. His sermons pushed listeners to think about missions, and when freedom came, he did a preaching tour to help promote the work of the Light of the Gospel mission. Kevin called him "the grandfather amongst indigenous mission leaders."

The second promoter of missions was Johannes Reimer, an evangelist who preached about the need for missions. Reimer also published a book called, *Operation Soviet Union: How to Pray for the 160 People Groups in the USSR*, raising awareness of ethnic groups in the Soviet Union that needed to hear the Gospel. Through these people and sources, some of the ideas and enthusiasm for missions were generated.

Enthusiasts for Christ

Ukrainian evangelical missionaries were enthusiasts for Christ since they really wanted to serve God, but they often didn't know how. Yulian described the situation during Soviet times:

> There weren't any interesting ideas of what do in church. They needed some kind of idea. Then the idea of missions came up. This was a new idea for people that was natural for the youth in church because the young people were bored. . . . For young people it was like a fresh wind, a gulp of fresh air.

The idea of missions made sense to these enthusiasts, but they were still looking for a way to get started. Almost any kind of a motivation or provision was enough of a push to send these Ukrainian evangelicals to the mission field.

Evangelical young people during Soviet times lived in a very different world than that of today. David shared that whereas today people are taught that they need "more prosperity, more success, more influence, then people were taught humility and obedience. In other words, we wanted to be obedient to God." In Soviet times, evangelicals didn't have many options open to them for making plans for the future. Instead, they had a "strong, hot" faith, as Ruslan shared, and were willing to take big steps of faith as opportunities arose.

Many had prayed for years for freedom to come, for the chance to do ministry freely, so they jumped at the chance to go into missions and share their faith. Some had read Oswald Smith's books on revival and missions—things that were previously thought of as impossible, but had now finally become possible. Scott shared a story about the tremendous dedication some of these young evangelicals had:

> You know, I can remember, I can remember being somewhere in the Volyn Oblast and . . . this group that we were with, you know basically, we gave them a speaker system and they were going out every day . . . preaching the Gospel morning, noon, and night, and someone said to them, "You guys ought to slow down. You're going to kill yourselves." And they said, "You know, we've been, we've had 90 years where we hadn't had a

chance to do anything. We may be dead tomorrow. This is the time to work."

Despite lack of experience and training

The Ukrainian evangelical missionary surge of the 1990s was basically a movement of amateurs. Many of those who went had gifts and some experience in ministry, and those in the first generation of missionaries who had grown up in Soviet times were often "spiritually mature and dedicated," as Stepan shared. Yet, even they didn't understand much about mission or have any experience or training. Very little training had been available in Soviet times and mission was not even a familiar word to most people.

Ukrainian evangelical missionaries realized that they weren't necessarily prepared, but they wanted to go anyway. For many, leaving for the mission field was a spontaneous decision. Sometimes the young Ukrainians didn't plan to be on the mission field for very long. The missionaries often learned how to preach and minister to people as they went. But, there was such a thirst in people for the Gospel that even the simplest efforts at sharing it were often successful, and thus, even amateur missionaries succeeded. And because of the ongoing need, many missionaries stayed much longer than they had originally intended. In some cases the missionaries' lack of experience and training was a positive thing, making them more adaptable to new situations, as Daniel concluded in retrospect. Radislav summed up the situation like this:

> None of the missionaries, by and large, was really ready. Each one who went in the 1990s went in his own way, making his own mistakes, making his own attempts at ministry. But, as someone said, the Lord is doing an amazing thing through the Holy Spirit: He takes all of our faults, He fills in the gaps, He multiplies our efforts. And when we are weak, it's really true, the Lord is strong.

Despite lack of resources

Ukrainians would often go to the mission field without any support—just by faith and with perhaps enough money to reach their destination. They were so focused on the ministry that they often didn't think about how they would be provided for. Miroslav looked back at those years in this way:

I now look back and think, if it were today, I couldn't leave like that. And many of my friends who are missionaries say, "If it were now, we would have thought, what will we live on? Even more so, in a time of crisis. How will my family be?" But we left for an absolutely new place. Yet, we didn't think about anything except sharing the Gospel. I think that it was an unusual moment in history, in the history of the Soviet Union.

An inner calling and dedication kept missionaries going despite hardships and difficulties. Gleb shared how his family moved 25 times in eight years. Yet, they were dedicated to the ministry and kept working. He even called that time "the best years of my youth, those years spent in Siberia."

In those days, having people of faith was far more important than having financial resources. Damian explained the unusual situation:

> During that period of time financial resources, as strange as it is to say, did not mean nearly as much. . . . They weren't the most important thing. The most important thing was human resources because there was a huge enthusiasm in believers to go and preach God's Word, to plant churches in new places. Today I'm really amazed that we didn't think at all about the financial side of things. It was a work of faith, it was a movement of faith. The people who became our first missionaries left so easily just taking some potatoes and a small amount of food. In other words, you need to start and God will take care of you when you get there.

The general attitude of many of the missionaries was, first you take a step of faith and then you see the Lord provide for you. Of course, many of the missionaries were young and had fewer needs, or at the very least, they didn't worry much about them. But even with this caveat, faith in God's provision was a big factor in many going to the mission field. Scott described how "they just had a missionary spirit about them and a faith to believe that God wanted it done and He'd take care of them."

Perhaps because they often lacked resources the missionaries developed a greater dependence on God and then had more success on the mission field in those years. Those who couldn't live by faith in God's provision eventually left the mission field. So, in some ways, the lack of resources was a test. Ruslan analyzed those years in this way:

> I observed that God always met us halfway. We built a church and did some other projects and saw God's hand, and that did it. So, on the one hand, maybe we could complain: why didn't we get what we needed to live on? But, on the other hand, maybe it

was really thanks to that that we learned a different way: a way to depend on God and not on the budget of a mission organization.

So, a lack of resources did not stop the enthusiasts for Christ; it appeared simply to increase their faith.

Despite opposition and dangers

To get to the mission field, Ukrainians often faced opposition at home as well as on the field, and sometimes dangers. Many evangelical missionaries in the 1990s were not blessed by their home churches and some were even excommunicated for leaving as missionaries. And some traditional evangelical churches even on the mission field worked against missionaries who were trying to start a new church.

New missionaries knew that they would face some dangers on the mission field, but many didn't know what they would be. Young women showed courage in traveling to faraway places like Siberia, trusting in unknown colleagues, and serving among new people. Of course, the KGB was a danger, but that proved to be less and less of a problem as time went on. Missionaries did face opposition from the Orthodox Church and sometimes danger from other religions and cults. Yevgeny shared:

> Once some young people stormed up to us aggressively. They were Muslims and they said, "Water baptism—that's the price of your life. If you hold a water baptism, we know each of you and we will kill each of you. We will even receive a reward for killing unbelievers." And looking at those young men, it was clear that they were capable of doing what they said. And each of us, we, when we returned after the service, they couldn't do anything to us. The people protected us. God was at work.

In other cases, Ukrainian missionaries understood the dangers and went anyway. Scott shared a story about the new missionaries coming to replace a pastor who had just been killed:

> On Sunday afternoon, the pastor and the head of the oblast, who's a Ukrainian guy, gets a phone call from a school in Moldova, in which a Ukrainian guy with a family says, "We're coming up on the train tonight, and we'll be there Monday morning to take this pastor's place and keep the church going." So, this guy had gotten killed, you know. He was a single guy, didn't have a family. But this Ukrainian guy, with his wife and three kids, will be up. "We're coming up on the train right now. We'll be up

there Monday," like Monday night, they got there. I remember picking them up at the train station, saying, "Aren't you worried? They just killed the pastor here! Aren't you worried, that, you know, if you come in here?" He says, "Well, you know, if God wants to do that, that's up to Him." Again there was always that spirit of trust and faith and entrepreneurial-type spirit.

Ukrainian evangelical missionaries were so committed to the idea or cause of missions that they would not let dangers stand in their way.

Spiritual Romanticism

Despite the fact that the word enthusiast has less of an emotional side to it in Russian than it does in English, some of the participants in the Ukrainian evangelical missionary surge of the 1990s did refer to a more emotional vision of the mission field and a more spontaneous decision, even using the term *spiritual romanticism*. Philemon shared, "It's like a first love, like romance with Jesus. You don't really think about consequences, or what awaits you, okay—either what you're going to eat, or what you're going to be dressed or what dangers [are] over there." Other participants pointed to the ideas of trying something new, testing one's abilities for ministry, and traveling to new places. Oksana called it the "human factor."

Spiritual romanticism had its good and bad sides. Oleg shared how God used it:

> In general, it was people who had probably heard God's voice, but maybe in a few cases it was just romanticism. I think that there were both cases. But nevertheless, it was, I would say, a spiritual romanticism. It wasn't simply romanticism to visit Russia. It was connected with, all the same, the work of God's Spirit. And people packed their bags, gathered their kids, not having anything, and left for Russia.

Yet, there did seem to be cases of Ukrainians leaving for the mission field just on the basis of romanticism, and as Timofey pointed out, those who didn't have a "personal call" from God were forced eventually to leave the mission field. They just didn't have success, and in some cases, even caused harm. Thus, God's call to the mission field was another vital element in the Ukrainian evangelical missionary surge, and I will turn to that next.

Vision 2: God's Call and Answered Prayer

The second way that Ukrainian evangelical missionaries gained a vision for the mission field was through some type of communication from God. As Gennady shared, "I am absolutely sure that God worked in our hearts." This communication came in various forms, such as a call, a sign, or an answered prayer. Interestingly, both Baptists and Pentecostals, in fairly equal measure, reported this factor as being important. This factor went beyond the simple idea or cause of missions, because it was personal—a personal invitation or commission from God to go to the mission field.

Inward Call From God

First, I want to focus on the more traditional, inner calling that participants experienced through feelings, circumstances, and relationships with other people. This type of call was mentioned the most frequently by far, sometimes in conjunction with one of the other types described below. Sometimes participants in the missionary surge felt God's call at a typical church service. Sometimes the call came through an invitation or through an experience of short-term missions. In any case, "God led people" in a way that Miroslav described was "phenomenal in the history of the evangelical movement on the territory of the Soviet Union."

The call of God was often referred to as a very important factor—more important than even the missionary organization, according to Oksana. The call was the work of the Holy Spirit, working in individual lives in different ways, but leading many to the same mission fields. Since the call seemed so important, Ukrainians were willing to go to great lengths and take great risks as missionaries. For example, Filipp explained his calling this way:

> But I understood that God was calling me into ministry and I didn't have an answer for Him. I felt fear and I thought, okay, even if I have to go to prison for some number of years, however much time we have to work, we will do whatever is possible. Well, it seems that for more than 20 years we've had enough freedom to work and plant churches and a whole movement and we believe that this may influence, possibly, if it is pleasing to the Lord, if He wants it, this may influence the fate of Russia. It is already a Russian movement that can continue without Ukrainians participating.

One other aspect that is important to understand is that this inward call from God was based on a strong relationship with God, but it often did not include many details about what to do. I've decided to describe this calling as vision because it gave an idea as to what to do and was based on a clear connection with God, but it might be considered more of a motivation since it didn't give a very clear picture of exactly what to do. Fyodor explained:

> At least later, when we got an education and learned all of those things like what a vision is. . . . Then, we didn't even know those words. At that time we were ready for completely different things—to go to prison, to suffer for Christ, to stand in faith under extreme pressure. Those were our purposes. Then, no one even thought about mission. It came unexpectedly. Therefore, we didn't have any vision, any understanding of any kind of what to do. Missionary work in the first years was very primitive—as primitive as you can imagine. The one thing that was true for everyone who went into missions, practically speaking, was that they had a deep personal relationship with God. And for them, to hear God's voice, to discern that God is sending you, for them, that was practically clear. And therefore, if God told you to go, you went, not knowing where, not knowing what you would do.

In some cases, this close relationship with God would mean that He would continue to speak until the person finally agreed to go. Yevgeny shared how God called him originally at the age of 12, sent him on a short-term mission trip, and then continued to tell him things such as "it is your place, it is your time, but you have to make the decision yourself," until Yevgeny finally left. Thus, missionaries had a choice, but the inward call from God was a strong force in pushing them toward the mission field.

Outward Sign From God

Participants recalled several cases of outward signs from God that they should go to the mission field. These signs came to both Baptists and Pentecostals in fairly equal number, although they were much less frequent than the inward call described above. In some cases, it was connected to a prophetic word or some kind of revelation from the Holy Spirit that they should go into missionary work. For example, Miroslav shared that about a year before the Iron Curtain fell, a prophetic word was shared in his church that "there is coming a time when I will take people, and you will leave your homes, you will leave everything, and you will go and preach the Gospel."

In other cases, an outward sign revealed that God was giving the same inner call to different people at the same time or a sign was an answer to prayer. David shared that both he and his wife individually received God's call to go to the same city, thus confirming each other's calling. Georgi had long wanted to go to the mission field, so he sat down to pray for God's direction after graduating from school, and a knock at the door revealed someone with an invitation to serve on the mission field in Russia. There were also a couple of times when a person was given an idea connected with missions, which he or she wrote down, and then it was confirmed by another person who had never seen what had been written down. Thus, there were a number of times when outward signs from God helped give vision and motivation for the Ukrainian evangelical missionary surge of the 1990s.

Prayer Leading to Mission Work

Prayer was another important factor that influenced Ukrainian evangelicals, both Baptists and Pentecostals, to go to the mission field. In fact, there were interdenominational prayer meetings in the mid-eighties that Mikhail noted were one of the factors that influenced the Ukrainian missionary surge. And overall, prayer was mentioned as an important factor behind the surge.

A number of participants specifically noted the importance of prayer and fasting. Often the dedication people had was reflected in increasing amounts of evangelistic and missionary activity parallel with prayer. Dmitro shared about their dedication to prayer and fasting:

> There were fasts. There were fasts and prayer up to 10 days and more. These were not fasts like, for example, not eating before lunch. We didn't even drink water. Several sisters started to lose their hair. Without food, without water they went to work, to the plants and the factories. After work they would still go to help someone.

And through prayer and fasting, God often offered guidance. Sophia shared from her experience as a student at Donetsk Christian University: "I don't remember one instance when people went for a different reason. I would pray, pray, pray and God would reveal to me what He wants: I need to go to this or that place."

In addition, praying for others often led those who were praying to become missionaries themselves. Ukrainians would pray for missionaries and decide to join them. Oksana shared that "someone would pray, pray, and then ask: maybe I should go? Maybe I can serve as a missionary, too?" Some Ukrainians would go on short-term missions trips and not be able to stop thinking about and praying for the people until they became long-term missionaries. Some Ukrainian evangelical churchgoers would pray for the many people groups without the Gospel and decide that they themselves must become missionaries to reach them. Thus, prayer was an important element in preparing and motivating Ukrainians to join the missionary surge.

Motivation 1: Need and Opportunity for Missions

Many participants were motivated by the incredible opportunity and need to share the Gospel between the late eighties and the late nineties. Something only dreamed about in Soviet times started to come true during *perestroika*, and many Ukrainian evangelicals weren't going to miss their opportunity to do evangelism and missions. They felt a responsibility to share God's love with the many unsaved people in Russia. In terms of responses, the opportunities and needs were mentioned about twice as often as were the idea of mission or God's call to mission, so this first motivating factor was a very important one. I will divide this motivation into three major parts: the spiritual vacuum, the greatest needs, and connections to places that led Ukrainians to the mission field.

Response to the "Terrifying Spiritual Vacuum"

As communism and atheism lost their authority in society, a "terrifying spiritual vacuum" was left in their wake, according to Filipp. The need to fill that vacuum led to the opportunity for evangelism and missions. Oles believed that this need was a major factor behind the missions surge:

> I think that the most important thing was the people's spiritual thirst. In that God's Word wasn't being shared, there were no preachers, there were no printed Bibles, no Gospels—the demand was huge.... People wanted to hear, wanted to receive the Gospel, they gladly came to meetings—that's a fact.

Participants in the missionary surge talked about the Holy Spirit opening the way, and they wanted to do something to provide answers for people's interest in spiritual things.

The spiritual vacuum was both significant and widespread. One measure of the need was the incredible demand for Bibles and Christian literature. Scott explained that "You couldn't get enough" and that "everything was flying off the shelves." Another measure of the significance of the interest was how easy it was to attract people. Rostislav shared from his experience:

> And we, as I already said, the whole missionary group, we lived in a house that I bought. And we were constantly being visited by people every evening. We talked with students. People came in order to receive the Gospel, in order to pray. It was a truly powerful movement. It was so open that we could preach openly in the squares. We didn't even need to ask for permission. You just start to preach, hold a Bible in your hands, and you'll gather about 1,000 people around you. It was just stunning.

And this incredible interest and openness was about the same all across the Soviet Union. As Miroslav remembered, you could go to practically any city or village, start a church, and find that "people were waiting for you there."

People across the Soviet Union had a great thirst for the Gospel, and evangelistic outreaches and the missionary surge attempted to meet that thirst. As Rodion described it, "The most important factor was the thirst for 'rain,' and then the rain came. So churches were opened everywhere and people, masses of people, came into the church."

Going to the Greatest Need

Ukrainian evangelical missionaries were drawn to the places and people with the greatest needs. Although the openness and interest were practically the same everywhere, there were many people who had very little opportunity to hear the Gospel, and missionaries wanted to go to them. In general, Ukrainian evangelicals were "burdened for the lost," as Samuel put it, but there were certain people who seemed more deeply lost than others.

Under this general heading, I noticed that Baptists and Pentecostals tended to express their understanding of the neediest people differently. I do not mean to say that Baptists and Pentecostals had contradictory motivations or that they would even disagree with each other on this point if asked. I believe that both sides would embrace all of the ideas about needs that follow. However, they did tend to emphasize needs differently, and this shows something about how they were motivated to go to the mission field.

Plant churches where none exist

There was a general understanding that Ukraine, especially Western Ukraine, was blessed with far more churches than Russia, especially far more than Siberia. Thus, when the idea of missions was embraced, many missionaries wanted to go plant a church specifically where no church existed. Of course, part of the reasoning for this focus was the fact that in Soviet times, one church per city was often considered enough (e.g., it was argued that there was only one church in Corinth, one in Ephesus, etc.) and many missionaries left for the mission field specifically trying to avoid splitting an existing church. But in addition to this reasoning, there was also the desire simply to provide a church for those who had none. Often Ukrainian evangelicals sought to learn about places that had no churches in order to go and serve as missionaries there.

Overall, the desire to plant churches where none existed was mentioned much more often by Baptists than by Pentecostals. In the few cases when Pentecostals mentioned this idea, they did support it, but perhaps Pentecostals mentioned it less due to the fact that Pentecostal churches generally supported Pentecostal missionaries more, and thus, the need to do ministry away from other churches was less of a motivation. David confirmed that the idea of needing to start new churches wasn't that well developed among Pentecostals at that time. For Baptists, however, there was a big push first to plant churches where none existed; only a bit later, as Stepan shared, did the Baptist mission Light of the Gospel move to the idea of starting new churches in big cities that already had churches, but needed more.

Go to the end of the earth

In Acts 1:8, Jesus said that his disciples would be his witnesses "to the end of the earth." For many Ukrainian evangelicals, the end of the earth was Siberia and the Far North of Russia. Therefore, they felt that real missionaries should go to those places. Mikhail explained:

> When missionaries left, and then our missionary expeditions traveled through northern Russia, we painted a picture in people's minds of what a missionary was like. He rides reindeer and is pulled by dogs; he is out there somewhere far away. Yes, that's a real missionary.

In fact, as Scott shared, it seemed as if Ukrainians intentionally chose to be missionaries in the "more difficult" places, in the places "farther out."

The vast area of Russia, especially Siberia, drew missionaries to come and bring the Gospel to places where it had never been. The size of the territory itself seemed to make it more attractive. And, in fact, the needs were great, and much of that territory had never heard the Gospel, but this kind of thinking led to many missionaries going to more exotic, more distant places and few going to more populated, nearer places, such as Central Russia, which also had huge numbers of people that needed to hear the Gospel.

In my research, the attraction of the end of the earth and the massive size of Russia were terms often used by Baptists, but not by Pentecostals. Baptists did concentrate some of their work along the Volga River, but to a much greater extent they saw their mission field to be the vast and sparsely populated areas of Yakutia, the Far East, and Siberian Russia in general. Pentecostals did send missionaries to these places as well, but generally didn't refer to the end of the earth as the Baptists did. Instead, they more often used the terminology of the next category.

Go to the unreached

From the vision trip that Vasily Boyechko made in 1960 to the spying trip made by Slavik Radchuk and Sergei Sharapa in 1985, Western Ukrainian Pentecostals had been exposed to and interested in the idea of unreached people groups. In Matthew 24:14, Jesus said, "And this gospel of the kingdom will be proclaimed throughout the whole world as a testimony to all nations, and then the end will come." These *nations* are usually understood to be people groups, and thus, many Ukrainian Pentecostals felt that missionary work should be focused on bringing the Gospel to the unreached people groups in the former Soviet Union, those that had not yet heard the Gospel.

I could see how this motivation was evidenced when Dmitro shared how the Pentecostals looked at the information they had about different people groups and decided to send missionaries to reach the people of Tyva and Khakassia. These groups were both unreached, which made them a priority. Plus, there was an advantage to doing missionary work among these peoples because the Russian Orthodox Church had less influence there than in places where more ethnic Russians lived.

Furthermore, Ukrainian Pentecostals divided up among their churches the people groups that they had learned about and prayed for them. And as they prayed, they were encouraged to send missionaries to reach those people, for, as David remembered,

> The brothers said, "If no one will go there, they will just die out and will only exist in history. Only in the history books will it be

written that those people once lived. And not one of them will be in heaven, even though, it is said that people from every tribe will be there. How can that be? Someone needs to bring them the Gospel."

Other Ukrainian Pentecostals didn't necessarily seek out unreached people groups, but they did seek to preach the Gospel in cities and villages that were unreached. Missionaries would spread out from a city to reach the surrounding villages. Oles explained that the mission Voice of Hope always tried to send missionaries into the deeper parts of Russia where there were no churches and no missionaries. These were places where unreached people groups often lived as well.

In contrast, the Baptists spoke significantly less about the idea of going to unreached people groups. In one of the few times that it was mentioned, Samuel characterized Baptist missionaries' focus in the following way:

> I think that there was just a real commitment to, you know, let's reach out to the unevangelized, unreached people, both ethnic Slavs, ethnic Russians, and tribal peoples. And so, I think a lot of the ministry that went on in Siberia, for example, was with this dual focus: reaching locals, peoples of indigenous groups, and reaching the large ethnic Russian communities that were also in those same places.

Thus, even when mentioning unreached people groups, reaching ethnic Russians is mentioned in parallel. So, it seems as if going to Siberia, the end of the earth, was more of a focus for Baptists. Then, missionaries would reach all of the people there that they could, without necessarily prioritizing one people group over another.

Let's look at the map

Maps were often used by Ukrainians to decide where to go as missionaries. Their use varied from the casting lots variety of pointing randomly to a place on the map to very calculated attempts by mission organizations to send missionaries to new and needy places. Shawn described the wide use of maps this way:

> Every Ukrainian I ever met always had a map of whatever region they were trying to reach, whether it was a whole oblast, a city, [or] just a part of an oblast. They always had a map and they always had pins in that map of where they had been or were doing ministry, or you know, planning to go. They always seemed

to have that, that vision of looking and seeing, where do we have to go next? What do we need to do?

Students preparing to be missionaries often used maps to decide their place of future missionary work. For example, at the Pentecostal school in Jelgava, one missionary simply chose a city because all the other cities on the map were already chosen by others. Denis shared how this missionary said that if no one wants to go there, "I lay hands on . . . [that city.] I will go." Similarly, students at the Baptist school, Donetsk Christian University, remembered using a map. Sophia shared how there were 20 marked spots on the map where Light of the Gospel mission wanted to send missionaries. Students prayed about those places, and "we naturally chose from those 20 spots."

Thus, needs and opportunities motivated many Ukrainians to become missionaries. Maps were helpful instruments in this process, but the main idea was to find places that needed missionaries, whether among unreached peoples or at the end of the earth.

Connections to Places

A significant number of opportunities for mission work came out of historical or current connections to a particular mission field. Of course, in several cases, the connections were just a simple invitation from a mission agency; the mission agency suggested that someone go to a particular place, and he or she went. In a few other cases, Ukrainians served in the Soviet Army somewhere, and after finishing their service, they decided to stay and do mission work. But in addition to these examples, there were three other kinds of connections worth noting that played a role in getting Ukrainian evangelicals to the mission field.

Short-term missions

The most commonly mentioned connection that influenced Ukrainian evangelicals to go to a particular mission field was having been there on a short-term mission trip. Very often, just going to a place and seeing the needs and opportunities there connected Ukrainians to that place in such a way that they felt that they just had to go back. For example, Rostislav shared his experience:

> And each time after we showed the [Jesus] film, we gave a call to repentance. A huge number of people came forward to repent.

THE STORY OF THE UKRAINIAN EVANGELICAL MISSIONARY SURGE   115

> This was a witness to the fact that this was really God's calling because if people hear and accept the Gospel, it means that this is something we need to do.... I planned to be there for only two months... but that thirst that people had for God's Word, it changed my intentions. I decided, okay, I'll go for two years. I returned home, I spoke with my wife. She said, "Yes, I agree." Our fourth child had just been born. And we, in 1991, with our four children, moved to the city.... Since that time, two years has already been stretched into 24 years.

A number of Ukrainian missionaries said that seeing what was happening on the mission field was enough for them to want to be a part of it. Oles also referred to the "thirst" in people, that in three to five minutes, you could gather a crowd of people to hear the Gospel. After seeing that, "We understood that we needed to organize something in order to preach the Gospel." That understanding helped start the mission organization Voice of Hope. Filipp spoke of what he saw on a short-term mission trip to Yakutsk: "A new movement, new churches. I encountered something that I had never seen before." And he, and many others, wanted to be a part of it.

Family and friend connections

Sometimes Ukrainians went to the mission field because they knew someone who was already there or was going there—family members or good friends. Those connections were more important than the place itself. For example, Yevgeny's friends were going to a city that he had never heard of. He asked them where it was and they told him that it was the place where they made a particular kind of truck. That was all he needed to know in order make the decision to go.

Or, in a greater number of cases, it was family that did the inviting, often initially for a short period of time or for a short-term mission trip. Yaroslav shared how he first went to the mission field:

> My cousin left for the Ural Mountains in Russia in 1990. He just planned to build himself a house there. He had been gone for a month when he returned and told me that there were many people there who had never heard the Gospel. I was the leader of a youth group.... And we decided to go.... There were about half Slavic people that held to Orthodoxy or atheism. And there were Muslim peoples—Bashkirs, Tatars, and other peoples of Islam. We went there, a group of eight people—three sisters and five brothers. I organized the group and we went to preach the

Gospel there. We went for three weeks. . . . It was amazing how God worked in the hearts of people. And people turned to Jesus Christ. These were the first to hear God's Word. After these people repented, a question touched my heart: who will stay with these people and go further with them? Who will help them get established in their faith and later baptize them? And when we left, they gave us their addresses, prayed, and we said we would write. God laid it on my heart that I should move there for at least a year until someone else could help them grow further.

Thus, both family connections and short-term missions played a role in motivating Ukrainians to go and serve on the mission field.

Prison connections

The last kind of connection, which in some ways is the most interesting, was the way that many Ukrainian evangelicals went to serve as missionaries in places where their relatives had served time, and in some cases, had died in prison. These prisoners of faith broke the ground for future missionary work, or as Dmitro said, they were "unofficial missionaries" themselves. Those prisoners shared their faith and planted God's seeds before the Ukrainian evangelical missionary surge of the 1990s even started.

Those places of suffering seemed to attract missionaries. As Tristan shared,

> "The blood of the martyrs is the seed of the saints." In other words, the places where our brothers' and fathers' blood was shed. Where did they suffer? They were sent to the Far East, they were sent to Yakutia, they were sent to Komi, they were sent beyond the Urals. Go there, where our fathers suffered. And where blood was shed, there will be an awakening. In other words, that was a strong motivation.

Thus, many missionaries followed this idea, going to the places where their fathers, grandfathers, and great grandfathers had suffered in prison because of their Christian faith.

There was a whole network during Soviet times connecting prisoners in Russia with their relatives in Ukraine. Vincent explained that

> the *Bulletin of Prisoners' Relatives* was giving information about many places where there were congregations that were isolated. They were giving information about the places where there had been prisons that these people had been at. So, going back to

my place of imprisonment, to share the Gospel to that place and maybe to the prisoners, once they started letting people come into the prisons with some religious presentations. That was certainly a focus drive. And that would be the reason why they go to very specific places rather than to others because they knew about them—if not personally, but somebody in their circle said, "I've got the addresses and phone numbers and go there and they'll tip you off of where to go next."

Rostislav added the important idea that "when brothers began to return from prison, they brought the idea of freedom, religious freedom. Freedom to preach, freedom to do missions. And this added up to a wave, and a new movement." And as Oles shared, this idea of freedom and these former prisoners of faith helped "form" missionaries. Thus, missionary work became focused on these places of imprisonment, and in some cases, the former prisoners of faith helped mentor younger missionaries and motivate them to go there.

Motivation 2: Inspiration From Missionaries

One of the biggest factors that influenced the Ukrainian evangelical missionary surge, at least in terms of numbers of responses by participants, was inspiration from missionaries. Inspiration came from stories of and visits by foreign missionaries. Even more inspiration came from the example of and invitations from national missionaries. Although they all brought some measure of inspiration, the degree of influence they had varied according to whether they had initiated mission, they were inviting others to join them in mission, or they simply served as examples to others. In some cases, missionaries inspired in all three ways, but I will generally focus on the category in which particular missionaries had the greatest degree of influence.

Initiators of Mission

Initiators of mission were generally the most famous people in the Ukrainian evangelical missionary surge of the 1990s—those who were the first to go as missionaries and/or the leaders of the most influential missionary organizations. These initiators tended also to be both good examples and recruiters of missionaries. They were often innovators, trying new methods or opening up new places for missionary work. Thus, these initiators were often mentioned as influencers of the Ukrainian evangelical missionary surge.

Baptist initiators of mission

Although Light of the Gospel was clearly the largest and most active Baptist mission during the surge, let me first mention one Baptist initiator of mission who worked outside of Light of the Gospel. His name is Ruvim Voloshin, a Moldovan who was one of the first Baptist missionaries in Chita, Siberia, first visiting in 1987 and then moving there in 1988.[6] He worked together with Ukrainians and recruited Ukrainians both as an independent missionary and later, in the mid-nineties, as a representative of the Russian Baptist Union. His example and his recruitment influenced many Ukrainians to become missionaries.

Moving on to Light of the Gospel, beyond the motivation of Franz Shumeiko, mentioned earlier, the first leaders of the mission were Sergei Tupchik, Oleksii Melnychuk, and Taras Pristupa. Bogdan described Sergei Tupchik as the "integrator" and Taras Pristupa as the "communicator" for the mission. Thus, Tupchik brought together various initiators and innovators and helped integrate them into one organization. Pristupa became better known as the recruiter for the mission, so I will discuss him at greater length below. Oleksii Melnychuk took initiative particularly in the area of establishing the training center for the mission, Donetsk Christian University.

Other initiators and innovators involved in Light of the Gospel were Vasily Davidyuk in Kyiv and Sergei Guts, Leonid Kartavenko, and Pyotr Kislyak from the Donetsk Oblast. Davidyuk helped start a new denomination of missionary churches near Kyiv, demonstrating how new churches could be planted in Ukraine and setting an example for others in mission work. Kislyak came up with the innovative art exhibition method of evangelism that was used to help start mission work throughout the former Soviet Union. Kartavenko started his own mission in Makiivka, which eventually joined Light of the Gospel, and, as Samuel shared, was innovative in mission work both locally and in later Siberian expeditions. Finally, Sergei Guts not only recruited numerous Ukrainians for the mission field, he helped establish a new denomination of churches near the Volga River in Russia. As Radislav shared, he had the vision to start churches in the cities with a population over one million. All of these men both set an example for missions and enabled others to go and be successful as missionaries.

---

6. Voloshin, "Sviditel'stvo Ruvima Voloshina."

Pentecostal initiators of mission

Moving to Pentecostal initiators of mission, I need to look at the initiators of the major Pentecostal mission organizations plus one evangelist: Vasily Boyechko and Slavik Radchuk (Good Samaritan mission), Waldemar Sardachuk (Nehemiah mission), Vladimir Franchuk (Possibility mission), Nikolai Sinyuk (Voice of Hope mission), and Pyotr Serdichenko (evangelist). Even though Nikolai Sinyuk could be included here, he was described more often as an organizer of mission than as an initiator, so I will describe his role in more detail below in connection with the Voice of Hope mission.

Vasily Boyechko, as noted above, was probably the first Ukrainian initiator of mission in the latter half of the twentieth century and was certainly one of the main initiators in the founding of Good Samaritan mission. Roman shared how Boyechko "got very excited about missionary work," and how he "worked very well with different pastors from Rovno [Rivne], from Belarus, from Brest, from Minsk. I'm not even including Western Ukraine because they worked well together. I think that as an engine for all of this, God used Vasily Boyechko." He helped teach new missionaries and establish them on the missionary field. Boyechko made a great impact on the development of Ukrainian Pentecostal missions.

Slavik Radchuk was one of the first spies, or explorers, among the unreached peoples of the Soviet Union. Roman described Radchuk as a "generator of ideas" and a "motivator for missions." As the first president of Good Samaritan mission, Radchuk was a key recruiter and organizer of missionaries. Since Radchuk was well known, not just as one of the first underground missionaries, but also as a preacher and evangelist, he was an effective recruiter and example for others thinking about missions.

Waldemar Sardachuk and Vladimir Franchuk also made significant impacts for Ukrainian Pentecostal missions. These men were very active in the mission organizations Nehemiah and Possibility, respectively, helping to recruit and send out Ukrainian missionaries, as Rodion and David explained. Their impact may not have been as great as the two initiators connected with Good Samaritan mission, but they still significantly helped promote the Ukrainian evangelical missionary surge of the 1990s.

Finally, Pyotr Serdichenko helped promote evangelism and missions throughout the former Soviet Union. He held one of the first open evangelizations in Odessa in 1988 in connection with the Millennium celebration. This event helped embolden others to engage in evangelism. Serdichenko continued doing evangelism around Ukraine and Russia in coordination with the singing group Emmanuel and, as one of the leaders of the newly formed Pentecostal Union, helped promote mission work. In addition, Serdichenko founded the Odessa Missionary School, as Damian explained. So, even though Serdichenko was not a leader of a mission organization, he helped connect Pentecostal leadership, evangelism, and training to missions.

An Invitation from Missionaries

It probably comes as no surprise that an invitation from missionaries or mission leaders to go to the mission field was another influential factor that motivated young Ukrainians to become missionaries. Missionaries attracted missionaries, friends invited friends, and the number of Ukrainian missionaries swelled. Missionary conferences, with powerful testimonies and invitations to the mission field, made a powerful impact—even more than the endorsement of church leadership, Damian suggested.

Invitations came in many places and in many forms. In some cases, Ukrainians arrived for a short-term mission trip and were then invited to stay or to quickly return. In other cases, there were requests for help from people in Russia. For example, one man who came to Christ in Yakutia asked Light of the Gospel for help—to send people who could minister, since he was limited in ministry as his family would not accept his conversion to Christianity. Stepan explained that as he shared this need with others, two young women answered this need, moving to Yakutia as missionaries and helping to establish a new community of believers there. Thus, invitations to the mission field played an important role in the Ukrainian evangelical missionary surge. As was shared earlier, often young Ukrainian evangelicals didn't need much beyond a simple invitation to pack their bags for the mission field.

Invitations to Baptists

In addition to many informal invitations, there were at least two groups among the Baptists extending formal invitations to people to become missionaries: Light of the Gospel (from 1989) and the Russian Baptist Union (starting in the mid-nineties). Recruiting was done in churches and at the Light of the Gospel school, Donetsk Christian University. A number of people were involved in recruiting missionaries, but the two most prominent ones whom research participants mentioned were Ruvim Voloshin for the Russian Baptist Union (who was discussed above) and Taras Pristupa for Light of the Gospel.

In my interviews, Taras Pristupa was mentioned the most often by far. Pristupa was the head of the missionary department of Light of the Gospel from 1991 to 1993 and was responsible for recruiting, preparing, sending, and caring for missionaries. Bogdan described him as "a person who always had lots of information; he always heard everything and always knew everything. As I said, he was a communicator." Yulian remembered how Pristupa would travel to churches and share "a new vision" for missions. In addition, Pristupa connected people to study at Donetsk Christian University, from which many would later become missionaries. Thus, the active recruitment of Baptist missionaries, in addition to many informal invitations to the mission field, helped increase the Ukrainian evangelical missionary surge.

Invitations to Pentecostals

There was also active recruitment for missions among Pentecostals, often in conjunction with churches. As initiators of mission, Vasily Boyechko and Slavik Radchuk also stood out as key people who invited many Pentecostals to become missionaries, and there were a number of others as well who travelled around Ukraine recruiting missionaries. There were also calls from the classrooms at Jelgava Bible School to go to the mission field. In addition, radio preachers challenged young people to become missionaries. And as more Pentecostals became missionaries, there was a snowball effect, with current missionaries inviting new ones. As Daniel explained:

> Those people who had already left for the mission field later returned and traveled around Ukraine, saying: "Brothers and sisters, Russia needs to be saved! Come back with us!" I think that this was the biggest flow of movement, so that more people went, yes? When people gave their testimonies about what was happening on the mission field, it inspired young people, especially young people. Older people didn't want to go anywhere, but young people wanted to do something.

Thus, invitations from current missionaries played a significant role in motivating more Pentecostals to go into missions.

The Example of Missionaries

In thinking about factors that influenced the Ukrainian evangelical missionary surge, Gleb said: "I believe that personal example played the biggest role. When we came back after trying for three years to return to Rovno [Rivne] and traveled around Ukraine and shared about the need, it was the best advertisement." From the perspective of the listener, Gennady claimed that stories about missionaries and their testimonies "really, really inspired us" to do missions. Ukrainian missionaries perhaps served as the best kind of example, but there were other examples of missionaries that were effective in motivating young Ukrainians into missions as well.

Examples of foreign missionaries in other countries

Even before *perestroika* and the Fall of Communism, some Ukrainians heard about foreign missions. They heard stories of George Müller's ministry and the five missionaries killed by the Auca Indians in Ecuador. Filipp shared how much the story of foreign missionaries trying to reach the Auca Indians affected him:

> My father had an old radio, and I think Yakov Shalenko simply read the book on the radio. I leaned close and listened to the story with a heavy heart, the story of those five missionaries. There was Jim Elliot, and all of those five brave men were killed in the fifties. And then God spoke to me, and I felt God's call. ... "You must become a missionary!" But around me there were no examples.

Oles explained that to many Ukrainian evangelicals, doing the kind of missions that foreigners did seemed impossible:

> We lived dreaming about some kind of awakening. We lived, saturated with ideas of missionary work. We took in all the information we could, from places like America, to learn about missionaries. I remember sometimes hearing about Luis Palau and other missionaries, Billy Graham, and other evangelists. It was very interesting for us. And when we heard information that somewhere a thousand people repented in a stadium—that was something! For us, it was beyond understanding.

All these stories were inspiring, although for many, it was hard to imagine that such mission work would ever be possible in the Soviet Union. Then, with the opening provided by the Millennium celebration of the baptism of Kievan Rus', foreign missionaries actually came to the Soviet Union—openly.

Examples of foreign missionaries in the former Soviet Union

Of course, there were a few foreign missionaries working secretly before 1988, but the floodgates really opened that year. Some of them were able to show to national evangelicals that a new level of openness had truly come. Just the fact that they could openly preach was a shocking development and an answer to prayer. Some of those that stood out were evangelists like Billy Graham and astronaut Charles Duke. As mentioned earlier, the famous radio preacher Earl Poysti was able to come to the Soviet Union and help prepare the way for the missionary work of Light of the Gospel. Finnish evangelist Kalevi Lehtinen, who like Poysti, could speak in Russian, was constantly doing ministry in the Soviet Union and Russia. Johannes Reimer helped motivate Ukrainians to become missionaries. Ray Prigodich helped in the education and preparation of Ukrainian missionaries, especially through Donetsk Christian University. And of course, there were many more whose examples and ministries, at least in some cases, helped both provide a model for Ukrainian missionaries and prove that missionary work was now possible, unlike in the past.

Examples of national missionaries in the former Soviet Union

Many national missionaries, both Ukrainians and those from other parts of the former Soviet Union, played a role in setting an example for others to go into missions. Joseph and Andrei Bondarenko's mission out of Latvia, as mentioned earlier, helped inspire others to go into missionary work. Simon Borodin of Russia helped start the Evangelical Christian Missionary Union that did a significant amount of missionary work in Southern Russia. Mikhail Trubchik from Belarus, upon finishing his army service in the Russian Far East, decided to stay as a missionary. Trubchik was known as "the apostle of Yakutia" (as Mikhail called him) since he opened various mission fields in Siberia, eventually joining Light of the Gospel mission and leading its missionary work in Yakutia. Or, perhaps one might say that Light of the Gospel joined him!

Many Ukrainian missionaries were influential through their examples as well. Valentin Nikonenko was mentioned a number of times as a leader of Light of the Gospel's missionary work in Yakutia. Yuri Morokhovets was an example for missionaries, serving both in the Ural Mountains and then later in the Russian Far East for Light of the Gospel. Pavel Radchuk, Slavik Radchuk's brother, was an active missionary in Chukotka, Siberia, but died in a tragic plane crash, as Denis and Rodion shared. His service is still fondly remembered by many. Pavel Bak played a role in starting Voice of Hope mission as well as in starting mission work in the Ural Mountains. Pyotr Yarmolyuk was one of the first Pentecostal missionaries sent out to the Russian Far East. These and many other missionaries helped motivate Ukrainians to go into missions.

The example of missionaries made an impact in several different ways. Missionaries sometimes visited and shared with young people at schools (sometimes as students themselves!) such as Donetsk Christian University. Sometimes missionaries spoke to youth groups or shared at missionary conferences. In some cases missionaries, especially women, went to the mission field in "chains," as one missionary inspired another, and that one another, etc., as Nancy explained. The example of missionaries had an ever-widening sphere of influence.

Missionaries' testimonies were often very powerful and attractive to Ukrainian youth. Missionaries would preach about their personal experiences on the mission field, about the vast needs, and about God's incredible work. Gennady remembered when missionaries shared with his youth group:

> And for us, of course, for our youth in a big church, it was interesting, but for several young people it really touched them personally. These testimonies—they were like a seed that fell on the ground, in the soil, and they didn't allow one to feel peace. It was that way for me and for several of my friends: when we heard about it, we still didn't understand ourselves, but the idea was somewhere deep in our hearts, and we started to think about it. And we began to pray about it for awhile.

Thus, the idea of missions and the calling to missions would have their effect—but often only after seeing the example of a missionary.

Means 1: Tools for Ministry

Moving from motivation to means, one area that wasn't brought up a lot but is worthy of mentioning was tools for ministry. These were things that helped Ukrainians do missions, and although they were probably not a major factor in the missionary surge, they did make doing missions a bit easier and more successful. As mentioned earlier, many Ukrainians didn't really know how to do missions—they were amateurs—so being given tools for ministry made the prospect of becoming a missionary a good bit more feasible.

Bibles and Christian Literature

Perhaps the most basic tool for ministry is the Bible, and after that other kinds of Christian literature. As mentioned above, Christian literature was in short supply during most of the history of the Soviet Union. Some Christian literature was smuggled in and some was produced on illegal printing presses, but the amounts were generally still quite limited until 1987. As Tristan shared, that was the year that the limits were removed on the amount of literature from other countries that could be received, and thus, the floodgates to Christian literature were opened—at least for those Christians who were willing to risk asking for Christian literature in Soviet times.

Many foreign groups started sending in Bibles and other kinds of Christian literature. In 1988, the United Bible Societies, according to Vincent, "brought in a massive amount of Bibles." Furthermore, Vincent postulated that "they were also the ones who were probably most active from the West in producing literature," although other groups such as Slavic Gospel Association were also active. In addition, Emmanuel mission[7] both used the television program Superbook and distributed Christian literature as part of its mission, often working with Pentecostal groups out of Kyiv, according to Grigory and Daniel.

Finally, the German mission Light in the East sent large amounts of Christian literature to Light of the Gospel mission, which then sent it on to individuals, churches, and other ministries in addition to using it for their own missionary ministry. Grigory said that thousands of packages of literature were sent to far-away places like Kamchatka and Sakhalin. And, as Stepan shared, the literature provided "a very big impulse" for the development of missions.

Christian literature was the basic tool that many of the first Ukrainian missionaries used for ministry. In some cases, as Oles shared, mission organizations couldn't provide much, but they could at least provide some Christian literature for their missionaries to use. And, as Yevgeny explained, some missionaries who didn't officially work with any mission organization could still turn to mission organizations for Christian literature, and in his case, he and his team were given "as much as we could carry." Thus, Christian literature helped facilitate the effectiveness of the Ukrainian evangelical missionary surge of the 1990s.

---

7. This foreign mission should not be confused with the Emmanuel evangelistic singing group out of Odessa, Ukraine.

Evangelistic Methods and Projects

For not having any prior experience as missionaries, evangelicals in the Soviet Union were still quite creative. One of the very first methods of evangelism used in Ukraine and Russia during *perestroika* was traveling Christian libraries. As more Christian literature became available, evangelicals decided to share what they had with the public. Vincent explained why this method was so effective:

> These reading libraries that sprang up, where did that idea come from? I think that's probably very indigenous, but I don't know for sure because I haven't heard of that as much in other places. But it wasn't just in Makiivka, where they have these libraries standing there. And people would borrow and go back. It's a reading public. The, the Soviet Union, compared to most other places that weren't terribly mission driven, was a very literate public. To read was just natural. And so now we've got some religious books that you can borrow to read, and you haven't been able to do that [in the past]. It just makes so much obvious sense to have people read that and wait and see how they want to talk about it. . . . And wherever those missionaries went up, way up into northern Siberia, they had these reading libraries as one of their devices.

A whole network of these libraries was developed, and out of these developed conferences for library readers, and out of these Bible study groups, and finally, new churches. As Stepan shared, it was the "first help for beginning missionary ministry."

A second method that helped the first evangelical missionaries during *perestroika* and beyond was the Jesus Film, often provided together with a film projector. Often foreign missionaries provided this equipment to eager young evangelists. One way that these tools were transferred was through the Lausanne Conference in 1989. As Mikhail recalled, different young ministers in the Donetsk Oblast shared the equipment with one another and showed the Jesus Film thousands of times in all of the cities that they could. Gerhard remembered how Ukrainian evangelicals were able to show the Jesus Film in institutes and universities, and through the film at least eight churches were planted around Kyiv. Rostislav said that the German mission organization Nehemiah also provided the Jesus Film to Ukrainians on the mission field and Yevgeny added how effective the Jesus Film was in leading people to God.

One method that was mentioned earlier as being used specifically by Light of the Gospel mission was the art exhibition ministry, The Life of Jesus Christ, started by Pyotr Kislyak. This method was mentioned by a number of participants connected with Light of the Gospel as being an effective tool for ministry that often prepared the way for long-term missionaries. As Stepan explained, the art exhibition would often be sent to a city to be shown for one month, and out of that would usually come a small group of people interested in studying the Bible. Then, long-term missionaries could work with the Bible study group, which would eventually lead to a new church in a new city. Much of the mission work of Light of the Gospel was started in that way, especially in the cities near the Volga River, as well as in Elista in Kalmykia, Russia.

Finally, various evangelistic projects prepared the way for long-term mission, as in the case of the art exhibition. For example, in one case, a boat called *Christ for the Nations of Siberia* travelled down the Ob River. Every time the boat landed, a team would go out to evangelize the city. So, as Oleg explained, his Ukrainian church chose one city and sent long-term missionaries there to work with those who were interested after the evangelization. In another case, Mikhail shared how Ukrainians organized an expedition across the far north of Siberia in order to share the Gospel with isolated people groups, visit long-term missionaries, and inspire other Ukrainians to go into missions. Mikhail evaluated the expeditions:

> How did the expeditions help? Well, first, we visited missionaries. Second, for all those missionaries this was a kind of breakthrough. He [a missionary] had been working in a place for five years by himself, with his wife, and he had built up a group of 10 people. And they met together. The nearest church was 700 kilometers [435 miles] away through the taiga and the mountains. Getting there was just not possible. Perhaps a missionary was able to leave once a year to visit with other Christians in Yakutsk, but the Christians in this little village had never in their lives seen other Christians. They were closed off from the rest of the world. All they knew were 10 Christians. They would sing and preach. And then, the expedition team came, and they wouldn't let us sleep. They would hold services for six hours straight.... That was the kind of real thirst people had.

Thus, projects like these helped long-term missionaries and inspired and enabled others to go as missionaries as well.

Means 2: Missionary Structures

A key factor in helping Ukrainian evangelicals get to the mission field was the existence of missionary structures. Of course, having a missionary structure was not absolutely necessary, as evidenced by the number of independent missionaries who went out during the surge. However, the existence of missionary structures definitely played an important role for a great percentage of the Ukrainians who joined the missionary surge of the 1990s.

In considering missionary structures, I noticed a number of important parallels and contrasts between the Baptists and Pentecostals. As Fyodor shared, in some ways the Baptists and Pentecostals "mirrored" one another. While the two groups weren't very "friendly" with each other, they also didn't "confront" one another. They both focused on the mission field in Russia. They both had relationships with foreign mission organizations and created their own national mission organizations. Yet, there were a number of important contrasts as well, and I will detail these as I discuss the varying kinds of missionary structures below.

National Churches

One of the striking contrasts between Baptists and Pentecostals can be found in the relationships between national Ukrainian churches and Ukrainian missionaries. Although there were exceptions, Pentecostals seemed generally to have better relationships with and more blessing from their home churches in Ukraine than Baptists did during the 1990s. This difference meant that Pentecostal national churches played a greater role in the Ukrainian missionary surge than Baptist national churches did.

Baptist national churches

Regardless of the problems among Ukrainian Baptist churches, there were a number of individual Ukrainian Baptist churches that supported missionaries in the 1990s. Generally, the autonomous Baptist churches tended both to produce the greatest number of missionaries and to be the most supportive of missions. These churches, as Vincent explained, had less of a hierarchy and more openness among the leadership to discuss "pastoral and missional and theological issues," leading to more openness to and interest in missionary work. Tristan added that leaders from free, independent churches were the main "impulse" behind the mentoring of missionaries and the creation of missionary structures. However, there were exceptions, such as the Baptist

Union church in Chernivtsi, which not only supported missionaries but had a good relationship with Light of the Gospel, according to Stepan.

The level of support from individual churches varied from a simple blessing upon the missionary's departure to support through the sending of short-term mission groups and some limited financial help. The number of Baptist churches that supported missionaries in the 1990s was small. Oleg looked at missions-oriented churches as being "mature" and explained that "there was only a small percentage of mature churches in the 1990s. It was a very small percentage. But, over those 10 years, the percentage rose a little bit."

Unfortunately, in my interviews I heard a significant number of times how Baptist churches and Baptist church leadership were against missionary work in the 1990s. As Stepan shared, they would not support missions financially or spiritually and "turned people in their churches against missions." In some cases, it was due to a lack of understanding—why do we need more churches? In other cases, it was because church leaders feared losing people to mission work. For example, Mikhail shared how one time he was threatened with being beaten up if he came to hold a missionary conference at a church! He wasn't actually beaten up, but it was clear that missionary work was a threat to many churches.

Thus, as might be guessed, the official Ukrainian Baptist Union does not appear to have been active in doing mission work outside of Ukraine in the 1990s. The only mission work of any kind that I could find was connected with Ukrainians who emigrated to Western Europe and planted churches there, but as Scott analyzed that situation, he believed that it was the individual initiative of those Ukrainians and not really something organized by the Baptist Union. In any case, the Ukrainian Baptist Union was not involved in the Ukrainian evangelical missionary surge of the 1990s to Russia and other parts of the former Soviet Union.

On the other hand, the Russian Baptist Union, by the mid-nineties, did start inviting Ukrainians to do mission work in Russia. As Tristan explained:

> The Union, if we talk about the Russian Baptist Union, noticed the tendency toward active work done by those invited from Ukraine and Moldova. I repeat, I was not then a member of the Union, but in fact it was clear that many missionaries were working well in new regions—they were missionaries from Moldova and Ukraine—and they became the heads of all the churches in those regions.

Yulian explained that the Russian Baptist Union leadership in Moscow started taking a more active role in inviting missionaries, especially from Ukraine. He even called it a "Macedonian call." The Russian Baptist Union invited Ukrainians to work especially in Central Russia, as it had been bypassed by the first wave of missionaries who went to the Volga River, the Ural Mountains, and of course, Siberia. Thus, Baptist churches' involvement in missions was limited to rare, individual church support and to the Russian Baptist Union in the latter half of the 1990s.

Pentecostal national churches

Ukrainian Pentecostal churches tended to be more positive about missions than Baptist churches in the 1990s. Miroslav even said that the "motivation in churches to do missions" was probably the most important "human factor" behind the missionary surge. Pentecostal churches were interested in missions even before they were able to establish their own union of churches, as Pentecostal church leaders met, discussed missions, and sent out missionaries through the unofficial Good Samaritan mission in the mid-eighties. When Pentecostal churches were officially given permission by the government to form their own Union (the Union of Churches of Christians of Evangelical Faith), they acknowledged the importance of missions by setting up a missions and evangelism department, with Pyotr Serdichenko, Vasily Boyechko, and Slavik Radchuk all helping promote missionary work.

However, there was some disagreement in the leadership of the newly created[8] Pentecostal Union as to whether Pentecostals should have one overall missionary organization (like Good Samaritan mission) or let groups of churches form separate, more regional missionary organizations. Damian explained that a compromise was reached for a time between these two ideas with Pyotr Serdichenko becoming responsible for evangelism projects while Vasily Boyechko became responsible for missions of mercy and good works. Yet, eventually, the separate, more regional missionary structures were accepted as the way Pentecostals would do missions.

Pentecostal church leadership thus supported each of the major Pentecostal missionary organizations, including Good Samaritan mission in several Ukrainian oblasts, Voice of Hope mission in the Volyn Oblast, and Possibility mission in the Donetsk Oblast. Many of the local churches in

---

8. Damian explained that the process of forming Pentecostal unions in each of the territories of the Soviet Union and then forming an umbrella union over them took several years, from 1988 to 1991. So, the "creation" of the Pentecostal Union was a long process.

those oblasts were very active in supporting missionary work as well, as David and Damian explained. There were also cases, as Oles shared, that individual churches sent out missionaries without any mission organization. The amount and kinds of support that churches offered varied, and this issue will be discussed further below.

On the other hand, there were some cases, as Daniel recalled, when Pentecostal churches either didn't bless missionaries, or even called missionaries "rebels." Damian pointed out that this position was understandable considering the sacrifice that it was for churches to send missionaries:

> There was not a surplus of human resources. There were no people in churches "without work," without some kind of church ministry. . . . Therefore, every missionary project was a great sacrifice! The very best people left churches to go into missions, and these people were really needed at home!

Rodion estimated that only about 50% of churches were really ready to send missionaries. Therefore, Pentecostal church leadership, including both denominational leaders and missionary organization leadership, worked with pastors and individual churches to convince them of the importance of missionary work, as Rodion and Damian explained.

Yet, there was some missionary work that was associated with additional controversy. Jelgava Bible School, which was founded by Americans, was associated with foreign, charismatic teaching. Traditional Pentecostals were skeptical about this teaching, and thus, were also skeptical about the mission work associated with it, as Daniel shared. David recalled when, amidst this controversy, the Pentecostal leader Vladimir Murza came to the school and spoke to the students tenderly, like a father, and was able to find a middle ground so that the school could continue its work and the students could continue to be part of the Pentecostal Church. Rodion concluded that despite any controversies associated with the school, the graduates' success as missionaries was without question.

Independent Missionary Work

In many cases, Ukrainian evangelical missionaries went to the mission field independently—with little or no mission structure behind them—especially in the early years of the missionary surge. Scott went so far as to say that

> missions is the work of apostolic people. . . . That apostolic spirit breaks boundaries, doesn't know restrictions, has that impatience to do things. And so, I would say that all those people

that left, you know, what motivated them? It was the Spirit of God speaking through their apostolic spirit to go. So God [was] the only sender in those early years, as far I can determine.

Though perhaps Scott's assessment is a little too strong in light of the work that was already going on among both Baptists and Pentecostals, it was certainly true that most Ukrainian evangelicals went out with much less missionary structure than Western evangelicals have usually had. In any case, I will now turn to some specific examples of more independent missionary work.

Baptist independent missionary work

It makes sense that since Ukrainian Baptist churches often did not support missionary work, many Ukrainians went to the mission field independently. Yulian characterized many of the first missionaries as going "spontaneously," following a personal call. As mentioned earlier, some missionaries had already started working during *perestroika* before the mission agency Light of the Gospel existed, so they really had no choice but to go independently. And, in the years before the Soviet Union fell, it was easier to move and get a job to support oneself to do independent mission work.

In any case, missionaries who went independently had a certain spirit about them. Fyodor described them as "being ready to go no matter what happened." Fyodor further explained that "you simply need to be sure that you have a real relationship with God, and that it is the Lord speaking, and that He will take care of you in everything." That assurance led Baptist missionaries to go wherever they had a connection. If they had a connection with Light of the Gospel, they would go with them; otherwise, they would go wherever they could find some kind of connection (e.g., through friends, family, work, etc.) in a place that needed the Gospel. They were dependent on God with or without a missionary structure. Thus, missionary structures were not influential factors for everyone involved in the Ukrainian evangelical missionary surge of the 1990s.

Pentecostal independent missionary work

The lines between independence and missionary structures for Pentecostals seemed to be a bit more blurred than for the Baptists. In general, Pentecostals seemed to have better relationships with their home churches but many missionaries left not really associated with a particular mission organization.

Thus, they were independent but often had some kind of intermittent support from their home churches.

Certainly many of the first Ukrainian Pentecostal missionaries went out independently, and in Soviet times, that was easier. As Roman shared,

> There weren't any particular missionary structures. Everything was based on sincere prayers and a relationship with God. Our pastors motivated people to become missionaries and people went not really counting the cost about what it means to be an independent missionary. They went to a new place to live and [find] a new job. And then, you see, it was Soviet times, when everyone had a job working for the government. There weren't any missionary structures. But, praise God, then God worked in a special way to motivate many people to the work, to missions.

Independent Pentecostal missionaries supported themselves through money they had saved or through jobs on the mission field. A mission organization might help provide them with literature, but as Tamara shared, she saw very few connections between Pentecostal missionaries and any kind of support from the West.

Foreign Mission Organizations

So, what kind of role did foreign mission organizations play in the Ukrainian evangelical missionary surge of the 1990s? As it turns out, not a very big one. Despite the fact that thousands of foreign missionaries and hundreds of foreign mission organizations descended upon the former Soviet Union, it is remarkable how little foreigners were involved in the Ukrainian evangelical missionary surge. Tristan characterized the role of foreign missionaries in Russia this way: "They were never first; they always worked after the Russian missionary, helping support his [the Russian's] work." In some ways, Tristan's description is one of the better examples in which Westerners and nationals successfully worked together. In many cases, however, foreign missions did not work with national believers in the former Soviet Union at all, and thus, were unrelated to the Ukrainian evangelical missionary surge.

Regardless of the negative examples, some foreign missions did play a role in the missionary surge, so it is important to explain their influence. Overall, foreigners helped the most in the areas of education, offering new ideas about missions, providing Christian literature, and donating equipment for evangelism. In addition, foreigners also provided some financial support for missionaries, and two mission organizations in particular helped send out Ukrainian missionaries. So, I will next explore ways in which foreign mission organizations impacted Baptist and Pentecostal missions, focusing on four missions in particular that made a special impact. The parallels between the groups are rather striking.

Foreign missions working with Baptists

The mission organizations Slavic Gospel Association and Russian Ministries (today known as Mission Eurasia) were mentioned as influential organizations, and they had the advantage of having recent immigrants working for them. Stanislav specifically mentioned the mission organizations Light of the Gospel, Russian Ministries, and the Bible League as being the most influential in the missionary surge. The Bible League's main contribution was through providing Christian literature and Russian Ministries was described by Stanislav as a "locomotive," providing education and holding various conferences and events.

Denver Seminary: Americans facilitating education for Baptists

The American school Denver Seminary was noted several times as being influential as well. The Seminary developed and administered the first programs at Donetsk Christian University, starting in 1991, and initially provided most of the teachers for the school, according to Samuel. Grigoriy recalled how hundreds received training in missiology in addition to other important subjects, thanks to Ray Prigodich and other teachers from the Seminary. Denver Seminary's partnership with Donetsk Christian University helped train missionaries for Light of the Gospel mission and provided vision and inspiration to missionaries as well.

Light in the East: Germans equipping and sending out Baptists

The German mission Light in the East was mentioned far and away the greatest number of times by participants as being the most influential foreign mission. Vincent explained that they had an advantage in that they had many immigrants from the former Soviet Union who knew the language and culture well. According to Stepan, they sent the largest amounts of Christian literature to Light of the Gospel. As Gerhard explained, Light in the East also looked for national missionaries who were already planning

THE STORY OF THE UKRAINIAN EVANGELICAL MISSIONARY SURGE   135

to become missionaries and offered some support—sometimes individual support and sometimes through a mission organization like Light of the Gospel. At one point, Light in the East supported 70 to 80 missionaries with Light of the Gospel, Grigory recalled. Gerhard explained that Light in the East did not believe in tight control over missionaries they supported, but believed more in a partnership model, asking to meet with its missionaries once every two years for sharing and prayer. Thus, Light in the East was effective in supporting both individual missionaries and the Ukrainian mission organization Light of the Gospel.

Foreign missions working with Pentecostals

There were also a number of foreign mission organizations that worked with Pentecostals. Light for the Peoples was involved with the first vision trips that Pentecostals made in the 1980s and it continued to help support Pentecostals in the 1990s through Christian literature and seminars, according to Dmitro and Vincent. Emmanuel mission made an impact through its Superbook program and by providing Bibles. Vincent also pointed out that "the Assemblies of God of America and some Pentecostals conferences in Germany and Britain had ties to Pentecostal churches in this region." Overall, however, Pentecostal missionaries seemed to be less connected to foreign mission organizations than Baptists were.

CALVARY INTERNATIONAL: AMERICANS FACILITATING
EDUCATION, SENDING OUT PENTECOSTALS

The center for missionary development at Jelgava Bible School worked through the foreign ministry Calvary International, which served as a missionary structure as well. As noted above, about 25 to 30 missionary teams were sent out from Jelgava Bible School. Missionaries were asked to commit to serve for at least one year and Calvary International promised to provide support for the year. In addition to providing financial support, Calvary International would send short-term mission teams to help the new long-term missionaries and provide funds for missionaries to return to Jelgava once per month to report on their ministry, Daniel and David shared.

The amount of support missionaries received varied. Steve Bradcovich sought American sponsors for each of the missionaries and one American church provided each missionary team with a sound system to use for evangelism. The first group of missionaries went out in 1991 when the Soviet Union was still intact. At that time support of about $30 per month and $1,000 to buy an apartment was a reasonable amount, Daniel shared. But some missionaries received no regular support; they just received an initial gift to reach the mission field and get established in ministry, David remembered.

After the Soviet Union fell at the end of 1991, prices rose tenfold and the support that Calvary International budgeted just wasn't enough. Missionaries who went out through Calvary International needed to find another way to survive or go home, which numerous missionaries did, as Daniel recounted. But those missionaries who did find a way to continue in ministry essentially became independent. David concluded that the lack of support was actually a blessing, as it forced missionaries to trust in God and teach new believers to tithe.

The breakup of the Soviet Union led not only to economic difficulties, but logistical ones as well. It became more difficult for people of the former Soviet Union to travel between the new countries, and thus, traveling to Latvia for school became problematic. Therefore, Calvary International moved the school to Moscow in 1993, but the new school didn't seem to have as much of a missionary vision, Daniel shared.

Nehemiah mission: Germans equipping and sending out Pentecostals

The German missionary organization Nehemiah helped Pentecostal missionaries in a number of ways, both equipping and sending out Ukrainians for missionary work. Nehemiah mission helped provide equipment such as the Jesus Film and provided New Testaments for missionaries and evangelists, as reported by Rostislav and Damian. Nehemiah also gave sound equipment and a van for the Ukrainian evangelistic singing group Emmanuel to use, as Rodion shared.

Nehemiah mission also both recruited and supported Ukrainians to go into missions. Waldemar Sardachuk, representing Nehemiah mission, traveled around Ukraine, recruiting missionaries to go to Russia, David explained. Rodion added that the mission held seminars to inspire young people to become missionaries. Sardachuk gained the trust of many Pentecostal leaders, who helped assemble teams of Ukrainians that Nehemiah would send out and support. The mission sent teams to Smolensk, Moscow, and all the way out to Irkutsk Oblast in Siberia, David recalled. Overall, Nehemiah was involved in a significant amount of Ukrainian missionary outreach.

National Mission Organizations

In considering national mission organizations, there were a number of contrasts between Baptists and Pentecostals. Daniel noted that the Baptists tended to work more closely with a mission organization (mainly Light of the Gospel) whereas the Pentecostals were more independent. I would add that the Pentecostal national churches seem to have had better relationships with Pentecostal mission organizations than the Baptist churches had with Light of the Gospel. Thus, the Baptist missionary structure of Light of the Gospel was critical for the success of Baptist missions in the 1990s whereas Pentecostal missions, while certainly facilitated by Pentecostal mission organizations, could often draw more help from Ukrainian national churches than Baptists could.

In the 1990s, there were many small mission organizations. Kevin described

> a phenomena of local mission agencies that have been springing up. And many major cities had them. So, based on that, we started contacting these mission agencies. Some of them were registered . . . [and some] unregistered. They didn't really know what a mission agency was, but they'd seen Westerners come and say, "I'm not part of a church, I'm part of a mission agency." So they went out and tried to make the best of what they thought Western mission organizations were [like].

Fyodor estimated that there were around 20 missions that did work regionally. Of all the missions, Oleg believed that the mission Light of the Gospel was the most active. It was certainly the most active Baptist mission. So, I will now look more closely at and analyze the influence of the largest and most active of the national mission organizations: Light of the Gospel, Good Samaritan, Possibility, and Voice of Hope.

Baptist national mission: Light of the Gospel

As explained earlier, Light of the Gospel was formed in 1989 by a number of young leaders from different Baptist churches, primarily from autonomous Baptist churches, the most prominent being Sergei Tupchik, Oleksii Melnychuk, and Taras Pristupa. As Bogdan recalled, those young leaders had been thinking about new ministry, including missions, from 1986 to 1988 and were finally able to organize a mission in 1989. As Grigory described them, in Light of the Gospel "visionaries" gathered whom

> God prepared, and who simply gathered as friends in order to think about how best to do [missions], without ambition. . . . But then God gathered people who really burned for the Lord and therefore God blessed them, God gave them some kind of understanding, God gave them unity, and then the people began to work.

These leaders began to do research as to how best to do missions. First, they contacted existing missionaries working in Siberia and met with them. After getting to know each other, they decided to work together. As Stepan shared, they "learned the process of missions together." Or, as was Scott's impression, "They were simply facilitating what God was doing. . . . You really had that sense that God was doing some special things."

The first missionaries from Light of the Gospel were sent out in response to the request of a woman in Kyiv. As Stepan shared, one of the leaders of the mission was speaking about missions at an event at a large Baptist church in Kyiv when a woman came up to him who had once been a high government official. She was from the Far East of Russia, from a large non-Christian family. She had visited them the previous summer and knew that there was no one near who could preach the Gospel to them. Could Light of the Gospel help?

Light of the Gospel had no partners at the time, so they had to be completely self-sufficient. Stepan explained what they decided to do:

> We had an idea that two teams would go. One team would have people who would work and feed themselves and the missionaries, and the other team would minister. . . . The woman suggested that the region was famous, it was praised, it was known throughout the whole world for its quality honey. So she suggested that if people went there to produce honey . . . if they would collect and sell honey, that would generate enough money for those collecting and for those ministering nearby. . . . They gathered a team and left. Several families left. They went to collect honey and there were those who went to be missionaries.

As Bogdan shared, the leaders didn't really know how to organize a mission, but they did their best to create their own missionary structure. This structure included the founding of a training school, Donetsk Christian University, which was described earlier. Light of the Gospel started attracting more new missionaries and sending them out to the mission field. As Mikhail observed, it was the first Baptist mission to send out national missionaries in the Soviet Union. Other missions, such as Latvian Christian Mission, did more humanitarian work or worked more locally, but sending out national missionaries was distinctive of Light of the Gospel. As the mission became more known, it attracted more and more young Baptists interested in missions and became the main missionary structure for Baptists.

Many young Ukrainians had a great desire to go to the mission field, and Light of the Gospel facilitated that longing. As Grigory shared, people "called, visited, asked, and did everything they could, and then they were sent." As Oksana recalled, often Baptist churches refused to help their members become missionaries, so many turned to Light of the Gospel for help in reaching the mission field. Light of the Gospel offered direction for those who were seeking it, as Grigory explained, and that was all that many people needed in the 1990s to become missionaries.

An independent spirit reflected both the missionaries sent and Light of the Gospel mission itself. This independent spirit meant that the mission was not well connected to Ukrainian churches, as Kevin shared, which resulted both in more freedom and a lack of accountability. The missionary teams or branches of the mission tended to be loosely connected, as Bogdan and Samuel noted, which would eventually lead to splits. But, in the first years of *perestoika* and after the break-up of the Soviet Union, flexibility allowed for quick growth. As Vincent analyzed:

> So, Light of the Gospel for example, had an early experience of a network of cohesion. And [they] managed to settle their competitive leadership issues for quite a long time internally. Not everybody else was like that. They relied more on regional centers of strength and trust with each other. And so that meant that the Ukrainian kind of mission could more easily reach out to long distant places, far away that were obviously more needy than Ukraine.

In 1993 a split took place in Light of the Gospel in which separate organizations were formed, although they were still connected through an overall association, as explained earlier. The reasons for the split were surely multiple, but the key issue here is how the split affected the facilitation of the missionary surge. Clearly the split, which drew the leaders of Light of the Gospel into different spheres, allowed each of them to fulfill more of their personal visions and ambitions. On the other hand, Stepan lamented that the split meant that some fruitful connections were lost.

The missionary surge continued, but with varying levels of success. As Nancy shared, more missionaries were sent out to support existing work and fewer to start new work. Another reason that the work didn't continue to expand was that the quality of new missionaries in the mid-nineties was lower overall than it had been during the first wave of missionaries, according to

Stepan. They were not prepared in the same way that the earlier missionaries had been during Soviet times, plus the issues of money and potential immigration to the West affected some new missionaries. Stanislav reported that some branches of Light of the Gospel fared better than others, particularly praising the Good News branch on the Volga River under Sergei Guts and Gospel to the East in the Russian Far East under Yuri Morokhovets. These missions, according to Stanislav, were able to plan for the long-term more effectively. Thus, facilitation of the mission surge continued under the successors of Light of the Gospel, but with varying levels of success.

Pentecostal national mission: Good Samaritan

Continuing its story from the timeline above, in 1989 Good Samaritan mission started functioning in conjunction with the Pentecostal Church with Slavik Radchuk as president, establishing branches in Rivne, Lviv, Ivano-Frankivsk, and Odessa with the main center in Rivne. From that point on, as Dmitro explained, they had the right to do ministry, distribute literature, or invite foreign missionaries anywhere across the Soviet Union. The Rivne branch was the most active in the 1990s, sending missionaries, according to Denis, "from Ukraine to Central Asia, Siberia, the Far East and Ukraine—Crimea, different places." They also held Bible schools and crusades which often led to new church plants, used various kinds of media, and distributed a lot of Christian literature, as shared by Denis and Yevgeny.

Thus, Good Samaritan mission had a great impact both within and outside of Ukraine, and was especially involved in sending Ukrainian missionaries through its Rivne branch. They had the advantages of good support from the Pentecostal Union and some star power in Slavik Radchuk, who was a very successful evangelist and influenced people to become missionaries. David called him one of the key people, a "giant" in terms of evangelism and missions. Thus, Good Samaritan mission helped both to motivate Ukrainian Pentecostals to take part in the missionary surge of the 1990s and to facilitate their involvement.

Pentecostal national mission: Possibility

On December 9, 1989, Possibility became the first official Pentecostal missionary organization in the Soviet Union under the leadership of Vladimir Franchuk, a Pentecostal pastor in Mariupol, as Rodion shared. A group of about 70 church representatives met in Donetsk and founded the mission.

As Damian looked back at that time, he explained why it was necessary to form a mission organization:

> The creation of the Christian mission Possibility was not a success, but was really a sad event. . . . The reason [it was created] was as a compensation for the lack of missionary vision in local churches. . . . Our local churches, unfortunately, did not have unity. I'm ashamed to say that in our churches there were debates, there were people who didn't understand, there were pastors who were against missions. . . . The mission was born in grief.

Therefore, Possibility mission played a key role in helping facilitate Eastern Ukrainian Pentecostals to go to the mission field since Eastern Ukrainian Pentecostal churches were not willing to take such a step.

Possibility mission never became very large, but Damian believed that it served as a "push" for other missions and missionaries to start working. Between 1989 and 1999 Possibility sent out 10 missionary families from the Donetsk Oblast to various places in Russia. Damian explained that the "ministry was oriented to the east from Mariupol, which included Buddhist Kalmykia, and . . . pagan Udmurtia, and unreached Siberia." The mission also worked with local churches so that their missionaries would receive a blessing from them as they went to the mission field. Eastern Ukrainian Pentecostal churches did not have the human resources that Western Ukrainian Pentecostal churches did, so the mission sent only mature, active believing individual families to the mission field, whereas bigger missions like Voice of Hope could send out whole teams. Yet, Possibility experienced significant success by sending missionaries to areas that had no Christians and then planting churches and founding Bible schools there, as Damian shared. David added that the mission gave Russia missionaries with influence. Thus, Possibility helped enable a number of missionaries from Eastern Ukraine to go to the mission field and the mission served as an example to other missions and missionaries, helping push the Ukrainian evangelical missionary surge a little bit further.

Pentecostal national mission: Voice of Hope

The first organizers of Voice of Hope mission were Nikolai Sinyuk, Pavel Bak, and Sergei Linnik. When first thinking about organizing a mission, some of the leaders actually visited Light of the Gospel mission and spoke to President Sergei Tupchik in order to learn from its good example, according to

Oles. The mission was founded in 1990 and then reregistered in 1991 to work throughout the Soviet Union, as Oles shared. Miroslav explained that Voice of Hope mission was founded to help support missionaries from the Volyn Oblast who were already on the field. After that original, simple goal, they expanded to offer more training and financial support. Rostislav explained that by creating a new missionary structure, it was hoped to improve the spiritual and financial care of missionaries. Thus, the missionaries actually preceded the missionary structure, although the structure proved useful in supporting and continuing the Ukrainian missionary surge.

Leaders from Voice of Hope, especially Nikolai Sinyuk, who continued to lead the mission in 2015, recruited new missionaries and visited those already working on the mission field, as Miroslav and Denis shared. In the 1990s, about 90% of the missionaries sent out went to Russia, mainly to central and northern Russia, according to Oles. In terms of size, Voice of Hope was probably the largest Pentecostal missionary sending organization, as Damian concluded.

Voice of Hope did not have a strict hierarchical structure, but wanted to be more like a family, knowing and supporting one another. They intentionally did not provide full financial support so that missionaries would always have to pray and live by faith, Oles shared. This loose structure seemed quite effective at getting missionaries to the mission field and keeping them there, even during difficult times. And so, this is a good point at which to turn to the question of finances and their impact on the Ukrainian evangelical missionary surge.

Means 3: Financial Support

The role of finances in the Ukrainian evangelical missionary surge of the 1990s is another important factor to consider. Missionary support moved from 100% local to more and more Western over the course of the 1990s, as Grigory shared. A key date in the transition from local to Western funds was December 25, 1991, when the Soviet Union was dissolved, resulting in different currencies in different countries of the former Soviet Union, hyperinflation in some countries, and general economic chaos. When this happened, the ability of national believers to support missionaries or even for missionaries to support themselves became much more difficult, and in many cases, the West stepped in to help. Yet, even with these difficulties, financial support was not often considered by research participants to be an important factor, positive or negative, in the missionary surge. Perhaps this perception was due to the fact, as Damian explained, that evangelicals were simply used to being poor under communism.

Finances Before the Fall of Communism

During Soviet times, finances were often not an issue since work was guaranteed, salaries were standardized, and costs were stable and low, as Bogdan explained. For example, a flight to the Russian Far East cost about 35 rubles (or about 60 dollars) and a flight to Alma-Ata (presently called Almaty), Kazakhstan, cost only about 5 dollars, according to Fyodor and Gerhard. As Nancy shared, missionaries often could easily find a job during this period in a new location—perhaps not as good a job as back in Ukraine, but a job by which one could support oneself. Thus, for many people, finances were not the barrier to missions that they have been for many missionaries in other places at other times. This fact in itself is significant and certainly helped give the missionary surge its initial push.

In addition, Ukrainian local churches and believers could more easily help support missionaries at this time. As explained earlier, many were against the idea of missions, but even a few could gather a significant amount of support, as Fyodor shared. Mikhail explained further how churches often had "too much" money:

> In general in Soviet times churches never had a problem with finances. I remember that our pastor sometimes said, "Brothers and sisters, please don't give so much." We didn't have any large expenses, we had nowhere to use the money. According to Soviet law, the church wasn't allowed to use money to help the needy. Only social services could help them. It was even a criminal offense for us to help them. . . . Several times a year, the tax department would come to our church and audit our accounts. If they decided that we had too much money, they forced us to "voluntarily" give (then everything was "voluntary") to the Gravestone Foundation, to the Foundation for the Protection of our Country, to the Foundation for Wildlife, or to the "Red Cross." They would count how much was in our account and say, "Yes, you have a lot of money. Give away more than half."

Even so, many missionaries were self-supporting, either from money they had already saved or from work on the mission field. In one case, Oles shared how a group of missionaries in northern Russia became the "ministry of culture" for the province. Under the sponsorship of the government, the missionaries were able to travel to different villages along the river and give concerts, freely sharing about spiritual things and religion. In other cases, such as Timofey's, missionaries were 100% self-supporting. There were cases of Ukrainian missionaries getting in their cars with just enough finances to get to Yakutsk, Siberia, as Shawn shared, trusting in the Lord to provide from there, which He did.

Overall, I did not find any significant difference in terms of financial support between Baptists and Pentecostals during this time period. There were only a few reports of Western support. Interestingly, in all but one case these were connected with the schools Donetsk Christian University or Jelgava Bible School (for school resources or initial funds for missionary work after graduating, according to Bogdan and David). Otherwise, all Ukrainian evangelical missionaries were supported locally, whether through their home churches, a mission organization, or their own finances—most often, some combination of these. The picture would change significantly, however, after the Fall of Communism.

Finances After the Fall of Communism

Finances became a much more difficult issue after the Fall of Communism with the economies of Ukraine and Russia in upheaval. Gleb described the situation this way:

> I'll tell you honestly, there was no money for basic existence, nothing to live on, sometimes nothing with which to buy milk because we had no money. There was a new currency, we didn't have Russian citizenship, so we couldn't get a job. Even so, there was no work in Siberia. Everything had broken down. The factories and businesses had closed.

Rostislav explained further that the whole defense industry fell apart and hundreds of thousands of people lost their jobs as all the factories connected with defense shut down. As David shared, Russian citizens were given coupons (i.e., food stamps) with which they could buy food staples in order to survive, but Ukrainian missionaries had no access to such help.

Finding new financial support became critical to keeping the missionary surge going. It was at this point that the paths of Baptists and Pentecostals diverged a bit. As Daniel put it:

> Pentecostals—they went by themselves. Baptists were sent—the mission sent them, yes? Nobody sent the Pentecostals. People simply went on their own—to America or to Russia, yes?

Nobody sent them. Maybe some people looked for sponsors for themselves.

Perhaps Daniel exaggerated the situation for Pentecostals a bit more than was the case—and made the situation for Baptists look better than was often the case! But, Daniel did see some real tendencies that were developing in both groups and even highlighted the temptation that many faced— emigrate to America or become a missionary to Russia. All in all, finances after 1991 became an important issue.

Finances for Baptists after the Fall of Communism

Many in Light of the Gospel, and perhaps other Ukrainian missionaries outside the mission as well, had the philosophy of never asking for money. Quite possibly they got this idea from George Müller, whose life had impacted some Ukrainians interested in missions. This philosophy was changed, or perhaps was simply not promoted any longer after 1991, but it was difficult for many Ukrainians to make the transition to ask for support. As Filipp shared, he tried to avoid saying that he had any needs, but when pressed, he finally admitted to one German woman that he had no support. She both gave him money and found 10 others to help support him!

As the economy failed, mission organizations and missionaries looked to foreigners for support. As Bogdan remembered:

> Local support began to fall. The percentage of local support began to go down as hyperinflation began. If we take the years 1992–1993, people were made poor very quickly in the former Soviet Union. Therefore, hyperinflation had its effect, but it wasn't the only thing. Interest from Western organizations in the Soviet Union grew so that all the directors of mission organizations, initiators of different kinds of ministries, they all looked to partner with the West, and they already didn't pay as much attention to collecting the "kopeeks" from our local churches because it [foreign support] was easier to get.

Thus, both a push and a pull were involved. Less money was available locally; more money was available from the West and it was easier to get. So, it was very natural to neglect local sources of funds in order to seek out Western funds.

Many Western mission organizations were interested in supporting work at that time. But the interest had been building slowly. Bogdan remembered that Light of the Gospel worked alone in 1989. Then in 1990 it connected with Gospel for Asia and Interact, and then Light in the East. By 1993, Bogdan recalled a "line" of organizations and people waiting to talk to representatives of Light of the Gospel. Fyodor estimated that in the case of Light of the Gospel, about 50% of missionaries' support came through the mission and 50% from self-support. The Russian Baptist Union also got involved supporting Ukrainian missionaries in the mid-nineties. They, too, largely depended on foreign support, "farming out funds from Western mission agencies to church planting missionaries," according to Kevin.

Fyodor asserted that Western help in those economically difficult years was a "big, important support" for Ukrainian mission work. From a Western perspective, the needs weren't that large, so it was easy to help. As Yulian shared, "Then if you were given 100 or 150 dollars, that was great. For the West, it wasn't that hard to give—to support someone for 100 dollars. For us, that was a good salary."

A little bit of help could make a big difference. Shawn recalled the experience of some Americans helping a Ukrainian missionary family find a place to live:

> We had a team in Kazan, Russia and met a really lovely Ukrainian couple and their two kids—just drove from Ukraine, want to plant a church among the Tatar people. I said, "Well, where are you living?" And they said, "In our car." I said, "What do you mean?" They said, "Well we've been living for six months in our car." And I said, "Well winter's coming! It's going to be cold!" They said, "Well, we know, but you know, we don't have a place to live." And I said, "Well do you have a church?" They said, "Oh yeah, we've already planted a church . . . but we don't have a place to live." He said, "Maybe we can live in the church, you know, rent out a room somewhere." But anyway, these Americans actually helped them be able to get an apartment and be able to stay in the apartment. But again, that, that spirit of just going and not worrying about finance, not having to have a mission board behind you, not having to have an exact plan, just going to someplace, that this is what God's called me to do. And, there was just a spirit of wanting to go and to preach and to plant a church.

Even though finances had grown more difficult, many missionaries still had the attitude that not much was really needed, that God would provide, and that this was ministry, not a job, so a minimal amount of support would suffice. For example, Sophia shared that

> in principle, we had enough. We were young—what did we really need? We had all these trips to different places and probably the

mission paid for them. What can I say? Missionaries never lived well financially. It was always just enough for life, and that's it.

Mikhail, in retrospect, believed that this was a negative aspect of how Ukrainian missionaries looked at finances: the idea that a missionary received "support," not a "salary," and thus it should be minimal for survival and nothing more. Perhaps this simple and humble view led more Ukrainians to join the missionary surge, but it did appear to lead to disappointment later and perhaps was one factor in the surge ending by the end of the 1990s.

There were a number of sad and frustrating stories from Light of the Gospel connected with a lack of finances that certainly discouraged some Ukrainian missionaries. Fyodor shared how Light of the Gospel had to cut back on expenses to make ends meet, which was one reason they decentralized in 1993. Sometimes technical difficulties connected with the economic chaos played a role, too. Stepan shared one story about some missionaries in Siberia near the Mongolian border:

> They left from here in 1990 when there was still the Soviet Union. Or maybe 1991. And then, the Soviet Union collapsed. They received their support through a bank account. In short, we sent them money from here and they received it there. Other means of communication, such as there are now, didn't really work. Telephones were very bad. It was difficult to get through and sometimes it didn't work at all. As it happened, I traveled there and they complained to me that they had been living without a salary for four months. But I said, "We sent the money." They told me that, "When we go to the bank, they tell us no, and that's it. No, that's all." And I asked, "How are you living?" They told me that they have some people that they minister to. "We simply visit them in the evenings and have tea. They put out tea and cookies." And there you have it.... Later, the bank sent the money back, but in the course of those months, the value of the money fell from, say, 100 dollars to five or ten dollars. Inflation took the rest.

Thus, splitting up the mission into separate regions and countries was necessary to help combat these kinds of problems.

Some missionaries had their support cut back so that they needed to find additional jobs to support their families. Filipp shared how some missionaries lost all of their support. In some cases, missionaries were completely dependent on a Western sponsor, and if the sponsor decided to stop giving, there was nothing the mission could do to help further. For example, Stepan shared how one foreign mission organization agreed to support a number of Light of the Gospel missionaries for 50 dollars per month each. Stepan continued:

> Fifty dollars. At the beginning, we could support two missionaries for 50 dollars. But when inflation hit, that was it. In short, prices increased and changed the situation, and already 50 dollars wasn't enough to rent an apartment or find a place to live. We began to make an appeal. We asked: give more support or allow us to look for additional support elsewhere. They answered: we have our policy. And then we said, well, we have to look for additional support. We can't find a place for our missionaries in the East to live. We don't have enough money for them. They, without warning, simply cut off support. We were left like a "cow on ice." What could we do?

Although in most cases support was difficult and generally too low during the period after communism fell, there were a few cases in which support was actually too high, leading to very different consequences. As Mikhail shared, by about 1995, most support came from the West, and in contrast to very low local salaries, missionary salaries from the West could cost very little there and be worth a great deal in Ukraine or Russia. Thus, there was the temptation for some Ukrainians to become missionaries in order to receive a higher, more stable salary.

So, overall, foreign support for Baptist missions after the Fall of Communism was mostly a positive influence on the Ukrainian evangelical missionary surge of the 1990s. There were some exceptions, but in general, foreign finances played a role in keeping the surge going. Yet, it can also be said that finances were still not a major factor in the sending of missionaries. They played more of a role in keeping missionaries on the mission field, although in many cases in the 1990s, missionaries continued in ministry regardless of financial hardship, though they did complain about it some.

Finances for Pentecostals after the Fall of Communism

In contrast to the Baptists, who became more dependent, for better or for worse, on foreign support in order to maintain their missionary work, Pentecostals remained more dependent on local funds for their support. The economic situation was just as hard for them as for the Baptists, but Pentecostals seemed to have fewer connections with potential foreign sponsors. As Daniel shared, the Baptists had "very big financial opportunities" as opposed to the Pentecostals.

THE STORY OF THE UKRAINIAN EVANGELICAL MISSIONARY SURGE 149

What kinds of foreign support did Pentecostal missionaries have? Some got support from immigrants, or in other cases, Ukrainian immigrants raised support in America and then went to the mission field themselves in Russia, as Daniel recalled. Voice of Hope mission also raised some funds from foreign sources starting in 1993 or 1994, especially among immigrants in America, according to Oles. In other cases, money was raised from Germany or America, as Rostislav shared. The German mission Nehemiah's representative, Waldemar Sardachuk, recruited and sponsored missionaries, according to David, and the Ukrainian immigrant Vasily Botsyan raised money to support about 50 Ukrainian missionaries, as Daniel remembered. However, as Damian observed regarding immigrant support, "In time, the better they lived in America, the less help came from them." So, some foreign support helped, but it did not appear to play nearly as big a role as it did for the Baptists.

A greater amount of support for Pentecostal missionaries continued to come from local sources. Ukrainian churches continued to give to missions such as Voice of Hope in the midst of the financial crisis, as Oles shared. Ukrainian friends and relatives also continued to give. For example, as David recalled:

> My friends in Ukraine sent me not one but many packages with salo and cabbage—because cabbage and salo can last a long time without spoiling. It can travel for a week and it doesn't matter if it gets frozen. And we lived on salo, on cabbage, and on the tea we also had. We drank tea. That was our first winter.

In addition to gifts from others, many Pentecostal missionaries found ways to earn money on their own during those difficult economic times. For those who had a car, like David, they could earn some money as taxi drivers. Some, like Yevgeny, worked construction jobs. Others found more creative ways to make money, as Ruslan shared:

> I remember when we had just gotten there . . . we baked waffles. . . . All night until morning we filled a bucket full of waffles that we made in three waffle makers. I remember that for our work all night, when we sold what we had made at night, we earned 10 dollars.

Thus, missionaries found many different ways to survive during the difficult times.

The policies of the Pentecostal mission organizations seemed to provide for less financial support than Light of the Gospel. For example, Good Samaritan mission provided support in terms of literature and finances according to Yevgeny, but the financial support appears to have been temporary. Denis explained that after the Fall of Communism, the mission supported its missionaries for a few years. Then, it was expected that the missionaries would be supported by their church—either their Ukrainian sending church or the new church that they had planted.

Voice of Hope mission intentionally never supported their missionaries fully. As Oles explained, support went from 20 dollars per month to 35 to 50 to 100 dollars per month today, minus a tithe that the missionaries give for general expenses in the central office. Even today no missionaries are fully supported as it is the mission's intention to encourage missionaries to "pray, brothers and sisters, and God will help: God will meet your needs." Oles continued:

> But even so, churches are being built, Christian centers are functioning, very serious work is going on at schools, children's camps—lots and lots and lots of work. Of course, they look for resources in the places where they live through personal acquaintances, and somehow God sends the needed people, and so on. And the work continues.

The mission would help in ways other than finances as well, providing Christian literature and sending food and other supplies, Oles added.

In addition to raising some support in the West, as noted above, Voice of Hope encouraged national churches to give by producing a newspaper with information about the mission and the possibility to give, Oles explained. But even with these gifts, missionaries were encouraged to earn some money on their own. Despite the fact that missionaries were encouraged to be, at least to some extent, self-supporting and to depend on God alone for help, the leadership of the mission was intentional in making sure that they were taken care of. Rostislav shared how the mission cared for missionaries after the Fall of Communism:

> Giving in several regions was not very good and the missionaries there needed to be supported. Therefore, the mission held conferences and supported missionaries. Constantly missionaries needed to be visited in order to see how they lived and how their ministry was going. Different kinds of help were given. I think that the leaders of the mission were very mature brothers. Many of them were in prison during Soviet times. They knew about everything very well.

Thus, Voice of Hope mission seemed to do a good job of striking a balance between encouraging missionaries to be dependent on God and trying to make sure they were provided for as well.

Graduates of Jelgava Bible School, in some cases, got support from the school (through Calvary International in America) for a time. Daniel shared that some got support and some didn't, but the support that some did receive didn't increase as much as inflation did. So, for example, 30 dollars per month was good support in 1992 but already negligible in 1994. David shared that some got one-time support—enough for an initial place to stay and to live for a few months, but that was all. Daniel said that this situation led graduates either to start working to support themselves, to teach their new churches to tithe, or to leave the mission field.

As is perhaps clear from the previous references, teaching members of newly planted churches to tithe appears to have been one of the main strategies Pentecostal missionaries had to provide for missionaries long-term. As Daniel shared:

> We taught about the tithe and we immediately lived by the amount given, you see? As much as, well, pastors in Russia earlier never were paid a salary, you see? Earlier everyone was a volunteer, but we were the first who became professional pastors, so we received a salary and paid taxes to the government.... Yes, we had practically no other kind of financial help. We lived by the tithe, by faith, that God oversees everything, and of course, we taught a lot about the tithe. People accused us of teaching a prosperity gospel, but our teaching helped us just to survive.

Newer churches were open to teaching about tithing and providing a salary for the pastor, whereas older, more traditional churches considered it a scheme by the missionaries to get wealthy. In any case, it helped enable many Ukrainian missionaries to stay on the mission field and to establish new churches for the long-term.

Therefore, Pentecostal missionaries continued to be supported by local sources through the 1990s, and this fact seems to have been a positive factor in continuing the missionary surge. As participants noted, some missionaries were not able to survive financially, so they went home. Thus, certain missionaries were weeded out, whereas others' faith was grown. David even asserted that the less financial support missionaries received, the more successful they often were. Overall, financial support did not appear to have been a very important factor for the missionary surge in the eyes of my participants, but perhaps the Pentecostal missionaries' relationship to financial support showed how committed they were to the idea of missions and their calling to missions, two factors that were consistently noted as important.

Opportunity 1: Common Territory, Language, and Culture

As the Soviet Union became more open for mission work during *perestroika*, Ukrainians had a great opportunity and a number of advantages that made it easier for them to become missionaries and be successful on the mission field, thus encouraging more people to join the missionary surge. Before the Soviet Union officially ended and while *perestroika* brought new freedoms, Ukrainians could easily travel throughout the Soviet Union, not needing to deal with any borders, visas, or citizenship issues. Nancy characterized travel as a "cakewalk," with cheap flights to just about anywhere. According to Daniel, the train was even cheaper. Of course, geographic barriers still existed in the sense that Siberia and the Far North felt far away, but there wasn't the feeling that Russia was a different country, as Yulian shared. It was easier to make a long journey to faraway places in Siberia than it is now, according to Oksana.

At the time, there was more of a connection between different peoples of the Soviet Union. The people all had Russian as a common language. The Ukrainian missionary didn't need to learn a new language. The generally young Ukrainians who left were able to adapt easily to small differences in dialect and culture. People's mentalities were similar, even after the Soviet Union officially ended, according to Yulian. The needy in Siberia called to their Christian brothers in Ukraine to come help them. Yulian argued that this connection made a significant difference.

Furthermore, when the Soviet Union was still one country, it was fairly easy for Ukrainians to find a new job in another part of the country. Single young men could easily move to the Far North or to the Far East for work. It was a natural thing for them to do to make good money according to Daniel and Timofey. Of course, some of the locals might have had suspicions as to the true motives of the missionaries. Timofey humorously recalled:

> When I went to the police to deal with a certain question they tried unofficially to figure out why I had moved there. They finally decided that I must have done something wrong in my church and that they had sent me away in order for me to pay off my guilt.

So, it was fairly easy for Ukrainian missionaries to move to distant places in the Soviet Union during this period, which facilitated the missionary surge, even if some further explanation as to the reason for their move was still necessary.

Opportunity 2: Freedom for Missionary Work

In addition to it being easy to move, Ukrainian evangelicals had a great opportunity for success in missionary work because of the tremendous freedom which appeared during *perestroika* and after the Fall of Communism. Samuel went so far as to say: "Clearly, the chief catalyst for this and many other mission efforts at that time was the sudden burst of freedom. 'We can do things now that we could never do before.'" Ukrainian evangelicals took advantage of the new door that had opened before them.

But the new door didn't just open. It was more like a bomb going off, with all of the inherent chaos involved in such an event. As Grigory explained: "When somehow the whole system was destroyed, people who were ready started to do something, not knowing how to do it. . . . People simply started to move, started to do something, and God blessed them." In Soviet times, most of society considered Christians to be backward and passive and there was no interest in Christianity among the general educated population. Christianity was supposed to be a thing of the past. Yet, it seemed to be coming back. As Nancy described it:

> But, but I think, you know my feeling. One of the best ways that this has been described is, like somebody said, that a lot of the, you know, church in mission stuff in the Soviet Union, it's a little bit like after London was bombed, and then suddenly all these plants start appearing that everybody thought were extinct. And you've got flowers that haven't appeared since the great fire, growing on these bomb sites and so on. And so, it's like [the] Soviet period, like that's all sort of underground, but then, the whole thing breaks open and this stuff is, you know, sprouting up. Where are the roots? Where are the seeds? We don't know. We thought you were extinct. And, you know, and here it is.

Freedom allowed for Christianity to come above ground again, and Ukrainian evangelical missionaries took advantage of that opportunity. We can see two distinct phases of freedom in this time period, so I will examine how freedom affected the Ukrainian evangelical missionary surge both before and after communism officially fell.

Freedom Before Communism Fell

The period of *perestoika* brought new freedom in many different forms. Christian ministries and missionary organizations could finally exist legally. As Bogdan explained, getting registered in Rivne, a place where the local government had recently changed and become more anti-communist (and thus, more favorable towards evangelicals), allowed Light of the Gospel mission the right to work anywhere in the Soviet Union—although, it should be noted, Bogdan considered it a miracle that the mission organization was even able to be registered at that time in Rivne.

In other places, the government officials didn't change at all, yet they started allowing freedom where it had never been allowed before. Since Moscow had decided Christian preaching was now allowed, all local authorities had to follow suit, as Fyodor explained. Evangelicals could preach openly in the streets and squares and, as Rostislav pointed out, they didn't even need to ask for permission. Baptists, who used to be considered the lowest class of society, were now being accepted into places to which they never had access before. As Nancy remembered:

> One thing that was interesting to me . . . and got more interesting the more I thought about it that summer of 1989, that there were a lot of people who were trying to do sort of social service type ministry. Like, suddenly, it's like Baptists could present themselves to the local *dom malyutki* [orphanage] as they did in Zaporozhye and say, "Could we fix up your place? You need painting, your stuff needs to be repaired. We'd be happy to do that." And so they, they were doing those kinds of things, just offering their services. And also, you know, they're, they're, suddenly they have access to prisons or people could just have access to schools. And so on.

And of course, the new freedom allowed Ukrainians to go into missionary work. Some evangelicals had been thinking about the idea of missions for a while, so when the opportunity came, they jumped at it, as Grigory shared. Some activities were still technically illegal, but some Ukrainian evangelicals decided to test the boundaries. Samuel described the thinking at the time:

> Maybe we could get away with doing some more aggressive outreach—evangelism, church planting in areas that are really in need of the gospel. They said, "We know that legally it is still forbidden to do things like that, but there is *glasnost*, there is

perestroika. Maybe we should . . . test the waters and see just what we can get away with."

So, those who were willing to take some risks, those who took greater steps of faith, took best advantage of the opportunities available. And there was an ever growing number of opportunities available.

Fyodor made the case that there were actually more opportunities for ministry before communism fell than afterward. The problem, of course, was that many people didn't take the opportunities that they had during this first period, fearing retribution, thinking that the freedom was temporary and a trap to catch those interested in doing ministry. But for those bold enough to do ministry and missionary work, there were a number of advantages during this period. Fyodor pointed out that the politics and the economics were more stable—people didn't have to worry about them as they would after communism fell. Life was simpler and people could simply seek God and were interested in the Bible and spiritual things.

Freedom After Communism Fell

So after communism actually fell at the end of 1991, people started thinking more about politics and worrying about how to survive, as Fyodor pointed out. These changes meant that there was less time for thinking about spiritual things. Yet, these new political and economic problems also brought new opportunities. Those who had been hanging onto the idea of communism had to search for something else to believe and trust in.

With the end of communism, more Ukrainian evangelicals were ready to accept their new freedom as real. More Christians started to preach openly and support the idea of evangelism and missions. Fyodor added that, legally, more options were open to evangelicals than before in terms of registering organizations, starting Christian schools, building churches, etc. "It was like suddenly all the barriers fell down," Nancy shared. Everything was now possible, so what would Ukrainian evangelicals do?

This freedom prompted more Ukrainian evangelicals to get involved in the missionary surge. Missionaries went out to meet the great spiritual thirst that covered the former Soviet Union. As Oles pointed out, people longed for God's Word and to hear God's truth, and the new freedom allowed missionaries to share the Gospel with them. Denis emphasized the great interest there was among young people in becoming missionaries at this point: "And then freedom came. You know, information [was] going from place to place and young people ask[ed], how we can go to be, for missions, to be missionaries?" Yevgeny put it well when he said that the "wave" of missions came out of the "context of freedom." So, in conclusion, it is clear that the coming of freedom was a big influence on the missionary surge, but it is also important to look at the wave of the missionary surge itself.

Opportunity 3: God's Grace at Work

I looked earlier at the spiritual factors which more directly motivated Ukrainians and gave them the vision to become missionaries through God's calling and answered prayer, but it seems to me that there was another spiritual factor at work which provided the opportunity for the entire missionary surge to take place. This factor is hard to explain, and not many of the participants mentioned it, but several considered it to be important. Therefore, I wanted to put together some of their thoughts as to how God's grace was at work, providing the opportunity for the missionary surge to happen.

Participants pointed to spiritual factors that are hard to explain, but difficult to ignore. Radislav said that "God opened the doors, finally, to the socialist countries of the Soviet Union. In my opinion, personally in my life, these spiritual things played the primary role. The primary role. It certainly wasn't politics." Dmitro recalled how God performed miracles changing people's hearts, opening new doors for ministry across Russia. Some participants simply said that behind the missionary surge was a phenomenon that was impossible to explain. And Stepan concluded that it must have been God's grace since there was so much fruit despite the weaknesses of leadership, conflicts over theology and traditions, lack of mentoring, and lack of vision. Only God could bring good out of all of their mistakes and inexperience.

Fyodor simply believed that God changed the times. There was a time of persecution and then came a time of freedom for preaching the Gospel. Fyodor further described God's work as a wave:

> There was a time when God sent a wave to the former Soviet Union. It was a wave of repentance of non-Christians. It wasn't an awakening in churches, no. But it was a repentance of non-Christians toward God who had been raised in Soviet and communist ideology and ethics. God gave the opportunity to hear, to accept the Gospel, to believe. God gave the time, the wave of the Holy Spirit. And I've used the example, a stark example from life, like one of Christ's parables, the stark example of surfing. When a person takes the surf board and floats on the waves, when he takes that surf board and swims in the ocean and if you look at him, it really isn't impressive. The person floats like

a frog, something is bothering him under his arms. And what is he doing in the huge ocean? He is waiting for a wave. And when an ocean wave comes, it is big, huge—he must not miss the moment. He needs to stand on his surf board on the wave. Not too early, not too late. Only at the moment the wave comes. And what is the surf board? The surf board is, as the disciples said, five loaves of bread and two fish. It is our opportunities. Our education and resources are not important. They are nothing. But when God's wave comes from the Lord, we need to stand on the wave and bring what we have to Jesus.

Certainly many factors were involved in the Ukrainian evangelical missionary surge of the 1990s, but several participants noted an invisible wave behind them all.

Comparison of Findings With the Literature Review

The interviewing process clearly yielded many more factors behind the Ukrainian evangelical missionary surge than the literature did. Some potential factors suggested by the literature as being important did not turn out to be so. Looking at socio-political factors, the greater voice and important social networks that evangelicals had did not seem to be significant factors behind the missionary surge in the minds of interview participants. Considering the state of the evangelical church and missions, many of the leadership factors mentioned in the literature also did not seem to be that important. Although there were many mission leaders who did help facilitate the missionary surge, the surge was more powered at the grassroots level than by just a few leaders. Therefore, the more democratic and empowering style of leadership was, in fact, important.

A number of other potential factors suggested by the literature did turn out to be significant in the opinion of participants. Considering socio-political factors, the freedom during *perestroika* and the Fall of Communism provided an important opportunity for missionary work. The tremendous interest in everything spiritual was an important motivation for missionaries as well. Turning to the state of the evangelical church and missions, negative factors such as emigration and an inwardly focused church subculture were mentioned as real factors, but they were overcome by a number of other factors. A new source of missionaries among church youth was quite significant, as was the new availability of Bibles and Christian literature. It was also true that many young people went to the mission field because of a lack of opportunities in their home churches. Spiritual factors such as prayer and calling in addition to the need to spread the Gospel and see people saved were all very important.

Finally, it was unclear from the literature what kind of role finances played in the missionary surge. As it turned out, the answer was mixed, but overall, in the view of participants, finances seemed less important than many other factors in the surge.

Conclusions

In gathering and organizing the data from participants, I have attempted to tell the story of the Ukrainian evangelical missionary surge from 1989 to 1999. I have done my best to allow the data to drive my categories and conclusions about factors behind the missionary surge. Clearly, a lot of different forces were at work, so perhaps the order of the factors I have described could be changed (e.g., placing the opportunity categories earlier). In any case, I think that the categories I have used paint a fairly complete picture of the missionary surge following the "Who, what, why, how, and where?" questions.

It was interesting to note how Baptists and Pentecostals took quite different paths during the missionary surge but, for the most part, made many similar choices and had similar success. Table 2 compares the timeline of the key events and people among Baptists and Pentecostals in the missionary surge. Note their many differences which reflect the "big wall" that separated Baptists and Pentecostals at that time, as David shared. Yet, as Fyodor noted, the Baptists and Pentecostals often "mirrored" one another, as can be seen in the list of key factors behind the Ukrainian evangelical missionary surge in table 3.

Before considering the similarities of Baptists and Pentecostals, I should note that there were a few differences in factors that influenced Baptists and Pentecostals during the missionary surge as well. Probably the biggest difference between them was the importance of national Ukrainian churches and multiple mission organizations for the Pentecostal churches versus the importance of Light of the Gospel mission for the Baptist churches. There were also some small differences in motivations as well as a significant difference in the way financial support was given after the Fall of Communism.

Table 2. Timeline of Key Events and People in the Ukrainian Evangelical Missionary Surge

Year	Pentecostal event and people	Baptist event and people
1960	Vasily Boyechko sees the needs for missions in Siberia	—
1969	Vasily Boyechko goes to Czechoslovakia for missions conference	—
1972	Good Samaritan mission founded as an underground mission	—
1984	Leaders gather in Rivne to discuss mission to unreached peoples, send out spies to learn more	—
1985	Short-term mission to Uyuk, Tyva Republic	—
1986	Long-term missionaries sent to Siberia and the Russian Far East	—
1987	—	Mission established in Chita, Siberia by Moldovans and Ukrainians
1988	**Millennium celebration of the Baptism of Kievan Rus'—new freedom**	**Millennium celebration of the Baptism of Kievan Rus'—new freedom**
1989	Good Samaritan mission starts functioning in conjunction with Pentecostal Church under leadership of Slavik Radchuk in Rivne. Other branches established in Lviv, Odessa, and Ivano-Frankivsk	Light of the Gospel mission founded in Rivne under leadership of Sergei Tupchik, Oleksii Melnychuk, and Taras Pristupa
	Lausanne Conference in Manila, Philippines—not that helpful	Lausanne Conference in Manila, Philippines—helpful
	Possibility mission founded in Mariupol under leadership of Vladimir Franchuk	—

Year	Pentecostal event and people	Baptist event and people
1990	Lausanne Conference in Moscow—not that helpful	Lausanne Conference in Moscow—helpful
	Voice of Hope mission founded in Lutsk under leadership of Nikolai Sinyuk, Pavel Bak, and Sergei Linnik	Light of the Gospel first missionary conference in Rivne
	Odessa Missionary School founded under leadership of Pyotr Serdichenko	—
1991	Jelgava Bible College founded in Jelgava, Latvia under leadership of Steve Bradcovich and Calvary International	Light of the Gospel Bible College (later Donetsk Christian University) founded in Donetsk under leadership of Oleksii Melnychuk with help from Denver Seminary
	—	Light of the Gospel second missionary conference in Kyiv
	Fall of the Soviet Union—15 separate countries emerge	**Fall of the Soviet Union—15 separate countries emerge**
1993	Jelgava Bible School closed—school moved to Moscow, Russia	Light of the Gospel mission split into nine different ministries/missions with Light of the Gospel International Association connecting them
1997	**New law limited religious activity in Russia**	**New law limited religious activity in Russia**

Note. Items that are the same for both Pentecostals and Baptists are shown in bold face type.

— = No comparable event.

Table 3. Key Factors Behind the Ukrainian Evangelical Missionary Surge

Factor	Pentecostal churches	Baptist churches
Source	Families	Families
	Young, entrepreneurial spirit	Young, entrepreneurial spirit
	Western Ukrainian churches	Western Ukrainian churches
	Donetsk Oblast churches	Donetsk Oblast churches
	—	Light of the Gospel mission
	Schools: Jelgava Bible School, Odessa Missionary School	School: Donetsk Christian University
Vision	Idea of missions	Idea of missions
	God's call and answered prayer	God's call and answered prayer
Motivation	Go to the unreached	Plant churches where none exist
	—	Go to the end of the earth (Siberia)
	Connections through short-term missions, family, and friends	Connections through short-term missions, family, and friends
	Inspiration from missionaries	Inspiration from missionaries

Factor	Pentecostal churches	Baptist churches
Means	Christian literature and evangelistic projects	Christian literature and evangelistic projects
	Some church support	—
	Independent missionary work	Independent missionary work
	American mission facilitates education and sends out Ukrainian missionaries (Calvary International)	American mission facilitates education (Denver Seminary)
	German mission equips and sends out Ukrainian missionaries (Nehemiah mission)	German mission equips and sends out Ukrainian missionaries (Light in the East)
	Good Samaritan mission	Light of the Gospel mission
	Possibility mission	—
	Voice of Hope mission	—
	Local financial support before 1991	Local financial support before 1991
	Mostly local financial support after 1991	Foreign financial support after 1991
Opportunity	Common territory, language, and culture	Common territory, language, and culture
	Freedom	Freedom
	God's grace at work	God's grace at work

Note. Items that are the same for both Pentecostals and Baptists are shown in bold face type.

— = No comparable event.

In any case, the number of similarities between the Baptists and Pentecostals was much greater. Baptists and Pentecostals had very similar centers for missionary development, both geographically (in Western Ukraine and the Donetsk Oblast) and educationally (through missionary training schools that were aided in their founding by Westerners). They had extremely similar understandings of vision, both believing in the idea of missions and following God's calling. The opportunities for both groups were almost identical and many of their motivations and means were similar.

Thus, I concluded that the Ukrainian evangelical missionary surge should be considered one surge and not two separate ones, despite the differences between the Baptists and Pentecostals. See table 3 for a list of the key factors behind the Ukrainian evangelical missionary surge, including some comparison between Pentecostals and Baptists.

Overall, a number of factors emerged as most important in the Ukrainian evangelical missionary surge. Centers for missionary development were needed, which for both Baptists and Pentecostals included a school. The opportunities created by freedom and God's invisible hand of grace allowed the idea of missions and calling to missions to lead young entrepreneurial Ukrainians to the mission field, a place with great needs and some kind of connection. Missionary structures played a role in getting Ukrainians to the mission field, although not as much in the initial stages of the surge—more so in later stages.

But perhaps the biggest factor of all, at least according to the participants I spoke with, was the inspiration that came from missionaries. This inspiration, whether through direct recruitment or merely by example, helped the missionary surge to gather momentum as chains of missionaries were formed with one friend telling another and one relative inviting another relative, etc. The power of example was extremely important for the missionary surge, allowing it to spread through the grassroots of churches even though many church leaders were against it. The power of example allowed the cause of missions and the stories of missionaries to spread in natural and attractive ways, leading more and more young Ukrainians to the mission field.

In the next chapter, I will attempt to adapt the results of my study into a more generalizable model by comparing my results to existing models of change theory. My goal is to maintain the results of my data that emerged from the study while also finding more accepted and generalized terminology that could be more useful for future analyses of missionary surges.

6

Summary: A Model for the Ukrainian Evangelical Missionary Surge from 1989 to 1999

IN THE PREVIOUS CHAPTER, I attempted to gather all of the data from my research into a limited number of categories to explain the story of the Ukrainian evangelical missionary surge of the 1990s, moving from source to vision to motivation to means to opportunities. Now I would like to take out of that chapter the most important factors that I found behind the missionary surge and put them into a model that could help us to predict and/or influence missionary surges in the future. By most important factors, I mean those factors that were mentioned the most often overall and/or mentioned the most often as being specifically important. Of course, there may be other factors beyond those mentioned by participants, but I am trying to prioritize those factors that participants noted in this study.

In order to organize my data into a useful model, I have analyzed various models for culture change to see how the data can best be expressed in terms that would be more broadly understood and applicable. Specifically, I have looked at the classic 1962 model *Diffusion of Innovations* by Rogers, in addition to the models for change from Naylor, Rochon, Gladwell,[1] Crouch, Hunter, and Heath and Heath.[2] Tables C1–C4 in Appendix C show my comparison of these models with the model that emerged from my study.

---

1. Gladwell's model is enhanced by adding details from Heath and Heath, *Made to Stick*, and Collins and Porras, *Built to Last*.

2. Naylor, *Culture and Change*; Rochon, *Culture Moves*; Gladwell, *Tipping Point*; Crouch, *Culture Making*; Hunter, *To Change the World*; Heath and Heath, *Switch*.

The most helpful models for the data I have collected have proved to be from Rogers, Rochon, Gladwell, and Heath and Heath.[3] Rogers[4] provided excellent information for the basic components of change, including the more rational and emotional sides, as well as some very helpful ideas for communication and facilitation agents. Rochon[5] provided a good description of the importance of centers for change as well as adding some important nuances to Rogers's idea of the compatibility of change. Gladwell[6] provided additional helpful information for the components of change (with special help from Heath and Heath[7]), as well as new ideas for communication and facilitation agents and context. Finally, Heath and Heath[8] gave further ideas for developing the categories for change and context in ways that perhaps best paralleled my findings. In all, I have constructed a five-point model for the Ukrainian evangelical missionary surge of 1989 to 1999: centers for missionary development, the change itself (divided into two parts: the rational idea and the emotional motivation), communication and facilitation agents, and the context for missions. Where possible, I have chosen to use Rogers's[9] categories within my model since Rogers's diffusion model is so widely accepted and I am trying to construct the most easily understood and widely applicable model possible.

Most Important Factors in the Missionary Surge

Before explaining the model that I have developed, I would like to list the factors I found that were described as the most important by the participants in my research. These factors form the bulk of the model below, with only a few smaller factors included in cases where they enhanced the explanatory power of the model. The importance of a factor is determined by the number of times it was mentioned and/or participants specifically saying that a particular factor was important. It should also be mentioned that factors that were tied to Baptists had an advantage over factors related to Pentecostals since about twice as many Baptists were interviewed as Pentecostals.

---

3. Rogers, *Diffusion of Innovations*; Rochon, *Culture Moves*; Gladwell, *Tipping Point*; Heath and Heath, *Switch*.
4. Rogers, *Diffusion of Innovations*.
5. Rochon, *Culture Moves*.
6. Gladwell, *Tipping Point*.
7. Heath and Heath, *Made to Stick*.
8. Heath and Heath, *Switch*.
9. Rogers, *Diffusion of Innovations*.

In terms of the number of instances in which factors were mentioned, the most important factor was clearly inspiration from missionaries (Motivation 2). After this key factor were the following: Baptist centers for missionary development (Source), Pentecostal centers for missionary development (Source), the missionary structure Light of the Gospel (Means 2), enthusiasm for the idea or cause of missions (Vision 1), going where there is the greatest need to hear the Gospel (Motivation 1), God's call and answered prayer (Vision 2), and connections to places and people on the mission field (Motivation 1). Four more factors that were mentioned less frequently but still appeared to be significant were freedom for Christian missionary work (Opportunity 2), Pentecostal churches as a missionary structure (Means 2), response to the spiritual vacuum (Motivation 1), and family support for missions (Source).

As a different measure, I also noted when participants mentioned that a particular factor was important. This list turned out to be a subset of the previous one, with one addition. By number of times mentioned (with at least multiple references), the factors that were listed as most important were: going where there is the greatest need to hear the Gospel and responding to the spiritual vacuum (Motivation 1), God's call and answered prayer (Vision 2), inspiration from missionaries (Motivation 2), God's grace at work (Opportunity 3), enthusiasm for the idea or cause of missions (Vision 1), freedom for Christian missionary work (Opportunity 2), and Pentecostal churches as a missionary structure (Means 2). It is interesting to note that factors regarding tools for ministry, finances, and the common territory did not appear to be very important to participants, not having been mentioned as often or as specifically important.

These most important factors, with the exception of God's grace at work, have been organized into a five-point model elaborated below. I believe that God's grace at work should not be included in the model since it was not mentioned by that many participants and since it doesn't really fit into the model, but instead could be understood as facilitating the model as a whole.

The five-point model starts with centers for missionary development that include Baptist centers, Pentecostal centers, and family support. The rational side of change includes enthusiasm for the idea or cause of missions and God's call and answered prayer. The emotional side of change includes going where there is the greatest need to hear the Gospel and inspiration from missionaries. Communication and facilitation agents include Light of the Gospel, Pentecostal churches, and inspiration from missionaries. Finally, the context for missions includes freedom for Christian missionary work and connections to people and places on the mission field.

Centers for Missionary Development

One important point that came out of my interviews was the fact that there were particular centers that seemed to develop missionaries. The Baptists had centers where missionaries developed in churches in Western Ukraine and the Donetsk Oblast as well as in two institutions: Light of the Gospel mission and Donetsk Christian University. Similarly, Pentecostals had centers of missionary development in churches in Western Ukraine and in the Donetsk Oblast as well as at Odessa Missionary School and at Jelgava Bible School in Latvia. In addition, family influence was another kind of center of missionary development which was especially important, as most Ukrainian missionaries were young (under 35, many in their early twenties) and many were single.

For the new idea of missions to be considered and developed before it could be spread, it was important that smaller communities first grapple with it. Thomas Rochon asserted that

> the creation of new ideas occurs initially within a relatively small community of critical thinkers who have developed a sensitivity to some problem, an analysis of the sources of the problem, and a prescription for what should be done about the problem. These critical thinkers do not necessarily belong to a formally constituted organization, but they are part of a self aware, mutually interacting group.[10]

As Rochon further explained, it is in these smaller communities that "the incubation of new ideas" occurs.[11] Heath and Heath added that "if you want to change the culture of your organization, you've got to get the reformers together. They need a free space. They need time to coordinate outside the gaze of the resisters."[12]

Additionally, it was important that multiple groups develop missionaries and the idea of missions separately. Malcolm Gladwell explained that "small, close-knit groups have the power to magnify the epidemic potential of a message or idea"[13] and furthermore, "that in order to create one contagious movement, you often have to create many small movements first."[14] Of course, there were actually multiple small groups based out of different churches in Western Ukraine as well as the Donetsk Oblast, so the

10. Rochon, *Culture Moves*, 22.
11. Rochon, *Culture Moves*, 30.
12. Heath and Heath, *Switch*, 247.
13. Gladwell, *Tipping Point*, 174.
14. Gladwell, *Tipping Point*, 192.

Ukrainian evangelical missionary surge met the criteria well for developing the idea of missions.

Who was involved in these centers of missionary development? In general, it was young Ukrainians, some married and some single, generally not pastors of churches, but very active in ministry. They tended to be independent and entrepreneurial and they wanted to do more. James Davison Hunter said that "change is typically initiated by elites who are outside of the centermost positions of prestige."[15] That might be overstating it a bit, but it is true that the Ukrainian evangelical missionary surge was led by young leaders outside the center of power of evangelical churches. There were some pastors and church leaders who supported the movement, especially in Pentecostal churches, but generally, it was active non-pastors who led the way into missionary work.

What drove these centers of missionary development to dream about missions? Each of these small groups was dealing with a problem. Each of them had groups of people who had desired to do more ministry for some time (some might have called it missions, whereas some became familiar with the idea of missions only at the end of the eighties), but were restricted from doing so. To some, the main barrier was the State (a context change would help with this problem, which I'll discuss below). To others, the main problem was the church leadership itself, which was against many kinds of ministry, including missions. This latter problem was especially true in Donetsk Oblast Baptist churches.

This problem, this desire to do ministry and missions, helped drive Ukrainians in these centers to develop the idea of missions and send out missionaries. Of course, the context change (described below) was a major factor as well, but the

> change process always involves an innovator who generates an idea (through invention, discovery, borrowing) in response to a perceived need, followed by informal and nondirected interactions (associations) by which others, also responding to some felt need, simply copy a new belief, behavior, or product in a continually widening circle until the new trait is spread throughout the group. The trait may then spread to other groups based on their perceptions of its value as responding to their own needs, as keeping them competitive with others attempting to survive under similar conditions.[16]

---

15. Hunter, *To Change the World*, 42.
16. Naylor, *Culture and Change*, 66.

Rogers also concurred that the innovation process often begins in response to a problem or need.[17] Thus, these centers of missionary development each grappled with the problem of lack of ministry and generated a solution by doing missions.

Why missions? For Pentecostals, missions was something driven by many in church leadership, so when the context changed, it was natural to do missions. For Baptists, especially in the Donetsk Oblast, missionary work was the only possible solution since many in church leadership wouldn't allow new ministry locally. Naylor described what happened well when he explained how sometimes change agents and the focal groups that they are trying to change cannot agree upon a compatible change since, as in this case, the church culture considered their traditions and conservatism essential for their "continued survival."[18] Thus, missionary work outside of Ukraine was the best solution.

And missionary work was a creative solution. For many years, the idea of missions was unthinkable—something done in faraway, exotic lands and forbidden in the Soviet Union. Even doing ministry beyond the walls of the church building was a stretch for most Soviet evangelicals, so going to Siberia to do mission work was incredibly bold and creative. And creative thinking comes about best when responding to a problem. Matthew Syed explained that

> without a problem, without a failure, without a flaw, without a frustration, innovation has nothing to latch on to. It loses its pivot. As Dyson puts it: "Creativity should be thought of as a dialogue. You have to have a problem before you can have the game-changing riposte."[19]

So, these centers of missionary development creatively found a solution to many young Ukrainians' longing for ministry. The problem led to a dialogue which led to a "game-changing riposte:"[20] they would do missions at the ends of the earth—in the Far North and the Far East of Siberia.

Change: The Idea and Value of Missions

Regarding the change itself, I'd first like to address the rational side of the missionary surge. This category lined up well with the vision category that

17. Rogers, *Diffusion of Innovations*, 137–39.
18. Naylor, *Culture and Change*, 106.
19. Syed, *Black Box Thinking*, 196.
20. Syed, *Black Box Thinking*, 196.

I have been using and the idea of the *rider* in Heath and Heath's[21] model for change. Even though I could use either of these models to express my findings, I have decided to follow Rogers's categories below.

Relative Advantage

During the Ukrainian evangelical missionary surge, the people involved believed in the basic idea or cause of missions, and they were persuaded that its importance far outweighed the dangers involved and the fact that most had no training and no experience. Participants mentioned this reason for becoming missionaries a significant number of times and, multiple times, it was listed specifically as an important reason behind the missionary surge. Ukrainian evangelicals believed that their doing missions was God's plan for the world. The fact that Ukrainian evangelicals were willing to sacrifice so much in order to become missionaries shows how important they believed doing missionary work was. As Kevin shared, it was

> the desire to dedicate yourself to something and volunteer and not just go and get your high-income good education that will get you a good job, and say I'm dedicating myself to the Lord, [to] His kingdom, and to those who . . . aren't sheltered [the needy].

Believing in the relative advantage of a change is a fundamental reason for people to choose to change. As Rogers explained, "Diffusion scholars have found relative advantage to be one of the strongest predictors of an innovation's rate of adoption."[22] Why do people believe that a new idea is advantageous? First, they can see the *bright spots* of the change as opposed to focusing on all of the difficulties and problems involved.[23] As Sophia shared, "God is making an opportunity there, that we could go there and do missions. And somehow we all got excited about this idea, that we didn't have to just sit in church, but we could go somewhere." In thinking back on that time, a number of participants in the missionary surge said that they didn't really think about the difficulties that much—they just went on enthusiasm.

Secondly, an idea needs to be credible in order for it to be believed and acted upon, as Heath and Heath[24] elaborated upon Gladwell's[25] concept of the need for the *stickiness* of an idea in order to see change. Despite the fact

---

21. Heath and Heath, *Switch*.
22. Rogers, *Diffusion of Innovations*, 233.
23. Heath and Heath, *Switch*, 32–33.
24. Heath and Heath, *Made to Stick*.
25. Gladwell, *Tipping Point*.

A MODEL FOR THE UKRAINIAN EVANGELICAL MISSIONARY SURGE

that many in church leadership, especially Baptist church leadership, did not endorse missionary work, there were many young church leaders who supported missions and went as missionaries themselves. The issue of credibility is one area in which Pentecostals had an advantage over Baptists, but in any case, the fact that many were going to the mission field and reported success there swayed more Ukrainians to go. This issue will be further discussed in the Context for Missions section, where the importance of connections to the mission field is explained.

Compatibility

The idea of missions was not, for the most part, understood or accepted prior to the missionary surge, so what changed that made it compatible to so many Ukrainians, particularly young Ukrainians? Considering participants' observations from the surge, more Bibles and Christian literature became available in which people could read about missions. People received callings from God to go into missions. Freedom of speech and spiritual interest by masses of people encouraged Ukrainians to preach the Gospel openly. The Ukrainian evangelical church was finally able to communicate freely with the Global evangelical church, which had been doing missions for centuries. And finally, young Ukrainian evangelicals went on short-term mission trips, met other missionaries, and learned more about the mission field.

Rogers emphasized the importance of compatibility for how well a proposed change will be accepted and implemented. By compatibility, he meant "the degree to which an innovation is perceived as consistent with the existing values, past experiences, and needs of potential adopters."[26] Now, any change or innovation is based on some kind of values. As Rochon explained, "New value claimants are not considered in isolation, but are instead examined in light of those values already held."[27] Rochon further explained that one of three types of value change can occur: value conversion, value creation, and value connection.[28]

In the first case, value conversion "is the replacement of existing values with new ideas on the same topic about what is important, equitable, or legitimate."[29] As might be expected, Rochon claimed that "conversion is the most difficult and conflictual strategy for generating changes in group

---

26. Rogers, *Diffusion of Innovations*, 240.
27. Rochon, *Culture Moves*, 54.
28. Rochon, *Culture Moves*, 54.
29. Rochon, *Culture Moves*, 54.

identity."³⁰ J. D. Hunter wrote of the need for "cultural transformation," but he said that this transformation typically happens only "from the top down. . . . Change is typically initiated by elites who are outside the centermost positions of prestige."³¹ The missionary surge was, to some extent, a case of value conversion since it was a challenge by some younger church leaders to the main church leadership to change evangelical churches' values regarding missions. But, this challenge was difficult, especially for the Baptists, as Rochon predicted. Thus, I would argue that the missionary surge was not primarily a case of value conversion.

In the second case, value creation "is the development of new ideas, concepts, or categories of analysis that apply to situations that had not previously been the subject of explicit cultural values."³² Andy Crouch made the argument that this is really the only way to change culture: "to create more of it."³³ And, to some extent, the ideas of missionary work and doing organized missionary work were new things that brought about new values in some people. However, even as missionary work was new and exciting to some, historically, the evangelical movement in the former Soviet Union had always been "profoundly evangelistic," according to Nancy. Vincent added that Soviet evangelicals were constantly "finding ways to do mission." Thus, it is also hard to characterize the Ukrainian evangelical missionary surge as being the creation of a new culture, as Crouch³⁴ suggests, moreover a creation of new values.

Finally, Rochon described value connection as "the development of a conceptual link between phenomena previously thought either to be unconnected with each other or to be connected in a different way."³⁵ Rochon further explained that

> an alternative means of changing group identity that runs into less resistance is to change only the content rather than the boundaries of group identity. This is identity change by connection, which involves developing a link between a new critical community discourse and existing group identifications.³⁶

---

30. Rochon, *Culture Moves*, 107.
31. Hunter, *To Change the World*, 42.
32. Rochon, *Culture Moves*, 54.
33. Crouch, *Culture Making*, 67.
34. Crouch, *Culture Making*.
35. Rochon, *Culture Moves*, 54.
36. Rochon, *Culture Moves*, 108.

I think this idea of value connection best describes what happened during the Ukrainian evangelical missionary surge. Young Ukrainian evangelicals were connected to missionary work. Considering all of the points mentioned above, this connection happened on both an intellectual and experiential level. Thus, this connection provided the compatibility needed to make missions acceptable and a worthwhile change for the Ukrainian evangelical church.

Complexity

The Ukrainian evangelical missionary surge can be very well characterized as simple with the critical moves being *scripted* due to the large number of instances of missionaries receiving a calling from God and answers to their prayers regarding missionary work. Heath and Heath's model for change explained that "scripting the critical moves"[37] is critical since

> change begins at the level of individual decisions and behaviors, but that's a hard place to start because that's where the friction is. Inertia and decision paralysis will conspire to keep people doing things the old way. To spark movement in a new direction, you need to provide crystal-clear guidance.[38]

Numerous participants made a point of saying that the factors of calling and answered prayer were among the most important ones. In contrast to the massive amount of uncertainty in the days of *perestroika* and the fall of the Soviet Union, many missionaries felt certain of their calling from God to do missions work, and that was a major factor in keeping the surge going. Rogers[39] as well as Heath and Heath,[40] expanding on Gladwell,[41] pointed to the importance of minimizing complexity. The fact that missions offered a certain, simple path endorsed by God made its value very important.

---

37. Heath and Heath, *Switch*, 55.
38. Heath and Heath, *Switch*, 56.
39. Rogers, *Diffusion of Innovations*.
40. Heath and Heath, *Made to Stick*.
41. Gladwell, *Tipping Point*.

Change: Motivation for Becoming a Missionary

As Donald Smith said, "Both emotion and reason are necessary in effective communication."[42] The same is true for change, as Heath and Heath[43] described through the analogy of a rider directing an *elephant*. Both the rider (rationality) and the elephant (emotions) have to work together to move in one direction to make a change happen. As the rational side lined up reasonably well with what I called previously vision, the emotional side lined up fairly closely with what I called motivation. In order to unpack this emotional side of change in more detail, I have chosen to use the last two aspects of change that Rogers[44] used plus add a category of my own (inspiration) that is parallel with three aspects of stickiness that Heath and Heath[45] used.

Triability

Rogers explained triability as "the degree to which an innovation may be experimented with on a limited basis."[46] The Ukrainian evangelical missionary surge had a high level of triability through both short-term missions and prayer. Numerous participants cited the importance of short-term missions in their decision to become long-term missionaries. Even those who didn't become long-term missionaries were at least exposed to the missionary surge and could help support it better. In addition, many people in Ukrainian evangelical churches prayed for missionaries and for unreached peoples, especially in Pentecostal churches, and these prayers helped them identify with missions more through prayer and communication with missionaries on the field.

Identifying with missionary work in some way, whether through short-term missions or through prayer, changed the way many Ukrainians thought about missions. As Rochon shared:

> When people see their own fates as being inextricably tied to the fate of some larger group, and when the extent of solidarity in that group leads one to expect that others will participate in the movement as well, then the expected utility of participation in a movement is transformed.[47]

---

42. Smith, *Creating Understanding*, 163.
43. Heath and Heath, *Switch*.
44. Rogers, *Diffusion of Innovations*.
45. Heath and Heath, *Made to Stick*.
46. Rogers, *Diffusion of Innovations*, 258.
47. Rochon, *Culture Moves*, 97.

Thus, over time, as the missionary surge grew and was tried more and more, people began to identify with it more and more, and so, more churches began to support it and start their own missionary efforts.

Heath and Heath[48] explained that identity is something that is both crucial for making decisions and that can grow through small identifications. For example, "Any change effort that violates someone's identity is likely doomed to failure."[49] Yet, "Identities 'grow' from small beginnings. Once you start seeing yourself as a 'concerned citizen,' you'll want to keep acting like one."[50] So, the triability of the missionary surge led more and more people to identify with missions over time and to promote the surge further.

Observability

The missionary surge was very observable, especially as the surge grew. Rogers described observability as "the degree to which the results of an innovation are visible to others. Some ideas are easily observed and communicated to other people, whereas other innovations are difficult to observe or to describe to others."[51] The example of missionaries, whether through reports from the mission field or through their visitation of churches upon returning to Ukraine made a big impact on additional Ukrainians joining the surge. One of the most popular answers that interview participants gave as a factor behind the missionary surge was the example of missionaries, with three participants listing it as a particularly important factor. Thus, Ukrainian young people were easily able to hear about and understand the surge.

The Ukrainian evangelical missionary surge of the 1990s was also motivated by very concrete needs. A great number of interview participants noted the motivation to go where there was the greatest need for missions, including where they saw a spiritual vacuum. Five participants listed this factor as a particularly important one. Thus, Ukrainian evangelicals knew of specific places and people that needed missionaries. Heath and Heath[52] pointed out the importance of an idea being concrete so that it can be understood, remembered, and transferred to others. Yet, interestingly, potential missionaries didn't know very much about the mission field—which was probably good for the missionary surge, since too many details and knowledge of problems might have dissuaded some Ukrainians from going.

48. Heath and Heath, *Switch*.
49. Heath and Heath, *Switch*, 154.
50. Heath and Heath, *Switch*, 161.
51. Rogers, *Diffusion of Innovations*, 258.
52. Heath and Heath, *Made to Stick*.

Or, in Heath and Heath's terms, too many details of problems might have scared the "skittish" elephant.[53]

Finally, the missionary surge was facilitated by the fact that small, concrete steps were available to potential missionaries to take the journey to the mission field. Numerous connections to the mission field, whether from previous short-term mission trips or through relatives or friends, made it simple for many to go. In addition, the development of missionary structures, which will be discussed in more detail later, provided a means to go to the mission field. Heath and Heath's model for change pointed out the need to "shrink the change" into small, concrete steps that are easier to handle.[54] Thus, the observability and concreteness of the missionary surge helped enable it to continue.

Inspiration

Emotions played an important role in the Ukrainian evangelical missionary surge. Some participants called the idea of missions romantic or an adventure. In most cases this was not blind emotion, but an excitement over doing something they were convinced was right and in line with God's will—an enthusiasm for an important cause. Furthermore, missionaries and leaders of mission organizations came and shared emotional stories about what God was doing through missions and about the incredible needs on the mission field. Most young Ukrainian believers didn't need much more motivation than that. They didn't worry about how they'd survive or that they didn't know how to be a missionary (rational issues)—they were ready to take a leap of faith to serve God in a faraway and freezing cold land. It was easy for young Ukrainian evangelicals to identify with other young Ukrainians who had gone to the mission field and respond to their invitations to join them.

Considering these emotional motivations, I decided to add a category to the two offered by Rogers[55] in order to express the way inspiration affected potential missionaries. Of course, inspiration often happened in conjunction with triability and observability, but this category is meant to express more of the emotion that helped motivate Ukrainians to decide to become missionaries. It also includes some of Heath and Heath's[56] ideas about the stickiness of an idea, that emotions, stories, and unexpectedness can all have an important impact on whether a new idea is accepted and spread to others.

53. Heath and Heath, *Switch*, 7.
54. Heath and Heath, *Switch*, 136.
55. Rogers, *Diffusion of Innovations*.
56. Heath and Heath, *Made to Stick*.

Emotions are often the key to inspiring a decision to act. Lots of rational contemplation with no emotion often leads to no action, no matter how good the cause.[57] Kotter and Cohen's[58] large study also found that the most successful change efforts were driven by feelings, not analysis. The importance of emotions has been demonstrated both on an individual as well as a group level, especially as emotions tend to be held more uniformly across groups than logical reasoning.[59] One of the key reasons why emotions can more easily lead to change than rational thought is that emotions tend to lead people to identify with the person making the argument, whereas rational thought usually leads to calculating pros versus cons. The pros might win out in the end, but identification with a need or a challenge can lead to a much quicker decision.[60]

Another key to inspiration leading to change is the use of stories. N.T. Wright declared that telling stories was a key for "subverting" or changing worldview.[61] Like emotions, stories can help hearers identify with the speaker and the speaker's ideas better than mere facts can.[62] As Koehler explained, "A story becomes a doorway to a possible world because it offers the listener a glimpse of a future that is not simply a repetition of the past."[63] Thus, stories about missionaries, both foreign and national, allowed young Ukrainian evangelicals to enter into the world of missions and helped inspire many to join the missionary surge.[64]

Furthermore, the challenge and shocking nature of missions attracted many young Ukrainians into missionary work. Heath and Heath did a survey of inspiration stories and "came to the conclusion that there are three basic plots: the Challenge plot, the Connection plot, and the Creativity plot."[65] Clearly, much missionary work fell under the Challenge plot idea. Not only was the work hard and needed, but it often included miraculous, unexpected results as God provided for missionaries and led remote peoples on the tundra of Siberia to turn to Christ. This unexpectedness was another way that the idea of missions was sticky, memorable,

57. Heath and Heath, *Made to Stick*, 165–67.
58. Kotter and Cohen, *Heart of Change*.
59. Hollingworth, *Psychology of the Audience*, 137.
60. Heath and Heath, *Switch*, 109.
61. Wright, *New Testament and the People of God*, 40.
62. Heath and Heath, *Switch*, 103, 155.
63. Koehler, *Telling God's Stories*, 51.
64. Steffen, *Reconnecting God's Story*.
65. Heath and Heath, *Made to Stick*, 224.

and worth passing on.⁶⁶ Thus, inspiration from missionaries and from God's work on the mission field was a significant factor in the Ukrainian evangelical missionary surge of the 1990s.

Communication and Facilitation Agents

In order to promote the Ukrainian evangelical missionary surge, communication of the idea of missions and of examples of missionaries was vital. Rogers called communication channels one of the main elements in the diffusion of innovations. He defined communication channels as "the means by which messages get from one individual to another."⁶⁷ However, communication wasn't enough for the missionary surge to occur; facilitation, or the means that helped missionaries actually get to the mission field, was also an important factor in the surge.

Change does not spread just because some centers or critical communities decide to a take on a new, compelling idea. There need to be forces that help spread the change from the original places in which it was generated. Rochon explained that

> critical communities and movements are the key actors in the two-stage process of value generation and value diffusion.... Movements mobilize thousands of people behind the ideas of the critical community. In so doing, they cannot use the ideas developed in critical networks as off-the-shelf packages. Some critical ideas lend themselves better to mass mobilization than others; many critical ideas are destined never to be embraced beyond the restricted network of thinkers in which they originated. At a minimum, the ideas of a critical community must be repackaged in a way that connects them with mobilizable social groups.⁶⁸

Sometimes, the centers or critical communities can overlap with the communication channels or movements that spread them.⁶⁹ But in any case, the means of communicating and facilitating the spread of a change is an important part of the diffusion process. I will now turn to the agents that enabled both communication and facilitation in the missionary surge.

---

66. Heath and Heath, *Made to Stick*.
67. Rogers, *Diffusion of Innovations*, 18.
68. Rochon, *Culture Moves*, 51.
69. Rochon, *Culture Moves*, 52.

I decided to use some of Rogers's[70] categories which can be expressed more chronologically than the ones I came up with earlier (initiators, inviters, and examples). So, I will start with the *innovators*—the first group of those involved in the missionary surge. I will then move to *change agents*, who pushed the surge further and challenged the opinion leaders of evangelical churches. Then, I will look at the *opinion leaders* who influenced the movement, some of whom were change agents as well. And finally, I will look at those who helped organize the movement and at the missionary structures that propelled and sustained the surge through the 1990s.

Innovators

Innovators are the first people to take part in new ventures. In the Ukrainian evangelical missionary surge, there were a number of innovators who went to the mission field on their own before any missionary structures were created. Some were supported by their churches, especially in the case of Western Ukrainian Pentecostals, but many were not. They were willing to take big risks because they saw the great need to spread the Gospel among people who had never heard it.

According to Naylor, "The voluntary change process always involves an innovator who generates an idea (through invention, discovery, borrowing) in response to a perceived need."[71] An innovator is known for his or her "venturesomeness, due to a desire for the rash, the daring, and the risky" and is "able to come with a high degree of uncertainty about an innovation at the time he or she adopts."[72]

Some of these innovators were change agents (our next category), but some weren't. In the cases where missionaries were focused only on their own missionary work, they influenced other Ukrainians as good examples, but they didn't intentionally try to promote the expansion of the missionary surge. As Naylor explained:

> Ideas for change are always generated by innovators, for all change begins with innovation; but, as noted before, innovators are not always the agents of change. Thinking up a new or revised way of doing something is not the same as attempting to get others to adopt it.[73]

---

70. Rogers, *Diffusion of Innovations*.
71. Naylor, *Culture and Change*, 66.
72. Rogers, *Diffusion of Innovations*, 282–83.
73. Naylor, *Culture and Change*, 77.

Naylor elaborated on this process as being "informal and nondirected interactions (associations) by which others, also responding to some felt need, simply copy a new belief, behavior, or product in a continually widening circle until the new trait is spread throughout the group."[74] Even with this informal spreading of the missionary surge, others needed to come along as change agents to push the surge further. I will turn to this group of people next.

Change Agents

After the first group of innovators went to the mission field, missionary structures began to form and change agents started to invite young Ukrainians to go to the mission field. In terms of my previous categories, these were initiators (who were both innovators and change agents) and inviters (who were known for doing intentional recruitment of new missionaries). As mentioned earlier, many young people had been prepared to go to the mission field in their centers of missionary development by learning about the idea of missions and being motivated by the needs on the mission field and the examples of missionaries. But they still needed to be invited—and in many cases, as Stanislav shared, that was all it took for them to go.

Rogers explained that a change agent "is an individual who influences clients' innovation-decisions."[75] As mentioned above, innovators may or may not be change agents themselves. In any case, just making an innovation isn't enough to see it spread. As Naylor shared:

> Because something is invented, discovered, or borrowed does not mean that it . . . automatically becomes a culture change. Someone has to assume the responsibility or task of getting others within the group to accept the trait until it spreads to all, or at least to a majority of its members.[76]

Thus, change agents communicate an idea to others and try to convince them to adopt it.[77] And as Gladwell shared about change agents using his term of *salesmen*, what makes them unique is that they have "the skills to persuade us when we are unconvinced of what we are hearing."[78]

---

74. Naylor, *Culture and Change*, 66.
75. Rogers, *Diffusion of Innovations*, 366.
76. Naylor, *Culture and Change*, 51.
77. Naylor, *Culture and Change*, 89, 91.
78. Gladwell, *Tipping Point*, 70.

Despite the growing missionary surge, there was still some significant resistance in Ukrainian church leadership, especially in Baptist churches. The proposed change of sending people to the mission field ran contrary to the bunker mentality that numerous churches had after years of government persecution. This mentality was especially prevalent in those first years of the missionary surge before the Soviet Union collapsed. As Naylor explained, "All cultures have core systems that are essential to their continued survival,"[79] and since the stability and the safety of churches seemed threatened, many church leaders stood against the missionary surge.

Since many opinion leaders in Ukrainian evangelical churches did not endorse the change, the surge did not grow as quickly or as much as it could have. Rogers explained that for a change to be successfully adopted, it is vital that a change agent "works through opinion leaders."[80] However, many change agents did have wide contact with church youth in Ukraine—the source of potential missionaries. As Rogers noted, "Change agent contact is one of the variables most highly related to innovativeness."[81] Plus, as leaders of the missionary surge became more well-known and respected (at least among church youth), they moved from being just change agents to also being opinion leaders. Thus, the missionary surge continued as it had support both on a grassroots level and through its leadership.

Opinion Leaders

The Ukrainian evangelical missionary surge of the 1990s, as explained above, was both a grassroots movement and had the support of some opinion leaders. Western Ukrainian Pentecostal opinion leaders offered some support, as did some key Baptist leaders. For example, when the Pentecostals formed their own union, Vasily Boyechko, Slavik Radchuk, and Pyotr Serdichenko were each influential in promoting missions. For the Baptists, Franz Shumeiko encouraged several young leaders to form the mission agency Light of the Gospel and plant new churches. As an example of an outside opinion leader, Earl Poysti, the famous radio preacher widely respected by both Baptists and Pentecostals, encouraged missions through his preaching and did a preaching tour in the Soviet Union, specifically helping Light of the Gospel spread its work.

Rogers defined opinion leadership as "the degree to which an individual is able to influence other individuals' attitudes or overt behavior informally in

79. Naylor, *Culture and Change*, 106.
80. Rogers, *Diffusion of Innovations*, 388.
81. Rogers, *Diffusion of Innovations*, 382.

a desired way with relative frequency."[82] Opinion leaders have a large amount of external communication, which includes exposure to mass media and significant social participation,[83] similar to Gladwell's idea of *connectors*, who have their "foot in... many different worlds... bringing them all together."[84] Additionally, opinion leaders are often sources of knowledge, experts in a certain field or fields,[85] similar to Gladwell's idea of *mavens*.[86]

Opinion leaders play an important role in the diffusion of a change since they help give legitimacy to a change and their endorsement is particularly important in bringing early adopters to choose the change.[87] It is important that opinion leaders are mobilized by change agents if a change is to be diffused successfully.[88] In fact, J. D. Hunter argued that it is vital that opinion leaders be active in supporting a change since change almost always happens from the top down.[89] Opinion leaders don't have to be the top leaders, but they can have great influence, especially if there are opinion leaders from multiple areas.[90] Thus, opinion leaders did play a role in the missionary surge, but change came through the grassroots as well, as opposed to J. D. Hunter's[91] more extreme position.

Organizers and Missionary Structures

Whereas the previous agents discussed (innovators, change agents, and opinion leaders) focused more on communication of the idea of change, this category is focused more on facilitation of change. It's easy to believe in the idea of missions without actually becoming a missionary. What facilitated young Ukrainian evangelicals to take the next step?

The Ukrainian evangelical missionary surge had some support from above (especially Pentecostal church leadership) and some structures below (various missionary organizations) to help get Ukrainians to the mission field. The surge clearly had some talented organizers behind the establishment and growth of several missionary agencies, most notably Good

82. Rogers, *Diffusion of Innovations*, 27.
83. Rogers, *Diffusion of Innovations*, 316–17.
84. Gladwell, *Tipping Point*, 51.
85. Rogers, *Diffusion of Innovations*, 88.
86. Gladwell, *Tipping Point*.
87. Rogers, *Diffusion of Innovations*, 283.
88. Rogers, *Diffusion of Innovations*, 388.
89. Hunter, *To Change the World*, 41–42.
90. Hunter, *To Change the World*, 42, 89–90.
91. Hunter, *To Change the World*.

Samaritan, Light of the Gospel, Possibility, and Voice of Hope. Especially during the initial organization of Light of the Gospel and Voice of Hope, good organizational skills were needed in order to unite independent missionaries into one collective organization. In addition, Light of the Gospel went through another transition when it split into more regional ministries in 1993. The fact that the missionary surge continued through these transitions attests to the work of skilled organizers.

Collins and Portas explained how organizational visionaries who are able to build a structure and keep change going are actually more important than charismatic leaders in bringing long-term success.[92] In considering the Ukrainian evangelical missionary surge from 1989 to 1999, I was looking at a period of time, rather than just one point. I was interested not just in what got the surge started, but also in what kept it going through the 1990s. Thus, I felt it helpful to add Collins and Portas's[93] idea of *organizer* to Gladwell's[94] list of other change agents (connectors, mavens, and salesmen) and to Rogers's[95] categories.

Having a missionary structure meant that there were fewer problems to deal with in going to the mission field. Missionary structures provided (to highly varying degrees) connections with a place to go, a team to work with, training, and finances. As Heath and Heath explained, if you can shrink the change into smaller, more manageable steps, it is more likely people will accept the change.[96]

Light of the Gospel, in particular, was cited as a positive facilitating factor leading numerous missionaries to the mission field. The mission provided some level of financial support, had an associated training school (Donetsk Christian University), and connected potential missionaries with mission fields and missionary teams. The network within Light of the Gospel gave missionaries confidence and moral support in their work, even in faraway places. As Vincent shared,

> They relied more on regional centers of strength and trust with each other. And so that meant that the Ukrainian kind of mission could more easily reach out to long distant places, far away that were obviously more needy than Ukraine.

92. Collins and Portas, *Built to Last*, 22–42.
93. Collins and Portas, *Built to Last*.
94. Gladwell, *Tipping Point*.
95. Rogers, *Diffusion of Innovations*.
96. Heath and Heath, *Switch*, 136.

Missionary structures provided a collective identity in support of missions. The structures, although much looser, offered an alternative to the supporting church structures which missionaries gave up by leaving for the mission field.[97] When new missionaries joined a missionary structure, it changed the way they looked at missions, making them even more devoted to the cause and willing to continue in spite of difficulties.[98] As Rochon explained:

> When people see their own fates as being inextricably tied to the fate of some larger group, and when the extent of solidarity in that group leads one to expect that others will participate in the movement as well, then the expected utility of participation in a movement is transformed. The choices that are rational for an individual in an atomized environment are not necessarily the decisions reached by someone in an environment rich in organizational networks and group solidarities.[99]

The fact that missionaries were taking action together helped enhance the value of mission work.[100] These actions helped solidify the growing formal and informal networks that made up the missionary structures.[101] Thus, missionary structures made a big difference in facilitating the Ukrainian evangelical missionary surge of the 1990s.

Context for Missions

Context was another important factor behind the Ukrainian evangelical missionary surge. The success of changes depends upon "the conditions and circumstances of the times and places in which they occur."[102] The Ukrainian evangelical missionary surge was clearly influenced by the political changes that occurred during *perestroika* and after the fall of the Soviet Union. In addition, the connections that Ukrainian evangelicals made in the 1990s to missionaries and mission fields led many to become missionaries themselves. Therefore, I will now explore further how these issues of context affected the missionary surge.

---

97. Rochon, *Culture Moves*, 125.
98. Rochon, *Culture Moves*, 134.
99. Rochon, *Culture Moves*, 97.
100. Rochon, *Culture Moves*, 9.
101. Rochon, *Culture Moves*, 96–97.
102. Gladwell, *Tipping Point*, 139.

Environmental Change: Freedom

As freedom came to evangelical churches in the Soviet Union during *perestroika*, especially during the celebration of the 1,000-year anniversary of the baptism of Kievan Rus', evangelicals gained access to preach in public places. Later, after the fall of the Soviet Union, many of the social systems began to break down and evangelicals had even more opportunities to play a role in society, replacing much of the social safety net that the government used to offer. Thus, evangelicals gained access to an "institutional niche"[103] that helped give them a platform for increased missionary work. Or, using Naylor's terminology, many of the social "barriers" to missionary work fell and new "stimulants" appeared in the form of social and spiritual needs.[104]

The environment can play a major role in tipping the balance for change.[105] Heath and Heath also supported the idea that the contemporary situation can play a major role in people's behavior.[106] Even a small tweak in the environment can make a big difference in people's openness to change since culture is highly interrelated and changing one part can affect many others.[107] Crouch,[108] however, took a different view regarding the interrelatedness of culture, saying that culture's complexity means that people can only change the world on a small scale. It is certainly true that it is difficult to change culture, but it is clear that in this case, the combination of elements of the five-point model explained in this chapter seems to have brought about a surge of missionaries from Ukraine unlike that ever seen before in the former Soviet Union.

It is worth noting at this point something in the environment that did not immediately change that also made an impact. Before the Soviet Union fell in 1991, the country had financial stability and guaranteed employment, and these facts, combined with freedom, meant that missionaries could easily travel to different parts of the Soviet Union and find work there. Thus, finances were not a major concern for most missionaries during the early years of the surge. After 1991, finances became more of a problem, and thus, missionary structures became even more valuable to facilitate the missionary surge.

---

103. Rochon, *Culture Moves*, 169.
104. Naylor, *Culture and Change*, 192.
105. Gladwell, *Tipping Point*, 167.
106. Heath and Heath, *Switch*, 180.
107. Heath and Heath, *Switch*, 183–84; Naylor, *Culture and Change*, 180.
108. Crouch, *Culture Making*.

Connections to Missions

In the Ukrainian evangelical missionary surge of the 1990s, the most often-cited factor of influence was the example of missionaries. As more young Ukrainian evangelicals left for the mission field, whether as short-term or long-term missionaries, the more their peers' interest in missions grew as well. Furthermore, as connections were made between Ukraine and the mission field, whether through relatives, friends, mission agencies, or short-term mission trips, missionary work became more understood and accepted. As Heath and Heath explained the mere exposure effect, "The more you're exposed to something, the more you like it."[109] This exposure to missions affected not only the young people who were being drawn to the mission field, but Ukrainian evangelical church leaders as well, many of whom had finally accepted the validity of mission work by the end of the 1990s, according to Scott and Oleg.

The relationship that peers have toward a potential change is another important aspect of context that can influence change. As Rogers explained, "The fact that certain innovations are adopted by clusters of individuals suggests that interpersonal networks among neighbors are powerful influences on individual decisions to adopt."[110] Gladwell pointed out that peer pressure can be even stronger than family pressure.[111] Alternatively, Heath and Heath referred to the power of *peer perception*:

> We all talk about the power of peer pressure, but "pressure" may be overstating the case. Peer perception is plenty. In this entire book, you might not find a single statement that is so rigorously supported by empirical research as this one: You are doing things because you see your peers do them. It's not only your body-pierced teen who follows the crowd. It's you, too. Behavior is contagious.[112]

Thus, the context of one's peers greatly influences one's relationship toward change.

As the social structure of Soviet Communism broke down, missionaries were able to try to build something up. Perhaps their work, though far from professional in its beginnings, could be considered a kind of "faithful presence," as J. D. Hunter advocates Christians should be in society.[113] J. D.

---

109. Heath and Heath, *Switch*, 254.
110. Rogers, *Diffusion of Innovations*, 334–35.
111. Gladwell, *Tipping Point*, 167.
112. Heath and Heath, *Switch*, 227.
113. Hunter, *To Change the World*, 95.

Hunter also made the claim that "in our world today, less and less ties word and world together other than will and power."[114] In other words, the connections of people's relationships are incredibly important in determining what will change and what won't. Clearly in this time of chaos, the connections that led Ukrainians to the mission field and the further connections they built there had a very positive impact on the missionary surge.

Comparison With Other Historical Missionary Surges

The Ukrainian evangelical missionary surge from 1989 to 1999 had a number of things in common with other historical surges as well as a couple of unusual elements. I draw my comparison from the study of the history of missionary surges found in Appendix A.

In terms of commonalities, the centers of development of the Ukrainian evangelical missionary surge paralleled other historical centers such as Catholic and Orthodox monasteries. In addition, it was mainly young people involved in the Ukrainian evangelical missionary surge, much like many historical Protestant missionary surges that came out of student groups and missionary conferences.

The Ukrainian evangelical missionary surge also had some similarities with historical missionary surges in that it was driven by a desire to serve God in the cause of missions. In addition, many missionaries felt God's calling and believed that becoming a missionary was an answer to prayer. New information about missions helped promote the idea of missions, as did the printing and distribution of Bibles and Christian literature and new opportunities for Christian education. All of these elements can be seen in numerous historical missionary surges.

Furthermore, motivations behind the Ukrainian evangelical missionary surge were similar to those of previous surges in history. The motivation to meet the needs of those who hadn't heard the Gospel was a common historical motivation, as was responding to the testimony and challenge of other missionaries. Also, as has often happened in history, there was some impulse for missions from foreigners at the beginning of the Ukrainian evangelical missionary surge, even though the surge was mostly driven by nationals.

The communication and facilitation agents for missionary work during the Ukrainian evangelical missionary surge were mainly nationals working through missionary structures or working independently with some financial support from local sources and some from foreign sources. In many cases, Ukrainian missionaries were largely self-supporting.

114. Hunter, *To Change the World*, 252.

Numerous historical missionary surges were similar, although they tended to vary widely in terms of finances and logistical support.

The context for missions played an important role in the Ukrainian evangelical missionary surge, just as it often did in previous surges in history. The freedom that created a platform for missionary work and the connections that gave direction to it could be considered similar to other large changes in context that created a platform for missionary work such as the Industrial Revolution or the Reformation. Also, the Ukrainian evangelical missionary surge, to some extent, did come out of the fringes of the evangelical church, perhaps more so among the Baptists, making it similar to many other historical missionary surges.

There were also a couple of key differences that stood out in the Ukrainian evangelical missionary surge. First, it was unusual that a revival or awakening did not precede the Ukrainian evangelical missionary surge. It seemed more that certain groups of evangelical church youth were prepared to become missionaries and were simply waiting for the opportunity that finally came as freedom increased after 1988. Second, there were not just one or two key leaders behind the surge, as was often the case during historical missionary surges. The Ukrainian evangelical missionary surge was spread out across different churches and denominations and had numerous leaders (communication and facilitation agents) who could be called innovators, change agents, opinion leaders, and organizers. Yet the movement developed at more of a grassroots level than many other missionary surges.

Comparison With Other Contemporary Surges in Eastern and Central Europe

Finally, I would like to compare the Ukrainian evangelical missionary surge with missionary surges that took place at a similar time in Central and Eastern Europe (including other countries of the former Soviet Union). I am referring to the missionary surges analyzed at the end of Appendix A.

The Ukrainian evangelical missionary surge had a few things in common with contemporary surges in Central and Eastern Europe. There were clearly spiritual factors at work, including God's calling and answered prayer. Each surge had some type of vision or idea of missions. In terms of communicating and facilitating factors, there was some foreign influence that helped the missionary surge. Furthermore, short-term missions played a role in exposing to missions people who would get more involved in the surge in the future, similar to what took place in the movements in Eastern and Central Europe. The Ukrainian missionary surge was mainly made up of young people, as was true for the Evangelical Christian Missionary Union in Russia. Additionally, there was a context conducive to a missionary surge connected to the new freedom that came to Eastern Bloc communist countries in the late eighties. Due to the proximity of these places and the same time frame, this similarity of context is not surprising. Finally, the Ukrainian evangelical missionary surge did not seem to be significantly influenced by finances, which was also generally true of other contemporary surges.

There were also some significant differences between the missionary surges. The Ukrainian evangelical missionary surge was less dependent on just one key person. It was facilitated by a number of leaders and appeared to be more of a grassroots movement than the missionary surges in Central and Eastern Europe, being based more around centers of missionary development. Furthermore, the example of national missionaries seemed to play a bigger role in Ukraine than in other contemporary missionary surges. Finally, although there was some foreign influence and support, the Ukrainian evangelical missionary surge seems to have been more driven by nationals than the other missionary surges in the region which were more facilitated by foreign missionaries.

Conclusion

Thus, it seems that the factors behind the Ukrainian evangelical missionary surge that emerged in this study can fit into accepted categories for change. By using these categories, I have produced a simpler model for the missionary surge that is portrayed visually in figure 4.

So, the most important factors that I found to be behind the surge, the ones most necessary for the surge to occur, were connected to the five C's of my model: centers for missionary development, the change (rational and emotional sides), communication and facilitation agents, and context. In other words, if we would like to see another missionary surge happen from Ukraine, we should strive to create centers for missionary development. We need to explain the idea of missions, seek God's calling into missions, attempt to understand and retell the needs on the mission field, and seek inspiration from the example of missionaries. We need communication agents who can initiate and invite others into mission. We need facilitation agents who can organize and we need missionary structures. Finally, we need a context that is conducive to missions, which includes freedom to preach the Gospel and connections to the mission field. We should seek each of these factors as best we can and ask God to bring a wave of His grace to make it happen.

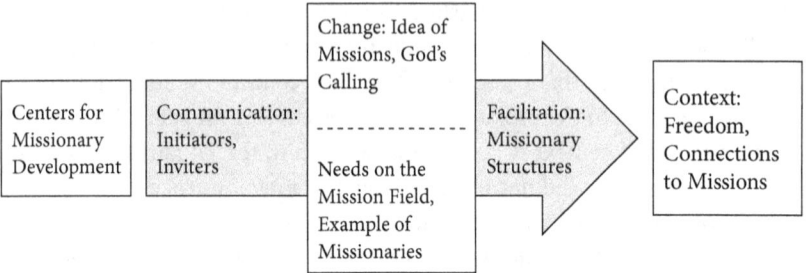

Figure 4. Model for the Ukrainian evangelical missionary surge from 1989 to 1999, showing the most important elements behind the surge. It portrays the flow of the missionary surge, from centers through communication agents to the change, through facilitation agents to the context.

Recommendations for Further Research

This study has been focused on qualitative research of the Ukrainian evangelical missionary surge over the period from 1989 to 1999. Over the course of this research, several issues emerged which deserve further study but could not be included within the scope of this paper.

First, there were some issues that fell outside the dates of this study. For example, how did the centers for missionary development come about? I was able to answer this question only partially since the factors behind the creation of these centers existed before the dates of my research topic. Furthermore, what factors caused the missionary surge to end? The surge seemed to be fading by the end of the 1990s, but some participants thought that it extended at least until 2004. In any case, the goal of my research was to find positive factors behind the missionary surge, and not negative ones that lessened the surge. I do think that the end of the missionary surge is a topic of interest, since a number of participants volunteered information about the problems missionaries faced, even though I did not really probe for such information.

Second, since this study was based on qualitative research, I did not collect quantitative and historical information that might be interesting to many who want to know more details about the missionary surge. For example, it would be interesting to collect statistics on the number of missionaries who went, analyze how the numbers changed over time and compare the work of the different missionary agencies and denominations. More accurate information on events and dates would be helpful as well, although I did my best to include what information I could, even though constructing a chronology of events was not a focus of my study.

Third, it might be useful to do a study of factors that influenced the longevity of missionary service for those involved in the Ukrainian evangelical missionary surge. It would be interesting to study the causes of early attrition across the various sending groups. Numerous participants talked about this issue, indicating that it was important to many people. Since longevity of service was not a focus of my study, however, I did not go into depth on this topic during the interviewing process.

Fourth, it would be interesting to study how the increase in missionary activity was reflected in the life of local churches. For example, how did the worship patterns in churches change, including references to missions in preaching and worship songs? What is the relationship between the promotion of missions in the local church and the level of missions actually being done?

Finally, it might be helpful to analyze how the model that this study has produced fits with other contemporary missionary surges. Is this model a fair predictor of missionary surges or is it limited to one time and one place? More comparisons between different missionary surges might produce a more accurate model that would be useful to missionaries in different parts of the world in the future.

Appendix A
The History of Missionary Surges

THROUGHOUT THE HISTORY OF Christian missions, there have been periods of increased missionary work, during which missionaries moved across cultural borders to evangelize and start new churches. These periods have varied widely in different places, times, and confessions or denominations. Yet, there should be some common factors behind them.

Typically, these periods are referred to as missionary movements. However, this term is not very precise, since it is used to refer to varying periods of missionary activity including the entire modern missionary movement, which some say continues to this day.[1] Therefore, we will specifically examine *missionary surges*, which are shorter periods of history during which a significant increase in the number of missionaries occurs, often at the beginning of a broader missionary movement. As an initial standard, we will look for surges of at least one hundred new missionaries over a span of twenty years or less.

Broader missionary movements have been analyzed in different ways in the past. For example, Johannes Van den Berg found ten main motivations behind missionary awakenings. These were political motives, humanitarian motives, ascetic motives, the motive of debt, romantic motives, the motive to promote the glory of God, the motive to help the unevangelized, the motive to plant churches, the motive to evangelize because the end will come soon, and the motive to follow Christ's command to do mission.[2] This analysis certainly has its merits, but we need to consider more than motivational factors.

Other authors have looked at more practical factors behind missionary movements. Paul Pierson suggested three factors that are necessary for a mission movement, with a fourth factor also usually being present.

---

1. Klingsmith, *Missions Beyond the Wall*, 11.
2. George, "Evangelical Revival," 58–63.

He claimed that these are a theology of mission, a spiritual dynamic, and a mission structure, with "leadership that communicates vision" also usually involved.[3] Similarly, Andrew Walls stated that what was needed was a competent group of people, an organization to send and support them, and Western access to a place for them to serve.[4] Lawrence Keyes specifically examined majority world missionary movements and found four different initiatives for mission: foreign influence, national influence, cooperative agreements, and individual service.[5] Steve Addison looked at Christian movements in general and concluded that the most important factors were faith, commitment to a cause, a network of relationships, rapid mobilization, and adaptive methods.[6] These authors give us a more comprehensive list of important factors to consider, but they still don't include broader historical, economic, and political factors.

Considering history, a few authors point out that mission movements usually arise on the fringe of the organized church.[7] Furthermore, Klaus Fiedler claimed that "nearly all missions trace their origin back to revival."[8] Other authors agree that revivals and awakenings usually precede missionary movements.[9] These insights are also important.

Scott Klingsmith[10] used another approach, adapting the "system of systems" idea from Paul Hiebert[11] for his analysis of missionary sending movements in East-Central Europe, focusing on spiritual, social, and cultural systems. This approach has the advantage of separating out broad, dynamic factors for analysis and points to the way that these systems interact with one another. However, Klingsmith's approach is more suited to analyzing a missionary movement as an ongoing system, whereas we want to examine a missionary surge as a more time-limited event.

Finally, we should consider some non-mission related research that analyzes change. Malcolm Gladwell[12] advocates the idea that a *tipping point* for change can be reached when there are certain kinds of people

   3. Pierson, *Dynamics of Christian Mission*, 210.
   4. Walls, *Cross-Cultural Process*, 200.
   5. Keyes, "Third World Missionaries," 91.
   6. Addison, *Movements that Change the World*.
   7. Addison, *Movements that Change the World*, 34; Johnstone, *Future of the Global Church*, 33; Pierson, *Dynamics of Christian Mission*, 32.
   8. Fiedler, *Story of Faith Missions*, 13.
   9. Johnstone, *Future of the Global Church*, 132; Lovelace, *Dynamics of Spiritual Life*, 21–22.
   10. Klingsmith, *Missions Beyond the Wall*.
   11. Hiebert, *Transforming Worldviews*, 75–80.
   12. Gladwell, *Tipping Point*.

(connectors, mavens, and salesmen) who advocate change, when the idea for change is sticky, and when the context allows for it. Everett Rogers[13] offers a similar idea, calling such people innovators. Chip and Dan Heath[14] did further research on what makes an idea sticky, or memorable, concluding that such ideas are simple, unexpected, concrete, credible, emotional, and told in stories. Some of these ideas are also quite useful, although they don't take into account some of the specific difficulties in producing a missionary surge (e.g., more than a good idea is needed to become a missionary since it is usually limited to Christians who have the capability to move to another place with a different culture).

Drawing from these various approaches, we will initially make use of six broader categories that focus specifically on an increase in the number of missionaries being sent (i.e., a missionary surge). These categories are a *source* for potential missionaries, a *vision* for the need to become a missionary, *motivation* to personally become a missionary, the *means* to becoming a missionary, *key leaders* who motivate and enable others to become missionaries, and the *historical opportunity* to become a missionary. These six categories may overlap to some extent, but we will attempt to treat them separately.

A few examples of these categories might be helpful. A *source* of potential missionaries can include such factors as church growth due to revival or awakening or the amateurization of missionary work such that there are more people qualified to go. A *vision* can include such things as new information about the mission field from books or news reports or a church developing a theology of mission. Personal *motivations* can include factors such as a spiritual call from God, eschatological motivation about the end coming soon, and altar calls at mission conferences. *Means* can refer to things like finances, education, transportation, and missionary agencies. *Key leaders* are people who help cast vision and provide motivation and means for new missionaries. Finally, *historical opportunities* can include events such as the opening of China to missionaries or globalization.

Historical Examples of Missionary Surges

It is difficult to make a comprehensive list all of the missionary surges that have occurred in history, but we will attempt to survey as many historical missionary surges as possible. The goal is to find as many factors as possible

---

13. Rogers, *Diffusion of Innovations*.
14. Heath and Heath, *Made to Stick*.

Early Monastic Missions (Fourth to Fifteenth Centuries)

For most of the history of the church, from the fourth through the eighteenth centuries, the vast majority of missionaries were monks.[15] Of course, the main goal of monasticism was not originally missionary work. Most people who became monks wanted to devote themselves fully and deeply to God, but it became natural for many to want to share the faith that they learned.[16] Those who intentionally set out to evangelize could sometimes receive financial support in their endeavors from local royalty, especially in England.[17] In other cases, monks sought solitude, but since they gained a reputation for holiness, they attracted visitors who were then converted.[18] Dana Robert called monks the "grassroots missionaries in the conversion of Europe."[19] So, many monks were initially motivated by a desire for spirituality, but ended up becoming missionaries.

Overall, monastic missionary surges reflect five of the categories we are exploring. Monasteries provided a source for missionaries; a vision to serve God; a motivation to share about God with others; the means to share, either through mutual support of the monastic community or through the resources provided by local royalty; and opportunities for success in missions as monasteries were established among non-Christians who often became interested in these apparently sanctified places. The only category that remains is key leaders, which will be discussed as part of specific monastic movements below.

Celtic Missionary Surge (Fifth to Ninth Centuries)

The Celtic monastic movement was founded by Patrick, a former slave in Ireland and later a missionary to that island. He was motivated by Scripture to reach the "barbarians who lived beyond the frontiers of the Roman

---

15. Latourette, *Expansion of Christianity*, 1:353; Pierson, *Dynamics of Christian Mission*, 65.
16. Latourette, *Expansion of Christianity*, 2:17.
17. Fletcher, *Barbarian Conversion*, 151, 174.
18. Latourette, *Expansion of Christianity*, 2:17.
19. Robert, *Christian Mission*, 25.

APPENDIX A: THE HISTORY OF MISSIONARY SURGES   197

empire."[20] Patrick was unusual in that he did not rely on Roman power to share the Gospel, but "lived and communicated the gospel in ways that connected and resonated deeply with Irish hopes and concerns."[21] Patrick formed monasteries and convents, inviting the most zealous of his converts (who were motivated), and then training them in the Bible and other learning (giving them vision) and sending them to continue the missionary work.[22] Patrick's results were tremendous, with an awakening of 100,000 converts to his credit. Ireland became a predominantly Christian island by the time of his death.[23] Patrick was a key leader whose example would be emulated and serve as a motivation for generations of Celtic missionaries to come. In addition, Patrick's successful ministry resulted in a great source for future missionaries.

Out of Christianized Ireland came the Celtic missionary surge. In fact, this was the first real "missionary thrust into the pagan world" in history,[24] and it came from the fringes of the Christian world.[25] As mentioned above, Celts often went on pilgrimage to a new land to live an ascetic life seeking God and ended up witnessing to the people around them.[26] Furthermore, thousands of missionary pilgrims in apostolic teams were sent from Scotland to Britain to Western and Central Europe.[27] It was called *white martyrdom* to leave the land of Ireland, which they loved.[28] But, the Celtic leaders believed that they were "chosen by God for mission to the 'barbarians' of Western Europe,"[29] and so they went—some as far as Kyiv.[30]

There were many other notable Celtic leaders who kept the missionary surge going. Columba founded a monastery on the island of Iona just off the coast of Scotland where he trained and then sent missionary teams to evangelize Scotland.[31] Other notable leaders were Aidan and Columbanus.[32]

20. Fletcher, *Barbarian Conversion*, 86.
21. Addison, *Movements that Change the World*, 19.
22. Pierson, *Dynamics of Christian Mission*, 72.
23. Tucker, *From Jerusalem to Irian Jaya*, 40.
24. Keyes, *Last Age of Missions*, 5.
25. Johnstone, *Future of the Global Church*, 33.
26. Bosch, *Transforming Mission*, 233; Fletcher, *Barbarian Conversion*, 94.
27. Hunter, *Celtic Way of Evangelism*, 35, 37; Johnstone, *Future of the Global Church*, 37.
28. Cahill, *How the Irish Saved Civilization*, 183–84.
29. Hunter, *Celtic Way of Evangelism*, 39.
30. Cahill, *How the Irish Saved Civilization*, 195.
31. Addison, *Movements that Change the World*, 21.
32. Cahill, *How the Irish Saved Civilization*, 200; Hunter, *Celtic Way of Evangelism*, 39.

Thus, the Celtic missionary surge lasted for centuries before it eventually faded as other Roman monastic orders took precedence.

Pope Gregory's Missionary Surge (Late Sixth to Early Seventh Centuries)

Gregory the Great was a Benedictine monk when he was called to become pope.[33] He had a heart for missionary work, and was aware of the potential source of missionaries in the monastic movement,[34] seeing it as a good means for missions. When Gregory saw English slave boys for sale in the marketplace, he asked who they were and was told they were Angles. Gregory said in response that they were "not Angles, but angels."[35] And then when he became aware of interest by the English to hear about Christianity,[36] Gregory responded by sending a group of monastic missionaries to England under the leadership of Augustine.[37] The monks were reluctant to go, actually going part way and returning before Gregory called them to go again.[38] After Augustine's initial success, Gregory sent more monastic missionaries to help.[39] Thus, Gregory's leadership was vitally important in this relatively small missionary surge.

So, again we can see the importance of a key leader who calls upon a source of potential missionaries to respond to a vision for mission work. He saw the potential of monasticism to produce and send missionaries, provided for their needs as pope, and motivated them to go upon learning of the opportunity to respond to those interested in hearing about Christianity.

Other Anglo-Saxon Monastic Missions (Seventh to Eighth Centuries)

Sometimes in connection with, sometimes in competition with Celtic missions, other Anglo-Saxons conducted important missionary work at this time. We have more isolated stories than clear evidence of a missionary surge, but it is still worthwhile to mention some of these monastic missionaries. Anglo-Saxon monks felt "an inward call of mission" to continental

---

33. Bosch, *Transforming Mission*, 235.
34. Robert, *Christian Mission*, 25.
35. Pierson, *Dynamics of Christian Mission*, 75.
36. Fletcher, *Barbarian Conversion*, 115.
37. Bosch, *Transforming Mission*, 235.
38. Neill, *History of Christian Missions*, 67–68; Pierson, *Dynamics of Christian Mission*, 75.
39. Latourette, *Expansion of Christianity*, 2:67.

Europe to which they responded.[40] Some of the better known monks were Wilfrid, Willibrord, and Boniface, all of whom conducted missionary work among the pagans.[41] Many of these monks belonged to the Benedictine order, which had "a 'missionary dimension' [that] permeated everything the monks did."[42] In time, other monastic orders would become the main missionary arms of the Catholic Church,[43] but for a period, Anglo-Saxons and Benedictines were the most involved in missionary work, producing small surges of missionaries.

Franciscan and Dominican Monastic Mission
(Thirteenth to Fifteenth Centuries)

In the thirteenth century, two new monastic orders were founded that would have a significant impact on missionary work for the Catholic Church: the Franciscans and Dominicans.[44] Founded by Dominic, the Dominicans were known as an order of preachers, whereas Francis founded the Franciscans in order to live lives of poverty and witness to the Gospel.[45] Dominic read his followers the Great Commission and Francis set an example by serving as a missionary in North Africa.[46] Thus, these founders set the missionary direction for their orders.

The pope supported both the Dominicans and the Franciscans, who sent out missionaries to Islamic lands, including North Africa, the Middle East, and Central Asia as well as to the Far East.[47] In the Middle Ages, the Franciscans conducted more missionary work than any other group. The Franciscans started out with a very simple and flexible structure, but eventually developed more control and support structures to support their mission work.[48] Thus, the Franciscans especially (and the Dominicans to a lesser extent) had a source for missionaries and a means to support them along with a vision and motivation to conduct missionary work.

---

40. Bosch, *Transforming Mission*, 235.
41. Cahill, *How the Irish Saved Civilization*, 205.
42. Bosch, *Transforming Mission*, 234–35.
43. Pierson, *Dynamics of Christian Mission*, 120.
44. Pierson, *Dynamics of Christian Mission*, 120, 124.
45. Pierson, *Dynamics of Christian Mission*, 120, 123.
46. Pierson, *Dynamics of Christian Mission*, 123.
47. Latourette, *Expansion of Christianity*, 2:288, 324; Pierson, *Dynamics of Christian Mission*, 123.
48. Pierson, *Dynamics of Christian Mission*, 123–24.

Renaissance/Enlightenment Catholic Missionary Surge (Sixteenth to Eighteenth Centuries)

With the discovery of America in 1492, a whole new era in Catholic missions began.[49] A vision was established to bring Christianity to the New World. Missionaries enjoyed the support of the Spanish and Portuguese governments, and could easily travel to new mission fields. Monastic missions continued, with Jesuits becoming the most active (see below), followed by the Franciscans and Dominicans.[50] Overall, support from the state (especially from Spain, Portugal, and later France) and the methods used generally reflected the pattern of previous monastic missions.[51]

However, some new factors emerged in the Catholic Church's mission work during this period. The first was the beginning of Protestantism, which actually seemed to motivate the Catholic Church to send out a new surge of missionaries. Roman Catholic leaders claimed that since the Protestants did not do missionary work, they could not claim to have true churches.[52] In order to have more centralized control over mission, the Propaganda Fide was established in 1622 to provide training for and administration over the increasing number of missionaries.[53] The Propaganda Fide was also meant to eliminate some of the rivalry between the monastic orders.[54] Also, monks received more specialized training for missionary work during this period, including study of the languages spoken on the mission field.[55]

Therefore, the Catholic missionary surge took place in response to two important historic events: the discovery of America and the Protestant Reformation. The key leaders came out of monastic orders, but there was new control from the pope himself. Learning that there were new peoples to evangelize in America brought a new vision and motivation to Catholic missionaries, who continued to have very good means for missionary work, being supported by the Catholic Church as well as by many European governments.

---

49. Walls, *Cross-Cultural Process*, 28.
50. Neill, *History of Christian Missions*, 177.
51. Latourette, *Expansion of Christianity*, 3:36, 39, 41; Neill, *History of Christian Missions*, 178.
52. Pierson, *Dynamics of Christian Mission*, 34.
53. Robert, *Christian Mission*, 37.
54. Pierson, *Dynamics of Christian Mission*, 176.
55. Latourette, *Expansion of Christianity*, 3:37.

Jesuit Missionary Surge (Sixteenth to Twentieth Centuries)

The Jesuit monastic order (The Society of Jesus) was established by Ignatius Loyola in the sixteenth century.[56] The Jesuits were to be an "army of the Church,"[57] ready to propagate the faith to pagans, heretics, or Protestants. They were very zealous for mission from the very beginning.

There were a number of key leaders in the Jesuit order who motivated others to become missionaries. First, Loyola himself wanted to become a missionary to Muslims.[58] Then, the most famous Jesuit, Francis Xavier, had a passion for missionary work that both bore tremendous fruit and inspired many others to become missionaries. Xavier was described as "a consummate example of the Jesuit ideal: fiery missionary spontaneity linked to uncompromising organizational obedience."[59] He served as a missionary in India, Indonesia, and Japan before dying on the way to China. Xavier inspired future Jesuits to continue his work and eventually reach China.[60]

The passion and boldness of Jesuits like Xavier inspired many to join the order. By 1626, "the Jesuits became the largest men's mission organization in the world, with 15,000 members and 440 colleges."[61] This incredible missionary surge was made possible through "personal, spiritual commitment to the overwhelming reality of God who created the world not by accident but with a purpose."[62] The Jesuits benefitted from the world situation and Catholic Church support described above, but what set them apart were their passion, creativity, and leadership.

Catholic Missions in the Nineteenth and Twentieth Centuries

A couple of events severely damaged the Catholic Church's ability to do missionary work. First, due to disagreements over methods and a fight for control, the Jesuit monastic missionary order was disbanded from 1773 to 1814.[63] This decision sent thousands of missionaries home. Secondly, since France was one of the main supporters of Catholic missionaries, the French Revolution (1789-99) almost completely stopped all Catholic missionary

---

56. Robert, *Christian Mission*, 38.
57. Pierson, *Dynamics of Christian Mission*, 168.
58. Robert, *Christian Mission*, 38.
59. Moffett, *History of Christianity in Asia*, 10.
60. Moffett, *History of Christianity in Asia*, 105.
61. Robert, *Christian Mission*, 37.
62. Moffett, *History of Christianity in Asia*, 9–10.
63. "Jesuit Missions in 1773," 316.

activity.[64] So, the nineteenth and twentieth centuries were a time when the Catholic Church was recovering and growing its mission work again.

Much of Catholic missions was controlled by the pope during this period. So, it was very important that after being freed by Napoleon, Pope Pius VII restored the Jesuit order in 1814.[65] The Catholic Church took back control of its missions from the governments of Spain and Portugal.[66] Later popes in the nineteenth century encouraged a new missionary surge which included a broader global network, more lay involvement, and a "new missionary spirituality."[67] As lay people got more involved, a great number of societies began raising money for missions, especially in the United States.[68] And, as Catholic missionaries faced persecution around the world, more Catholics became interested in getting involved in missions, which led to an increase in the number of missionaries.[69]

Therefore, the Catholic Church again experienced a surge of missionaries, primarily because they had lost so many missionaries at the end of the eighteenth century. Key leaders who helped bring about the new missionary surge were the popes of the nineteenth century. They increased involvement of the laity, which opened up a new source for potential missionaries and missionary support (means). A new missionary spirituality helped improve the vision and motivation for missionary work once again.

The White Fathers and Sisters Missionary Surge (Nineteenth and Twentieth Centuries)

Cardinal Lavigerie of Algiers founded the White Fathers in 1868.[70] He promoted missionary work in Africa, establishing a different kind of religious community. Instead of the vows that monks and nuns usually make, the White Fathers and White Sisters (a parallel organization) simply took oaths committing themselves to lifelong missionary work in Africa and

---

64. Iraola, *True Confucians*, 63.
65. Iraola, *True Confucians*, 64.
66. Moffett, *History of Christianity in Asia*, 184.
67. Iraola, *True Confucians*, 65; Latourette, "Christian Missionary Movement," 155–56; Moffett, *History of Christianity in Asia*, 184; Neill, *History of Christian Missions*, 250, 399–400.
68. Latourette, "Christian Missionary Movement," 155; Latourette, *Expansion of Christianity*, 4:59; Latourette, *Expansion of Christianity*, 7:44.
69. Iraola, *True Confucians*, 287; Neill, *History of Christian Missions*, 411.
70. Neill, *History of Christian Missions*, 399.

to obedience to their superiors.[71] However, despite these simple oaths, the White Fathers and White Sisters received very thorough training for missionary work, and they received talented seminary graduates as well, mainly from France.[72] This combination certainly impacted recruitment, which reached 2,000 ordained male missionaries and 1,200 female missionaries in 1957.[73]

Considering this missionary surge, it is clear that a key leader was behind it, casting vision through education and providing motivation for others to join. Getting approval from the pope to form the order provided the means for the missionary surge, and his source for missionaries was principally French.

Irish Missionary Surge in the Twentieth Century

Another place from which a missionary surge came in the twentieth century was Ireland, which experienced an increase from under 200 missionaries in 1900 to about 2,000 in 1935.[74] This great surge of interest seems to have been primarily motivated by two French missionary societies: Congregation du Saint Esprit and Missions Africaines de Lyons. The motivation included support for an anti-slavery campaign, support for poor missionaries, and the need to send more missionaries.[75] At this time, there was also a surge in growth of the Irish Catholic Church, which provided a source for potential missionaries.[76]

These French missionary societies effectively communicated their message through missionary magazines.[77] They publicized ceremonies for departing missionaries. They wrote about the adventure and romanticism of missions. They published statistics. They made spiritual arguments, pointing to the biblical command to go into all the world to help save desperate souls. They pointed to competition between Catholics, Protestants, and Muslims. They even explained how missionaries can play a key role in improving

---

71. Neill, *History of Christian Missions*, 425.

72. Latourette, *Expansion of Christianity*, 6:16, 38; Neill, *History of Christian Missions*, 425.

73. Neill, *History of Christian Missions*, 457.

74. Hogan, "Modern Irish Missionary Movement," 157.

75. Hogan, "Modern Irish Missionary Movement," 158–60.

76. Hogan, "Modern Irish Missionary Movement," 160.

77. Hogan, "Modern Irish Missionary Movement," 160.

the modern world.[78] Clearly, these provided a number of different ways for people to gain a vision and a motivation to become missionaries.

The Congregation du Saint Esprit (Congregation of the Holy Ghost) also offered missionary institutes to educate people about missions.[79] Eventually, it would become Ireland's largest missionary sending agency.[80]

Therefore, we can see that the Irish missionary surge was connected to a great deal of effort put into casting a vision and motivating through education and publications that seemed appropriate for the historical context. There was already a source for potential missionaries. Finally, the French missionary societies offered the means for becoming missionaries. Who the key leaders were is unclear in this case, although they may have been the leaders of these two French missionary societies.

Orthodox Missions (Ninth to Twentieth Centuries)

It is unclear if we can call any Orthodox missionary work a surge, despite significant results that led to the spread of Orthodoxy from Greece to Russia and into Siberia, Japan, and Alaska.[81] Much of the reported missionary work was done by small groups of missionaries. To contrast Catholic and Orthodox missions at the beginning of the twentieth century, Catholics had nearly 20,000 priests in missionary work in Asia and Africa whereas the Russian Orthodox had only about 400 in Asia.[82] In any case, there are a couple of examples of Orthodox missionaries that should be considered.

First, the missionary brothers Constantine and Methodius, who translated the Bible into Slavonic, had monastic missionary disciples who "trained hundreds in the tradition established by that apostle (Methodius) and his brother, and translated more of the literature of the Orthodox Church in to Slavonic."[83] This missionary surge, if it can be called that, came about due to the key people, Constantine and Methodius, who were well educated, theologically astute, and experienced in diplomacy. They also had the backing of the emperor, which provided the means for missions.[84] In addition, the brothers were fluent in the Slavonic language, which helped

---

78. Hogan, "Modern Irish Missionary Movement," 165–70, 173.
79. Hogan, "Congregation of the Holy Ghost," 2–4.
80. Hogan, "Congregation of the Holy Ghost," 13.
81. Gibson, "Russian Expansion," 134; Uspensky, "Orthodox Icon," 39.
82. Robert, *Christian Mission*, 51–52.
83. Latourette, *Expansion of Christianity*, 2:245.
84. Neill, *History of Christian Missions*, 84.

them translate the Bible well and pass on to others their translation skills and a vision and motivation for translation.[85]

Another possible missionary surge in Orthodox missions occurred after Russia accepted Orthodox Christianity. The state actively encouraged the building of monasteries and the sending out of groups of missionary monks.[86] In fact, Russian Orthodox missionaries received more government support in the nineteenth century than did either Roman Catholic or Protestant missionaries.[87] Missions and *"Russification"* became difficult to distinguish.[88] Thus, Orthodoxy and Russian nationalism became connected as well.[89] So, any missionary surges in Russia were supported by the state.

Church of the East (Nestorian) Missions (First to Twelfth Centuries)

Another Orthodox missionary movement was happening in Central Asia under the name of The Church of the East although it is better known in the West as the Nestorian Church. It is another example of missionary work happening on the fringes of the Christian church.[90] This is another case in which it is unclear if a missionary surge took place since the numbers of missionaries and the exact time frame are unknown. Nevertheless, some significant missionary work was happening.

The Church of the East, during a great portion of its existence, lived as a minority religion under Persian and Islamic rule. It first sent missionaries and expanded from Syria into Upper Mesopotamia, Arabia, Persia, and Kurdistan.[91] During the difficult period of the Middle Ages in the West, the Church of the East was a "missionary church *par excellence*," built on the foundations of theology, monasticism, and mission.[92] The Church of the East's greatest leader was the patriarch Timothy, who lived in the eighth and ninth centuries. Among Timothy's feats were the sending of monastic missionaries to the Caspian Sea in the West and to

---

85. Fletcher, *Barbarian Conversion*, 353.
86. Latourette, *Expansion of Christianity*, 2:254; Latourette, *Expansion of Christianity*, 3:67.
87. Latourette, *Expansion of Christianity*, 4:107.
88. Bosch, *Transforming Mission*, 206.
89. Bosch, *Transforming Mission*, 212; Neill, *History of Christian Missions*, 213.
90. Johnstone, *Future of the Global Church*, 33.
91. McDowell, "Ancient Nestorian Church," 69.
92. Bosch, *Transforming Mission*, 204.

China in the East and seeing the conversion of a Turkish king who ruled over a great portion of Central Asia.[93]

Overall, Church of the East missionaries had success among the Turks, Uygurs, Soghdians, and to some extent even among the Mongols and Tatars in Central Asia.[94] Some priests and bishops went as tentmakers (i.e., working menial trades) in order to spread the faith.[95] In addition to monastic missions, Soghdian merchants so often spread the Christian faith during their travels that "Syriac Christian writers used the word *merchant* as a metaphor for those who spread the gospel."[96]

Despite functioning as a minority religion, the Church of the East was able to establish an elaborate network of dioceses and to maintain its church and mission work with few difficulties up until the twelfth century.[97] Edessa was used as a training center and sending platform for many Church of the East missionaries. A school in Nsiblis, Mesopotamia, was also established for training in Bible, spiritual disciplines, and missionary work.[98]

So, the Church of the East was able to do significant missionary work on the basis of a large source for missionaries (both monastic and lay) through the means of a well-organized church with significant education and training. The key leader Timothy helped inspire a vision and motivation for missionaries who, for a significant period of time, had the opportunity to spread the Gospel in Asia.

Pietistic Missions (Eighteenth Century)

The first Protestant missionary surges came out of the Pietistic Movement. The Puritans also set an example for the later modern missionary movement,[99] and it can even be said that Pietism drew upon lessons from the Puritans.[100] However, the Puritans did not produce a large enough movement to be considered a missionary surge.

Pietism was started by Philip Jacob Spener who wanted to improve spiritual life in the Protestant churches.[101] The movement affected the

---

93. Jenkins, *Lost History of Christianity*, 8, 10.
94. Jenkins, *Lost History of Christianity*, 63.
95. Pierson, *Dynamics of Christian Mission*, 85.
96. Jenkins, *Lost History of Christianity*, 63.
97. Jenkins, *Lost History of Christianity*, 62–63, 110.
98. Pierson, *Dynamics of Christian Mission*, 52, 86.
99. Sweeney, "Introduction," 3.
100. Walls, *Cross-Cultural Process*, 221.
101. Pierson, *Dynamics of Christian Mission*, 182.

churches from both the top and bottom. In addition to getting the laity more involved in ministry and interested in missions, a second key leader, A.H. Francke, helped start a famous orphanage and the University of Halle which promoted Pietism and trained potential missionaries.[102]

As was the case in Catholic missions, Pietism tended to continue to connect support for missions with the state, despite increased interest, and even financial support in some cases, from the laity.[103] King Frederick IV of Denmark was behind the sending of the first Pietistic missionaries, taking them from Francke's school in Germany and sending them to the Danish territory of Tranquebar, India.[104] This is yet another example of missionaries coming from the fringe of the church.[105] The Danish Halle mission was thus founded, which sent out between fifty and sixty missionaries over the course of the eighteenth century.[106] In addition, the first Protestant student missionary group was formed at the University of Halle, the Order of the Mustard Seed, led by Count Ludwig von Zinzendorf,[107] who would later launch an even more significant missionary surge.

Thus, the first steps of Protestant missions were taken under the influence of Pietism. Perhaps these steps are too small to be called a surge, although it is clear that their vision for spirituality motivated them into missions, led by Spener and Francke. The means for missions continued to be primarily through the state, although the University of Halle and the Order of the Mustard Seed provided new, non-monastic sources for potential missionaries. Because the mission field tended to be limited to where there were Protestant governments, there were not many opportunities for mission, but this situation would change with the Moravian Brethren, who worked independently from the state.

Moravian Missionary Surge (Eighteenth Century)

Steve Addison put it well when he wrote that "the Moravians were the first Protestants to treat world missions as the responsibility of the whole church."[108] Count Zinzendorf was the key leader who helped bring vision

---

102. Bosch, *Transforming Mission*, 253; Tucker, *From Jerusalem to Irian Jaya*, 98; Walls, *Cross-Cultural Process*, 202.
103. Latourette, *Expansion of Christianity*, 3:50.
104. Neill, *History of Christian Missions*, 228.
105. Moffett, *History of Christianity in Asia*, 238.
106. Pierson, *Dynamics of Christian Mission*, 185.
107. Pierson, *Dynamics of Christian Mission*, 185.
108. Addison, *Movements that Change the World*, 42.

and motivation to the group. But first, he brought together a source of potential missionaries by inviting Protestant refugees (mostly from Moravia) to come live on his estate, which was called Herrnhut. After a period of internal conflict between refugees from different countries and denominations, God brought revival to the group of a few hundred in 1728. In weeping and repentance, they committed themselves to prayer, starting a prayer chain that would last for more than 100 years.[109]

In 1731, God gave the Moravians a specific vision for missionary work when in Copenhagen Zinzendorf met a former slave from the West Indies who begged Zinzendorf to send missionaries there. So, the Moravian Brethren sent their first two missionaries to the Caribbean.[110] Zinzendorf's conviction concerning missions was contagious, and Herrnhut became a center for sending out missionaries. Moravians had so much passion for God's mission that they were willing to go as self-supporting missionaries to some of the most hostile places on earth.[111] Moravians were provided only with enough support to reach their port of departure.[112] Their commitment to missionary service can be summed up by their maxim, "Where there is presently most to do for the Savior; that becomes our home."[113]

And thus, the first large Protestant missionary surge began. Over 20 years, the Moravians sent out more missionaries than all Protestants had sent out over the previous 200 years.[114] They had a tremendously active source for potential missionaries, sending on average two missionaries for every 58 of their members.[115] The Moravians really believed that "every Christian is a missionary."[116] This clear vision, along with continued spiritual motivation coming out of revival and prayer, helped support the surge. Zinzendorf was certainly the key leader in the movement, with the only negative being that missionaries had to provide most of their own means for mission. This weakness would eventually slow down the movement.

---

109. Irvin and Sunquist, *World Christian Movement*, 357; Johnstone, *Future of the Global Church*, 133.

110. Irvin and Sunquist, *World Christian Movement*, 358, 419.

111. Latourette, *Expansion of Christianity*, 3:47; Neill, *History of Christian Missions*, 237; Tucker, *From Jerusalem to Irian Jaya*, 99.

112. Addison, *Movements that Change the World*, 42.

113. Hinkson, "Missions among Puritans and Pietists," 39.

114. Tucker, *From Jerusalem to Irian Jaya*, 101.

115. Johnstone, *Future of the Global Church*, 133.

116. Tucker, *From Jerusalem to Irian Jaya*, 99.

The Great Century of Missions or The Modern Missionary Movement (Nineteenth Century)

There were a number of historical factors that made possible the *Great Century* of Protestant missions, or the modern missionary movement, in the nineteenth century. The Industrial Revolution in Great Britain, and to a lesser extent in the United States, helped improve the technology and wealth of both countries.[117] The wealth and the power that went with it led to colonial expansion, and along with it, the financing of missionary work.[118] Furthermore, improved technology led to the improvement of travel and communication at this time,[119] resulting in a measure of globalization. The nineteenth century was also relatively peaceful.[120] Each of these factors improved the opportunities for missionaries to travel and work.

In addition, people's worldviews broadened through hearing of the exploration and adventures of cartographer Captain James Cook.[121] Even William Carey was impressed by the new worlds described in Cook's travel narratives.[122] Learning of these new worlds suggested the possibility of new missionary work, for which people were ready to volunteer.[123] As trade and commerce increased following the circulation of Captain Cook's maps, missionaries were ready to follow.[124] People volunteered for missionary work, in some cases because they were interested in the adventure of travel.

Another issue also often linked commerce and Christianity. Many Christians were abolitionists and fought to end the slave trade throughout the world. Often these same Christians became interested in missionary work as one ministry involvement led to another.[125] Thus, promoting abolition ended up promoting missions as well.

In addition, the nineteenth century was a time of increasing literacy and interest in reading. Christians were very interested in reading about what God was doing both nearby and around the world.[126] So, missionary organizations began publishing magazines to share information about their

---

117. Latourette, *Expansion of Christianity*, 4:18–19.

118. Latourette, *Expansion of Christianity*, 4:18; Tucker, *From Jerusalem to Irian Jaya*, 119.

119. Latourette, *Expansion of Christianity*, 4:18.

120. Latourette, *Expansion of Christianity*, 4:19.

121. Robert, *Christian Mission*, 46.

122. Latourette, *Expansion of Christianity*, 5:202.

123. Bosch, *Transforming Mission*, 280.

124. Robert, *Christian Mission*, 46; Tucker, *From Jerusalem to Irian Jaya*, 118.

125. Stanley, "'Commerce and Christianity,'" 77; Walls, *Cross-Cultural Process*, 213.

126. George, "Evangelical Revival," 46.

ministries and connect with supporters.[127] Also, William Carey's pamphlet about missions and Jonathan Edwards's book on prayer became popular and motivated people to get more involved in missions.[128]

But, perhaps more than any other piece of literature, David Brainerd's diary (edited and published by Jonathan Edwards in 1749) about his missionary work among Native Americans motivated people to go into missionary work. Brainerd became the "patron saint of evangelical missionaries."[129] His life inspired key leaders Samuel Mills, John Wesley, William Carey, and Henry Martyn.[130] Brainerd's diary provided a powerful motivation for the missionary surge of the nineteenth century.

Finally, it is worthwhile to consider the theology behind the nineteenth century missionary surge which had a great impact on the vision and motivation of the people involved. People in the surge had "an evangelical vision of a world enslaved to sin, from which only the offer of salvation through Jesus Christ offered deliverance."[131] Individual conversion was the focus, which called upon missionaries to go and share the message with them. Because their mission work was based on salvation being a personal experience, they didn't think much about church structure.[132]

Many missionaries had postmillennial expectations, that Christ would be universally known prior to His return.[133] Missionary leader Rufus Anderson believed that the "fullness of time"[134] had now come, and he expected that missionary efforts would lead to the "conversion of the world."[135] Of course, these optimistic beliefs helped motivate missionaries to continue their ministry during difficult times.

This Great Century of missions, in fact, produced several missionary surges, each with numerous factors behind it. Since there was a lull in missionary activity about the middle of the nineteenth century,[136] it will be helpful to divide the century into two parts in order to see the way different factors had their effects.

---

127. Walls, *Missionary Movement*, 251; Walls, *Cross-Cultural Process*, 17.
128. Davey, "Literature in Missions," 148; George, "Evangelical Revival," 47.
129. Conforti, "David Brainerd," 310–11.
130. Conforti, "David Brainerd," 315–16; Tucker, *From Jerusalem to Irian Jaya*, 80.
131. Shenk, *Changing Frontiers of Mission*, 91–92.
132. Shenk, *Changing Frontiers of Mission*, 151.
133. Bosch, *Transforming Mission*, 314.
134. Shenk, *Changing Frontiers of Mission*, 109.
135. Shenk, *Changing Frontiers of Mission*, 110.
136. Stanley, "'Commerce and Christianity,'" 81.

First Half of the Nineteenth Century

In the year 1800, there were only about 100 Protestant foreign missionaries in the world.[137] However, the first Evangelical Awakening in Great Britain and America had laid the foundations for new missions, providing a source of and motivation for new missionaries that could be drawn from the laity.[138] The awakening provided the "logistic networks—interregional, international, interdenominational—that undergirded the movement" of missions in the nineteenth century.[139]

Over the course of the nineteenth century, Christianity would grow even more, from about 23% to almost 35% of the world population, the fastest growth seen since the early church.[140] By 1900, the number of Protestant missionaries on the field had grown to tens of thousands.[141] Thus, this incredible missionary surge happened after revival and in parallel with church growth, which provided a rich source for potential missionaries.

In addition to the historical, theological, and ecclesial factors described above, two more important factors need to be considered as well. *Concerts of prayer* for missions, established in the eighteenth century by Jonathan Edwards,[142] provided spiritual vision, motivation, and the spiritual means for a missionary surge. His book on prayer, first published in 1748, was reprinted multiple times in the nineteenth century as people sought revival and the expansion of the church.[143]

In addition to changes in Protestants' thinking about prayer, another important change in thinking that took place was that missionary work was no longer seen as being reserved for celibate monks. Now, people with families could become missionaries, as exemplified by the Moravians.[144] This change opened the door for many people to volunteer who would never have considered it in previous centuries. Thus, the stage was set for the growth of volunteer missionary societies.

---

137. Noll, *New Shape of World Christianity*, 40.

138. Bosch, *Transforming Mission*, 278–79; Latourette, "Christian Missionary Movement," 155–56.

139. Walls, *Missionary Movement*, 79.

140. Noll, *New Shape of World Christianity*, 41.

141. Actually, Johnstone, *Future of the Global Church*, has contradictory figures: 45,000 on p. 59 and 17,400 on p. 228. Perhaps the second figure is more accurate.

142. Pierson, *Dynamics of Christian Mission*, 334; Walls, *Missionary Movement*, 244.

143. Neill, *History of Christian Missions*, 239.

144. Robert, *Christian Mission*, 46–47.

Voluntary Missionary Society Surge (Late Eighteenth to Nineteenth Centuries)

The big innovation of the nineteenth century was the establishment of volunteer missionary societies separate from the main church body,[145] which was generally not interested in sending missionaries.[146] William Carey established the first such society, the Baptist Missionary Society,[147] as a new means to send and support missionaries. He appeared to have several sources of inspiration to take his first steps in sending missionaries, including Jonathan Edwards and the Moravian Brethren.[148] The volunteer missionary society was very practical, even "businesslike,"[149] providing a way for the laity to get involved in missions.[150]

But that was not all that Carey did. Between May 1792 and June 1793, Carey did four incredibly important things that helped start the missionary surge: He published a book, preached a sermon, organized a volunteer society, and went himself as a missionary.[151] Through his sermon, his book, and his personal example, Carey showed people that the main purpose of the Christian church is to evangelize the world. His book justified his vision for missions, that the church must use means to convert unbelievers. His sermon included the famous words, "Expect great things from God; attempt great things for God," neatly bridging the gap between Calvinism and Arminianism.[152] And finally, he set the supreme example, going as a missionary himself, saying, "I will go down, if you will hold the rope."[153]

Carey's bold steps influenced the creation of other volunteer missionary societies and the sending of more missionaries. Carey wrote John Garland, suggesting that he help form the London Missionary Society. The Church Missionary Society was formed a few years later.[154] In all, between 1792 and 1825, no fewer than 15 volunteer missionary societies were founded, primarily in England.[155] And as Carey sent reports home about

---

145. Walls, *Missionary Movement*, 239.
146. Neill, *History of Christian Missions*, 252.
147. Neill, *History of Christian Missions*, 262.
148. Pierson, *Dynamics of Christian Mission*, 214; Schattschneider, "William Carey," 9–10.
149. Bosch, *Transforming Mission*, 330.
150. Shenk, *Changing Frontiers of Mission*, 109.
151. Moffett, *History of Christianity in Asia*, 254.
152. Tucker, *From Jerusalem to Irian Jaya*, 122–23.
153. Moffett, *History of Christianity in Asia*, 255.
154. Pierson, *Dynamics of Christian Mission*, 204.
155. Keyes, *Last Age of Missions*, 6.

APPENDIX A: THE HISTORY OF MISSIONARY SURGES 213

his work on the mission field, they motivated more and more people to become missionaries.[156]

There were several reasons why the means of volunteer missionary societies were so effective. Before the nineteenth century, it was assumed that the state was responsible for administering society, including sponsoring missionary work.[157] The Enlightenment had brought about a paradigm shift in the way people thought, making society more individualistic, meaning that everyone was responsible to make his or her own free choices.[158] This change made people more open to volunteering to make an impact on society, so many volunteer organizations were started,[159] eventually including volunteer missionary societies. There was greater optimism about what common people could do.[160] Americans, in particular, felt a "sense of destiny, a feeling of opportunity and grave responsibility."[161] Thus, people's vision broadened as to what they could accomplish themselves.

Of course, not everyone was excited about these new volunteer missionary societies. The East India Trading Company, for example, did not like anything that might get in the way of their business. William Wilberforce and other evangelicals in the British Parliament forced a change in the charter of the Company in 1813 that allowed for more freedom for Christian missionary work,[162] which provided an historic opportunity for the missionary surge to increase.

Although most of the missionary surge came from Great Britain during the first half of the nineteenth century, the United States also started to send foreign missionaries, inspired by the key leader Samuel Mills.[163] In 1802, Mills felt a call from God to "preach the gospel to the nations."[164] In 1806, Mills became a student at Williams College to prepare for ministry. As he and some of his fellow students were on their way to a prayer meeting, a huge rainstorm hit, causing them to take shelter in the lee of a haystack. It was there that they promised to become foreign missionaries.[165] Mills himself

---

156. Addison, *Movements that Change the World*, 104.
157. Shenk, *Changing Frontiers of Mission*, 144.
158. Robert, *Christian Mission*, 46; Walls, *Cross-Cultural Process*, 201.
159. Noll, *New Shape of World Christianity*, 111.
160. Latourette, *Expansion of Christianity*, 4:18–19.
161. Gundlach, "Early American Missions," 87.
162. Latourette, *Expansion of Christianity*, 4:108–9; Moffett, *History of Christianity in Asia*, 263.
163. Pierson, *Dynamics of Christian Mission*, 215.
164. Hesselgrave, *Paradigms in Conflict*, 210–11.
165. Hesselgrave, *Paradigms in Conflict*, 210–11; Shaw, "Haystack that Changed the World."

would never become a missionary, dying in his mid-thirties,[166] but the promise from under the haystack would motivate many young people to become part of a missionary surge from the United States.

In 1808, the students founded the Society of Brethren with the purpose of spreading the Gospel around the world. They challenged their classmates as well to commit themselves to world missions after graduation, but they would only admit new members to the Society who were solidly committed to missionary service.[167] Two years later, the Society moved to Andover, the United States's first graduate seminary. Over the next sixty years, 527 students from Andover joined the Society with half of them later becoming foreign missionaries, including Adoniram Judson.[168] This growth of interest in missions helped inspire the creation of new missionary sending agencies as well.[169] In addition, the Society of Brethren encouraged the formation of the Societies of Inquiry on the Subject of Missions at several colleges and seminaries, the Young Men's Christian Association (YMCA), and the Philadelphian Society at Princeton College.[170] Each of these organizations helped recruit future missionaries.

Sierra Leone Missionary Surge (Late Eighteenth to Nineteenth Centuries)

One very interesting missionary surge that came about at this time started in 1792 when a group of 1100 people landed in Sierra Leone, Africa. William Wilberforce and the Clapham Sect had helped provide for the resettlement of this group of African American former slaves, British soldiers, and Canadian immigrants.[171] It is worth noting that this resettlement was one example of a broader movement of African Americans who specifically wished to reach Africans with the Gospel.[172]

---

166. Pierson, *Dynamics of Christian Mission*, 216.

167. Shaw, "Haystack that Changed the World"; Wallstrom, *Creation of a Student Movement*, 26.

168. Pierson, *Dynamics of Christian Mission*, 216, 246.

169. Gundlach, "Early American Missions," 67–68; Shaw, "Haystack that Changed the World"; Wallstrom, *Creation of a Student Movement*, 27.

170. Pierson, *Dynamics of Christian Mission*, 246; Wallstrom, *Creation of a Student Movement*, 28–29.

171. Pierson, *Dynamics of Christian Mission*, 290.

172. Killingray, "Black Atlantic Missionary Movement," 5–6.

What made this effort no ordinary resettlement was that the group already had its own preachers and churches.[173] They immediately began doing missionary work, both among Africans and among African Americans who were later resettled there. Over the next sixty years, the Sierra Leone settlement grew to a population of 50,000 and it provided one hundred ordained men to serve with the Church Missionary Society in addition to numerous other teachers and missionaries.[174] Their missionary outreach went as far as Nigeria and into Niger, led by Samuel Crowther.[175]

Thus, the Sierra Leone settlement had a source of trained and motivated missionaries. They had a vision to reach Africa for Christ and were provided with the means to be transported there. In terms of key leaders, their best example was Samuel Crowther, who was a gifted linguist and missionary.[176] Based on these factors, Sierra Leone had a small missionary surge.

Second Half of the Nineteenth Century

By the early to mid-1850s, missionary interest had died down. Other issues had taken precedence, including the Crimean War and the high prices and taxation that went with it.[177] Then, a number of events and actions occurred that stoked the fires of missionary passion once again.

In 1857, David Livingstone published his book *Missionary Travels and Researches in South Africa*. This book increased people's interest in missions in general and in Africa in particular.[178] Livingstone became famous in Great Britain, and as he gave speeches and published further, he continually appealed for more missionaries.[179] His appeal was heeded, as the London Missionary Society and Church Missionary Society saw significant increases in their missionary recruitment.[180]

Three events also helped encourage an increase of interest and possibilities in missions. The first was the Indian Mutiny against British control in 1857. This event shocked many British, encouraging them both to think about the needs of the world and to contrast some people's desire

---

173. Walls, *Missionary Movement*, 86.
174. Walls, *Missionary Movement*, 86–87.
175. Fiedler, *Story of Faith Missions*, 70.
176. Walls, *Missionary Movement*, 104–10.
177. Stanley, "'Commerce and Christianity,'" 81.
178. Neill, *History of Christian Missions*, 325.
179. Robert, *Christian Mission*, 84.
180. Stanley, "'Commerce and Christianity,'" 86.

for revenge against the Indians with the need to save Indians' souls.[181] The second event was the signing of a peace treaty between Great Britain and China following the Second Opium War. Missionaries had already begun to work on the coast of China following the end of the First Opium War in 1842.[182] But, in 1858, when the Tientsin treaty was signed, missionaries were finally allowed to enter the interior of China.[183] Of course, opium was allowed to be sold as well, which became a stigma in that it was associated with the coming of missionaries.[184] Each of these events stimulated renewed interest in missions.

Finally, the third event that impacted a renewed missionary surge was the Second Evangelical Awakening between 1858 and 1863. The Awakening began in the United States and spread to Europe and Asia, producing many new converts and increased interest in evangelism.[185] New missionary societies were formed on the heels of the awakening and the already-existing societies began to receive increased financial support and new recruits.[186] Many of these new societies were called *faith missions*, representing a modification of the earlier paradigm of volunteer missionary societies. They accepted people who had been motivated during the Awakening to enter into missionary work, but who did not meet the qualifications required for service with the older missionary societies. They also used a new mechanism for financial support.[187] The first faith mission, the China Inland Mission, will be described in more detail below. Thus, a new source of missionaries and motivation came about.

In addition, a new method of recruiting was first used in 1854. That was the year that Alexander Duff, Scottish missionary to India, traveled to North America and held a missionary conference. This method became a standard means of missionary encouragement and recruitment over the following years.[188]

A new key leader by the name of Dwight L. Moody also helped enable the missionary surge of the last half of the nineteenth century. He was involved in the Second Evangelical Awakening and began to lead revival

---

181. Stanley, "Commerce and Christianity," 86, 90.
182. Stanley, "Commerce and Christianity," 78.
183. Pierson, *Dynamics of Christian Mission*, 242; Wu, *Missionary Movement in China*, 24, 143.
184. Tucker, *From Jerusalem to Irian Jaya*, 177.
185. Johnstone, *Future of the Global Church*, 59.
186. Neill, *History of Christian Missions*, 324.
187. Fiedler, *Story of Faith Missions*, 125, 138.
188. Shenk, *Changing Frontiers of Mission*, 110.

meetings, leading people to Christ.[189] Initially, Moody was interested only in evangelism and not cross-cultural missions. However, some of his young converts changed his mind so that he expanded his goal from attempting just to save America to attempting to save the whole world.[190] To that end, Moody started holding student conferences that motivated many young people to go into missionary work.[191] In addition, he helped encourage business leaders to give financially toward missions.[192] Thus, Moody helped provide the means and motivation for a missionary surge.

Women's Missionary Surge (Late Nineteenth to Twentieth Centuries)

Women had already been taking an active role in Protestant missions since the Moravian missionary surge. However, single women had been excluded. In the 1860s, the Women's Missionary Movement began, with the creation of multiple women's volunteer missionary societies to send and support women in mission. There were more than forty such societies by the year 1900. This change led to the massive recruitment of single women missionaries, who already outnumbered men in Protestant missions by the early twentieth century.[193]

There were several factors behind this surge in missionary women. First, nearly all the single women who chose to become missionaries felt a calling from God and a sense that they could make an impact, helping women under pagan oppression.[194] Missionary wives often wrote letters about the needs of women in places such as Asia, and this motivated other women to become missionaries.[195] Married women were limited by their families' needs, so more single women were needed to minister to national women.[196] In addition, missions offered opportunities for ministry that most women could not obtain in their home country. Also, some women wanted to lead an exciting life, yet careers in the army, navy, and world exploration were closed to them.[197]

189. Pierson, *Dynamics of Christian Mission*, 242.
190. Varg, "Motives in Protestant Missions," 72.
191. Hopkins, "Kansas-Sudan Missionary Movement," 314.
192. Varg, "Motives in Protestant Missions," 73.
193. Tucker, *From Jerusalem to Irian Jaya*, 288.
194. Tucker, *From Jerusalem to Irian Jaya*, 289.
195. Moffett, *History of Christianity in Asia*, 437.
196. Pierson, *Dynamics of Christian Mission*, 255.
197. Tucker, *From Jerusalem to Irian Jaya*, 289.

It is interesting to note that women generally did not choose to become missionaries out of a commitment to women's activism in abolition or for women's rights. Most women followed Catharine Beecher's ideal to minister in the "traditional domestic sphere."[198] Thus, women did not go to the mission field to minister to men, but instead strove to help women and children there. In any case, women served in a large variety of roles, such as doctors, nurses, teachers, and social workers.[199]

So, a significant part of the renewed missionary surge during the second half of the nineteenth century was women missionaries. When the means of women's missionary societies was created, a huge new source of missionaries became available. Women were given a vision for missions by other women, and many were motivated to ministry out of a spiritual call and in response to the needs of other women. There were many women who led by example, but no key leader who stood out like William Carey or Dwight Moody.

China Inland Mission (Late Nineteenth to Twentieth Centuries)

Another significant part of the renewed missionary surge during the second half of the nineteenth century took place through the China Inland Mission. In 1865, Hudson Taylor founded this missionary society based on a profound conviction from God. His vision for reaching the interior of China drove him to start the mission with virtually no financial support. Taylor started the first faith mission, promising to give its missionaries only whatever was raised with no fixed salary. Taylor also *amateurized* his mission by not requiring applicants to have a special education or come from a particular denomination.[200] Thus, Taylor had a potentially larger source of missionaries than other mission societies of his day, even if he had less financial means to support them.

Clearly, God's hand was at work. Stephen Neill explained that "almost from the start [Taylor's] success was sensational. Recruits crowded to his doors."[201] Taylor's passion for China was palpable. Those who heard him pray for China said it was like hearing Spurgeon—it was "the experience of a lifetime."[202] Many people who had been saved during the recent revival

---

198. Parker, *Kingdom of Character*, 64–65.
199. Parker, *Kingdom of Character*, 75.
200. Pierson, *Dynamics of Christian Mission*, 243–44.
201. Neill, *History of Christian Missions*, 334.
202. Taylor and Taylor, *Hudson Taylor's Spiritual Secret*, 176.

resonated with Taylor's call since they "shared the religious convictions of Taylor."[203] Such a key leader certainly motivated many missionary recruits.

Furthermore, when the famous *Cambridge Seven* decided to join the mission, it attracted even more interest.[204] If they were willing to give up fame and fortune, answering God's call, why wouldn't someone with a lot less to lose? Certainly the need to share the good news about eternal life with the lost in China was enough motivation to go. Taylor didn't promise much in the way of money, but he delivered all that was needed through prayer.[205]

So, in 1900, the China Inland Mission accounted for about half of the 1500 Protestant missionaries working in China. In addition to the China Inland Mission's missionary surge, Taylor's focus on China helped other mission societies grow as well.[206] This surge was strong in the areas of source, key leadership, vision, and motivation. While the China Inland Mission did not have much in the way of financial means, perhaps a greater spiritual means made up for it.

Student Volunteer Movement Surge (Late Nineteenth to Early Twentieth Centuries)

The Student Volunteer Movement (SVM) probably facilitated the greatest missionary surge of all in the nineteenth century. Having been officially organized only in 1888, by the early twentieth century the SVM was responsible for recruiting approximately half of all Protestant missionaries.[207] Overall, it was involved in the sending of about 20,500 missionaries to the field.[208]

The SVM began informally in 1886 at a student conference in Mount Hermon, Massachusetts. Robert Wilder from Princeton organized some small informal meetings about missions, including *The Meeting of the Ten Nations*, in which students spoke of the needs in their own areas of the world. Missionary interest spread from person to person.[209] Then, on the final day of the conference, Wilder challenged students to commit themselves to become

---

203. Latourette, *Expansion of Christianity*, 6:326.
204. Neill, *History of Christian Missions*, 335.
205. Moffett, *History of Christianity in Asia*, 465–66.
206. Pierson, *Dynamics of Christian Mission*, 245.
207. Pierson, *Dynamics of Christian Mission*, 247–48; Tucker, *From Jerusalem to Irian Jaya*, 312.
208. Tucker, *From Jerusalem to Irian Jaya*, 312.
209. Parker, *Kingdom of Character*, 3, 13.

missionaries. One hundred students signed the *Princeton Pledge* that day, starting the missionary movement in earnest.[210]

Following up on this enthusiasm, Robert Wilder and John Forman toured over 160 colleges and seminaries during the 1887–88 school year, speaking about missions. This tour met with more success, recruiting 2,200 student volunteers for the mission field.[211] At most of these colleges, *missionary bands* were established. The enthusiasm snowballed, as just five years after the call to missions at Mount Hermon, already missionary bands had been established at 350 schools in the United States and Canada.[212] This was a particularly effective time to work among college students since colleges in the United States were experiencing massive growth, increasing from 23,000 undergraduates at 300 colleges in the 1870s to 100,000 students at 500 colleges in 1900.[213] Therefore, these new structures for mission came at just the right time in history.

In 1888, the SVM was officially organized, casting its vision in terms of the slogan, "The evangelization of the world in this generation."[214] More than at any other time, Christians believed that God's mission "depended on *them*."[215] The SVM involved young people in a starring role in that mission.[216] It emphasized that "only the present generation was capable of reaching its contemporaries, and that each day thousands of the unreached slipped haplessly and irretrievably into the eternal oblivion."[217] A premillennial emphasis made the missionary task urgent, especially since it was unclear how long this historical opportunity would remain available.[218] Thus, this vision for missions was incredibly motivating for young people.

In addition to belief that God was clearly behind its movement and the huge number of recruits, the SVM freely used modern business techniques to attract young people.[219] Moody was already using this approach, and the SVM extended its use. The mission "became highly organized and more professional.... Professionalization simply harnessed the latent

---

210. Tucker, *From Jerusalem to Irian Jaya*, 312, 320.

211. Parker, *Kingdom of Character*, xii; Pierson, *Dynamics of Christian Mission*, 247–48.

212. Parker, *Kingdom of Character*, 14, 17.

213. Parker, *Kingdom of Character*, 6.

214. Pierson, *Dynamics of Christian Mission*, 247–48.

215. Bosch, *Transforming Mission*, 334.

216. Robert, *Christian Mission*, 58.

217. Wallstrom, *Creation of a Student Movement*, 15.

218. Hesselgrave, *Paradigms in Conflict*, 286; Parker, *Kingdom of Character*, 85, 88.

219. Parker, *Kingdom of Character*, 30.

Christian commitment that was already present in the population."[220] Thus, the public relations methods used were able to hone the vision and motivation of the movement.

Furthermore, the SVM created a new image for missionaries that was very attractive to young people of the time. Michael Parker explained that the SVM promoted missionaries as having the "Victorian concept of character"[221] or, as some called it, a "muscular Christianity."[222] This "new breed of missionary" was noble and self-sacrificing.[223] The SVM actually promoted the difficulty of the missionary task, believing that the challenge was more attractive to middle-class, educated, idealistic young people.[224] So, these "university-educated 'gentlemen' . . . began to replace the previous generation of missionaries from humble backgrounds."[225] This vision for a new kind of missionary was very effective.

There were many key leaders in the SVM, but the most important was John Mott. He both promoted and ran the movement in North America and founded the World Student Christian Federation in 1890.[226] Working with Mott were a number of traveling secretaries who spent a year after graduating from college promoting missionary work before leaving for the mission field themselves.[227] They were particularly adept at recruiting new missionaries since they were peers of those to whom they spoke, who "could therefore encourage. . . [their] companions to 'come,' a much more persuasive request than 'go.'"[228] These leaders continued to cast vision and motivate the large source of potential missionaries at North American colleges.

In addition to human resources, the SVM was also successful in raising up financial and educational resources. Over the course of the movement, 100,000 students signed the Princeton Pledge to become missionaries, although only about 20,500 actually became missionaries. Those who stayed at home produced a financial and logistical support system for those who went.[229] Furthermore, there was a time of economic prosperity up until World War I and the Great Depression. Both Dwight Moody and John Mott

220. Parker, *Kingdom of Character*, 40, 42–43.
221. Parker, *Kingdom of Character*, xv.
222. Parker, *Kingdom of Character*, 29.
223. Walls, *Missionary Movement*, 106.
224. Parker, *Kingdom of Character*, 26, 97.
225. Bosch, *Transforming Mission*, 307.
226. Keyes, *Last Age of Missions*, 21.
227. Parker, *Kingdom of Character*, 17–18.
228. Wallstrom, *Creation of a Student Movement*, 14.
229. Parker, *Kingdom of Character*, 17; Tucker, *From Jerusalem to Irian Jaya*, 480–81.

were adept at raising support from a large group of wealthy Christian businessmen.[230] In addition, Moody helped develop "a network of institutions for education and missions training, including the Moody Bible Institute, and encouraged the growth of the SVM."[231] Thus, the means for the missionary surge were provided.

Finally, it is important to point out that missionary conferences were a very effective means that the SVM used to motivate missionaries and recruit new ones. Having been started at the Bible conference at Mount Hermon in 1886, the SVM reached its height when many of its members took part in the Edinburgh World Missionary Conference in 1910. It promoted long-standing themes of the SVM, including the idea that "the whole world is the mission field"[232] and the eschatological theme of the urgent need to reach the world in this generation.[233] Thus, there were numerous reasons why the SVM was responsible for a great missionary surge.

American Missionary Surge (Twentieth Century)

Although the nineteenth century was called the Great Century of missions by mission historian Kenneth Scott Latourette,[234] the twentieth century actually saw an even greater increase in the number of missionaries. According to Patrick Johnstone, the number of Christians in missionary work grew from 17,400 in 1900 to 43,000 in 1962 to 200,000 in 2000.[235] Through most of the twentieth century, the United States sent the majority of missionaries into the world, accounting for about two-thirds of the world total in the 1970s.[236] Therefore, it is important first to examine the factors behind this twentieth century American missionary surge.

The missions conference alluded to above at Edinburgh in 1910 was a turning point. Finally, American missionaries outnumbered British. One reason for this change was the advance in technology, which served to improve support for missionary work as well. Whereas Europe had led the way in technology for 200 years, America now took preeminence.[237] Furthermore, the business acumen of Americans, as exemplified by John

---

230. Walls, *Cross-Cultural Process*, 63; Walls, *Missionary Movement*, 230.
231. Beuttler, "Evangelical Missions in Modern America," 114.
232. Keyes, *Last Age of Missions*, 21.
233. Stanley, "Twentieth-Century World Christianity," 52–53.
234. Latourette, *Expansion of Christianity*, vols. 4–6.
235. Johnstone, *Future of the Global Church*, 228.
236. Noll, *New Shape of World Christianity*, 79–81.
237. Shenk, *Changing Frontiers of Mission*, 142, 172.

Mott and the SVM, also helped North America become the main source for missionaries.[238]

New historical opportunities for missions emerged at the end of World War II. In America especially, there was "a revival of religious fervor."[239] Christian literature was produced in huge amounts, encouraging more involvement in missions.[240] A new kind of Christian organization became popular as well, the parachurch agency, which engaged in specialized kinds of ministry, such as to students or for Bible distribution.[241] In addition, numerous new mission agencies were founded, providing the means for motivated Christians to go to the mission field.[242] The war had once again widened Americans' vision for missions, as soldiers traveled and people at home saw pictures and heard stories about places on the other side of the world. American Christians were motivated to take the Gospel to those places that had been visited, and in many cases, torn apart by war.

Although globalization had begun to some extent in the nineteenth century, it came to much greater fruition after World War II. It became much easier to travel and communicate across great distances.[243] Christians' vision for the world changed as they dreamed of "one world, one kingdom of God under Jesus Christ."[244] These factors provided an easier means for missions and a greater motivation.

Better and quicker communication brought both good and bad news to the United States. Hearing of missionaries being martyred shook the American church, such as in the cases of the five missionaries killed in Ecuador during Operation Auca and the murder of Chet Bitterman in Colombia a generation later. In addition to feeling sympathy toward their families, many people were motivated by these events to enter into missionary work, responding to these missionaries' courage and wishing to take their places.[245]

As had happened in the previous century, missionary conferences continued to be a source of encouragement and recruitment for missions. The twentieth century saw the first missions meetings of the Inter-Varsity

238. Walls, *Missionary Movement*, 235.
239. Tucker, *From Jerusalem to Irian Jaya*, 365.
240. Tucker, *From Jerusalem to Irian Jaya*, 365.
241. Beuttler, "Evangelical Missions in Modern America," 123.
242. Pierson, *Dynamics of Christian Mission*, 323.
243. Johnstone, "Next Forty Years for Christian Missions," 189; Pierson, *Dynamics of Christian Mission*, 316.
244. Robert, *Christian Mission*, 50.
245. Beuttler, "Evangelical Missions in Modern America," 110; Tucker, *From Jerusalem to Irian Jaya*, 359.

Christian Fellowship, which started in Toronto in 1946 but then moved to Urbana, Illinois.[246] The Urbana Missionary Conference became a regular event every three years, drawing thousands of students from across the world.[247] These conferences led to many young people, especially from the United States, becoming missionaries.

Another significant series of mission conferences started in 1974 with the Lausanne Congress on World Evangelization.[248] These conferences both served to motivate American evangelicals to go into cross-cultural missions as well as to energize non-Western missionaries.[249] The conferences helped missionaries and mission organizations to focus more strategically. It was at these conferences that the ideas of reaching *unreached peoples* and the *10/40 Window* were broached.[250] Out of Lausanne, many new missionary movements were started, including the AD 2000 and Beyond Movement, which purposed to have "a church for every people and the gospel for every person by the year 2000."[251] Thus, again, mission conferences served to improve the vision and motivation of potential missionaries.

Finally, it is worth pointing out that often the most significant missionary surges did not come from the main part of the church, but from the fringes. Wycliffe Bible Translators and Operation Mobilization are two good examples of that in the twentieth century.[252] We will briefly explore these two examples of missionary surges.

Wycliffe Bible Translators (Twentieth Century)

The Wycliffe missionary organization was founded by the key leader William Cameron Townsend and first sent missionaries to Mexico in 1935.[253] Wycliffe steadily grew into one of the largest missionary organizations in the world, having over 5,000 missionaries serving in 50 countries as of 2010.[254] This mission had the vision to translate the Bible into every language in the world. Capturing this vision, Townsend loved to say, "The greatest

---

246. Pierson, *Dynamics of Christian Mission*, 245.
247. Tucker, *From Jerusalem to Irian Jaya*, 481.
248. Tucker, *From Jerusalem to Irian Jaya*, 396.
249. Robert, *Christian Mission*, 72.
250. Beuttler, "Evangelical Missions in Modern America," 126.
251. Tarantal, "Networks in World Evangelization," 116.
252. Pierson, *Dynamics of Christian Mission*, 32.
253. James, "Turbulent and Transitional," 254; Pierson, *Dynamics of Christian Mission*, 245.
254. Johnstone, *Future of the Global Church*, 235.

missionary is the Bible in the mother tongue. It never needs a furlough, is never considered a foreigner."[255]

Although these are certainly eloquent words, it was the practical nature of the enterprise that attracted many Americans into mission.[256] Wycliffe proposed to do a task that was quantifiable and that had a clear beginning and end: first reduce a language to writing, then translate the Bible into this language, and then take the newly translated Bible as a tool that other missionaries could use to plant evangelical churches among the people.[257] This definitely appealed to the spirit of American entrepreneurship.

Operation Mobilization (Twentieth Century)

When George Verwer was sixteen years old, he received a Gospel of John. He read that booklet regularly for two years until he became a Christian at a Billy Graham meeting in New York City. These key events formed the foundation of the mission he would start which focused on "evangeliz[ing] with literature and personal testimony."[258]

Verwer founded Operation Mobilization in 1958.[259] This mission has not become as well-known as some, because it makes use of many "new forms of 'crazy' youth missions."[260] It was one of the first organizations to develop short-term missions, a topic discussed in greater length below. It has allowed people of all ages, with a variety of gifts, to join.[261] Not only has Operation Mobilization used this great variety of people and literature for ministry, it has significantly impacted those who came to serve, the missionaries themselves.[262]

Operation Mobilization has grown into one of the largest missionary organizations in the world, having 6,332 missionaries serving on 87 mission fields in 2010.[263] George Verwer has been the key leader of this mission. He is not only a very motivating speaker with a vision to reach the entire world for Christ, but he has also increased the source of potential missionaries by

255. Tucker, *From Jerusalem to Irian Jaya*, 379.
256. Walls, *Missionary Movement*, 235–36.
257. Noll, *New Shape of World Christianity*, 99.
258. Davey, "Literature in Missions," 144.
259. Tucker, *From Jerusalem to Irian Jaya*, 397.
260. Johnstone, *Future of the Global Church*, 228.
261. Maiden, "Life Well Lived," xi–xii.
262. Maiden, "Life Well Lived," xii; Tarantal, "Networks in World Evangelization," 120–21.
263. Johnstone, *Future of the Global Church*, 235.

accepting virtually anyone. As to means, Verwer has often used literature and a variety of so-called crazy methods. Verwer's faith and ingenuity have made a big difference in bringing about this missionary surge.

Pentecostal Missionary Surge (Twentieth Century)

Although the Pentecostal movement came out of the United States, it is so diverse and large today that it seems to need its own category. So, turning back to the beginning of the twentieth century, the Pentecostal movement officially began out of the Azusa Street Revival in 1906 in Los Angeles. The key leader was William Seymour, who "proclaimed that the end was near and that God was baptizing his people with tongues of the Spirit in order to raise up a mighty missionary force that would reach the world prior to the return of Christ."[264] So, quickly Pentecostal missionaries began sharing the Gospel, first in the United States and then moving on to Asia, South America, the Middle East, and Africa.[265] Then, in the 1960s, many Pentecostal denominations saw a missionary surge of over 50%, leading to significant church growth.[266]

There were a number of important factors behind this missionary surge. First, Pentecostals believed that Christ was returning very soon, so they felt the need to evangelize as many people as possible before he came.[267] Furthermore, they believed that God's grace was available to all, and so they had tremendous hope that many would be saved.[268] Early Pentecostal missionaries spread around the world, becoming known as the "missionaries of the one-way ticket" since they could often afford only a one-way ticket and since most believed Christ would return before they would need to go home.[269] This tremendous zeal motivated Pentecostal missionaries to do many incredible things.[270]

In addition, many Pentecostal missionaries gained their vision and motivation through their close relationship with God. Pentecostals sought "scriptural holiness."[271] Out of their close relationship with the Lord, many of the early Pentecostal missionaries believed that they had received a direct

---

264. Shaw, *Global Awakening*, 24.
265. Addison, *Movements that Change the World*, 44.
266. Tucker, *From Jerusalem to Irian Jaya*, 397.
267. Pierson, *Dynamics of Christian Mission*, 305.
268. Martin, *Tongues of Fire*, 28.
269. Pierson, *Dynamics of Christian Mission*, 311–12.
270. Addison, *Movements that Change the World*, 45.
271. Martin, *Tongues of Fire*, 28.

word from God to become missionaries.[272] This kind of call led people to go to the mission field with a willingness to endure tremendous difficulties.

In fact, Pentecostal missionaries believed that true faith required a spirit of sacrifice. Families would often sell all their possessions and leave for the mission field. Sometimes they would have little or no support, but they believed that God had called them and that He was the only means they required.[273] Some Pentecostal missionaries even took pride in their lack of support and organization, claiming that it proved that God was behind them.[274] That does not mean that Pentecostal missions were completely unorganized. On the contrary, often mission leaders would gather information about Pentecostal ministry around the world and publish it, encouraging more people to become missionaries.[275]

So, the Pentecostal missionary surge was driven by a very strong vision that Christ would return as well as by direct callings from God Himself. Missionaries had strong motivations, which often overcame a lack of means. There were many key leaders behind the surge, but we have considered only William Seymour, who inspired many of the first missionaries. As the Pentecostal revival spread, the source for missionaries increased as well.

Majority World Missionary Surges (Twentieth Century)

Finally moving away from the West, the twentieth century saw numerous missionary surges from majority world countries and peoples. Here, before turning to a number of specific cases, we will consider the general conditions and factors that helped drive these missionary surges.

The number of majority world missionaries has been increasing significantly, especially beginning in the second half of the twentieth century. Lawrence Keyes reported an increase from 3,404 missionaries in 1972 to 13,000 in 1980.[276] Larry Pate then put the 1990 total at 46,157 majority world missionaries out of 137,170 total Protestant missionaries.[277] Finally, of the 200,000 Protestant missionaries in 2000, about half of them were from the majority world, with the majority world finally sending the majority of

---

272. Pierson, *Dynamics of Christian Mission*, 312.
273. Pierson, *Dynamics of Christian Mission*, 305, 307.
274. Case, "Holiness Missionary Movement," 136.
275. Case, "Holiness Missionary Movement," 137.
276. Keyes, *Last Age of Missions*, 48, 61.
277. Pate, "Changing Balance in Global Mission," 58.

missionaries in the twenty-first century.[278] Therefore, the majority world as a whole is experiencing perhaps the largest missionary surge in history.

One factor behind this surge was the changing of Western attitudes toward majority world missions. The Lausanne Movement was an intentional attempt to help enable the majority world for mission. Luis Bush, who was born in Argentina, played a key role in promoting world missions and expanding the role of the majority world church. Bush was the one who promoted the vision of the 10/40 Window at the 1989 Lausanne conference and he also promoted the AD2000 & Beyond Movement.[279] Being himself from the majority world, Bush was an example whom many could look to.

Meanwhile, more fruitful partnerships were built between Western and majority world churches and missions. Western missionaries started encouraging the development of national mission organizations.[280] Then, two different paths were taken by Western groups. Some decided to help fund national missionaries. One of the biggest problems majority world missionaries face is funding, as about 35% do not receive the salary they were promised.[281] Back in 1983, one survey calculated that 91% of majority world missionary funds came from the majority world.[282] However, as the number of potential and new majority world missionaries increases, more funds are needed,[283] and many in the majority world look to the West for increased funding.[284] Thus, the question of means is a very important one.

Other Western missionary organizations decided not to support majority world missionaries financially. They were concerned about dependence, which can hinder the creativity and contextualization of majority world missionaries.[285] David Garrison noted that it is important on the one hand to mobilize and train lay missionaries while on the other not to create financial dependencies.[286] Majority world missionaries often have a different vision for missionary work that focuses more "from below"[287] than Western missionaries do. Although majority world missionaries do not always use the kinds of organizational structures that Westerners use,

---

278. Johnstone, *Future of the Global Church*, 228.
279. Tucker, *From Jerusalem to Irian Jaya*, 421.
280. Keyes, *Last Age of Missions*, 61.
281. Keyes, "Third World Missionaries."
282. Keyes, *Last Age of Missions*, 82.
283. D'Souza, "Role of the Two-Thirds World Church," 101.
284. Noll, *New Shape of World Christianity*, 29.
285. Keyes, *Last Age of Missions*, 75.
286. Garrison, *Church Planting Movements*, 14, 16.
287. Keyes, *Last Age of Missions*, 111.

often growth comes through their spontaneous ministry.[288] It is important for majority world missionaries not to lose the distinctives in vision and motivation that God has given them.

Finally, it is worth mentioning that majority world missionaries often get involved in diaspora and tentmaking mission work.[289] In these ways, majority world missionaries can either reach out to their own people in different contexts or use the work skills that they've gained at home in a new context. These mission methods provide a different vision, but one that takes advantage of the skills and means of majority world people.

Batak Missionary Surge (Early Twentieth Century)

The German missionary Ludwig Nommenson planted churches among the Batak people in Sumatra, Indonesia.[290] After experiencing an awakening in the 1880s,[291] the Bataks started conducting missionary work in 1899 among non-Christian Bataks.[292] The Bataks raised money for the mission work themselves, using an annual mission festival after the fall harvest.[293]

Over the middle portion of the twentieth century, Bataks began reaching out to other parts of Indonesia. In many of these cases, entire families or even colonies of a number of families would migrate to a new place, working the land and sharing the Gospel. These missionaries were often completely self-supporting, and in some cases even obtained positions of authority, then being able to help other migrant missionaries.[294]

Although it is not clear how many Bataks have gone into missionary work, it is clear that some kind of surge has occurred. The Bataks are particularly creative using various means to move to new places, to gain positions of influence, and even to reach out to (predominantly Muslim) peoples who have previously been closed to the Gospel.[295]

---

288. Keyes, *Last Age of Missions*, 55.
289. Keyes, *Last Age of Missions*, 79; Pierson, *Dynamics of Christian Mission*, 325.
290. Pierson, *Dynamics of Christian Mission*, 270.
291. Johnstone, *Future of the Global Church*, 134.
292. Pedersen, *Batak Blood and Protestant Soul*, 74–75.
293. Pedersen, *Batak Blood and Protestant Soul*, 76.
294. Pedersen, *Batak Blood and Protestant Soul*, 77.
295. Pedersen, *Batak Blood and Protestant Soul*, 77.

Melanesian Brotherhood Missionary Surge (Early Twentieth Century)

In Oceania in the 1920s, a very effective missionary organization called the Melanesian Brotherhood was formed.[296] It was started by a young Melanesian named Ini Kopuria who received a vision from God. Upon sharing this vision with a foreign missionary, he was encouraged to start a mission organization.[297] Another foreign influence that may have helped came from the fact that Melanesia had been evangelized by Polynesian missionaries, who had been encouraged by the British missionary John Williams.[298] Thus, a key leader with the encouragement of foreign missionaries was ready to spread a vision.

The Melanesians tended to be communal, and so when they accepted Ini Kopuria's call to mission, they supported one another and whole groups committed themselves to missionary work.[299] More than one hundred missionaries in the course of fifteen years were sent out in their long canoes to faraway islands.[300] The Brotherhood traveled in groups of eight to twelve to many dangerous islands. Some were martyred. But, God used them to lead thousands of islanders to Christ.[301] After a pause in their work during World War II, the Melanesian Brotherhood led thousands more to Christ from 1955 to 1975.[302]

So, again God used a key leader to set vision and motivate the beginning of a missionary surge. Because the Melanesians were communal, once some agreed to help, a source of great numbers of potential missionaries followed. The Melanesians used simple but effective means, traveling by boat to non-Christian peoples. Although the historic event of World War II caused a stoppage of their missionary work, the Melanesians were able to continue the missionary surge later on.

Korean Missionary Surge (Twentieth Century)

Over the course of the twentieth century, South Korea went from being a missionary receiving country to being one of the leading missionary

---

296. Keyes, *Last Age of Missions*, 20.
297. Keyes, *Last Age of Missions*, 95–96.
298. Davidson, "Pacific is No Longer a Mission Field?," 138–39.
299. Keyes, *Last Age of Missions*, 97.
300. Keyes, *Last Age of Missions*, 96; Pierson, *Dynamics of Christian Mission*, 324.
301. Keyes, *Last Age of Missions*, 95–96; Pierson, *Dynamics of Christian Mission*, 324.
302. Keyes, *Last Age of Missions*, 96.

APPENDIX A: THE HISTORY OF MISSIONARY SURGES   231

sending countries in the world. In 1907, Korea experienced revival, leading to significant church growth.[303] In the 1960s and 1970s, Korea had explosive church growth, which led to a surge of Korean missionaries.[304] There were 2,000 missionaries by 1980[305] and 8,100 missionaries by 2000.[306] Estimates of the current number of Korean missionaries vary widely from 15,000[307] to 21,000.[308] In any case, per capita, more missionaries are sent out from South Korea than from any other country in the world.[309] Korea has definitely experienced a significant missionary surge.

Again, there are numerous factors behind this surge. The most recent increase in missionaries can be connected to an historical opportunity: the 1988 Seoul Olympic Games led to the Korean government becoming more open politically.[310]

Globalization has increased the freedom granted to missionaries and Koreans' awareness of the need for missions around the world.[311] Increased wealth has provided more means to send missionaries.[312] Furthermore, the source for potential missionaries has increased following a surplus of graduates from seminary, meaning that some graduates cannot find ministry positions in South Korea.[313]

Korean mission organizations have had a tendency to prioritize increased recruitment, even if missionary care could not keep pace. Overall, the support structure of Korean missions is not strong. Often missionary organizations depend almost entirely on the vision and motivation of a charismatic leader, which can mean that the organizations die when their leader does.[314] So, much of the success of the missionary surge has depended upon key leaders, including vision and motivation, and these strengths have often overcome weaknesses in the area of means.

303. Robert, *Christian Mission*, 62.
304. Moon, "Protestant Missionary Movement in Korea," 60.
305. Johnstone, *Future of the Global Church*, 229.
306. Moon, "Recent Korean Missionary Movement," 11.
307. Moon, "Protestant Missionary Movement in Korea," 59.
308. Johnstone, *Future of the Global Church*, 229.
309. Shaw, *Global Awakening*, 34.
310. Cook, "Great Commission in Asia," 158.
311. Moon, "Protestant Missionary Movement in Korea," 60; Noll, *New Shape of World Christianity*, 161.
312. Noll, *New Shape of World Christianity*, 161.
313. Moon, "Protestant Missionary Movement in Korea," 60.
314. Moon, "Recent Korean Missionary Movement," 13.

African Missionary Surges (Twentieth Century)

Africa, as a continent, is sending more and more missionaries. Multiple missionary surges have been taking place. For example, Nigeria has sent out over 3,000 missionaries.[315] Ethiopia has sent more than 600 missionaries.[316] Overall, there are currently about 18,400 African missionaries.[317]

Since the very beginning of the twentieth century, all major missionary work in southern and central Africa has been done by Africans.[318] Since the 1980s, more and more Africans have become missionaries in Europe and the United States, reaching out to the African diaspora in cities like London, Berlin, New York, and Kyiv.[319] However, many Africans are planting churches that reach beyond the African community as well. Calling this *reverse mission*, the Redeemed Christian Church of God out of Nigeria has branches in 110 countries.[320] Certainly, these are multiple examples of missionary surges.

Turning to factors behind these surges, African missionaries tend to feel called, often turning to the Bible for guidance and looking at passages such as Matthew 28:19–20, the Great Commission.[321] The Bible has helped guide African missionaries with a vision for the Gospel being spread around the world as God blesses His faithful people.[322] As Africans have become more aware of the need for missions over the twentieth century through foreign missionaries and networks of church and mission leaders, they have gotten more involved in missionary training institutes, preparing for the mission field.[323] So, a number of factors have helped provide vision for Africans, and the means for going to the mission field have been improved through educational opportunities.

Africans have had some interesting sources for motivation as well. Out of communist persecution, the Ethiopian church has built a vision and motivation for missionary work.[324] Church ceremonies in Zimbabwe have connected annual celebrations and communion with motivation to go into

---

315. Johnstone, *Future of the Global Church*, 228.
316. Johnstone, *Future of the Global Church*, 167.
317. Barrett et al., "Missiometrics 2007," 31.
318. Robert, *Christian Mission*, 62.
319. Robert, *Christian Mission*, 74; Shaw, *Global Awakening*, 174.
320. Shaw, *Global Awakening*, 162.
321. Daneel, "African Initiated Churches," 202; Robert, *Christian Mission*, 75.
322. Robert, *Christian Mission*, 75.
323. Fiedler, *Story of Faith Missions*, 377; Tarantal, "Networks in World Evangelization," 122.
324. Johnstone, *Future of the Global Church*, 167.

missions, mobilizing entire churches to get involved. Sometimes, these ceremonies are connected with key people who have been examples for ministry and missions.[325] Thus, Africans often use creative and contextual means for motivating missionaries.

Latin American Missionary Surges (Twentieth Century)

Since the 1980s, a rising number of Latin Americans have become cross-cultural missionaries. As of 2007, approximately 44,000 Latin Americans are working as foreign missionaries. The countries of Brazil and Mexico are two of the largest sending nations, sending 21,100 and 4,800 missionaries, respectively.[326]

Brazil has had the most dramatic missionary surge, experiencing a huge increase in numbers since the 1980s, with the total reaching about 5,000 missionaries in 2000 and 21,000 by 2007.[327] These missionaries serve in a variety of contexts, including service by Brazilian Pentecostals in Muslim areas.[328] Over time, the missionary surge has slowed while becoming more stable with gifted and mature evangelists and church planters serving in over 100 countries.[329]

In 1987, the COMIBAM mission conference was held in São Paulo, Brazil, significantly increasing interest in missions. A network was created to provide support for missionary work. Out of this conference, Latin American missionaries began using creative means to serve, from pastors migrating together with their congregations to do missions to holding "evangelistic demon-fighting campaigns."[330] So, this conference helped increase the source for missionaries and provided a greater means for the missionary surge along with vision and motivation.

Indian Missionary Surges (Twentieth Century)

There are varying estimates as to how many Indians serve in missionary ministry today. Dana Robert puts the total somewhere between 40,000

---

325. Daneel, "African Initiated Churches," 202–3.
326. Barrett et al., "Missiometrics 2007," 31; Robert, *Christian Mission*, 77.
327. Barrett et al., "Missiometrics 2007," 31; Johnstone, *Future of the Global Church*, 153.
328. Robert, *Christian Mission*, 77.
329. Johnstone, *Future of the Global Church*, 153.
330. Pierson, *Dynamics of Christian Mission*, 326; Robert, *Christian Mission*, 77.

and 80,000 working just to reach other ethnic groups within India itself.[331] Certainly, the large numbers of Indian missionaries listed in some sources are almost all working among different ethnic groups in their own nation. In any case, the number of missionaries has definitely increased over the course of the twentieth century.

Indian Protestants have founded about 250 mission organizations.[332] The largest is Gospel for Asia, the second largest missionary agency in the world with 9,550 workers in 2010. Seven Indian mission agencies each have at least 1,000 missionaries.[333] So, it is appropriate to talk about Indian missionary surges in the plural.

One reason for the large growth in the number of Indian missionaries is the fact that many white missionaries have left India, opening the door for more national missionary work.[334] K.P. Yohannan, the head of Gospel for Asia, claimed that "the whole native missionary movement . . . is initiated by God."[335] Means for the movement have been largely provided by foreign support, while the source for missionaries for the movement has continually grown.[336]

Many Indians feel called to be missionaries to the unreached within India, and one example of a mission organization that works with the unreached is the Friends Missionary Prayer Band. This organization has had a fairly loose support structure, but it has recruited many Indians and has financially and prayerfully supported them. In contrast to Gospel for Asia, the Prayer Band receives no foreign support. In 2000, this group had recruited over 600 missionaries who were working with 165 different people groups.[337] Thus, there are multiple kinds of means being used in the different missionary surges of India.

Chinese Missionary Surge (Late Twentieth Century)

The Chinese church, especially the underground house churches, has undergone tremendous growth and revival since the coming of communism in 1949, even by conservative estimates growing to over 60 million

---

331. Robert, *Christian Mission*, 78.
332. Robert, *Christian Mission*, 78.
333. Johnstone, *Future of the Global Church*, 235.
334. Yohannan, *Revolution in World Missions*, 150.
335. Yohannan, *Revolution in World Missions*, 68.
336. Yohannan, *Revolution in World Missions*, 22–23.
337. Pierson, *Dynamics of Christian Mission*, 325.

evangelical Christians.[338] In the 1990s, the house churches decided to revive a vision that had been neglected for years, the *Back to Jerusalem* vision.[339] This vision is "for the Chinese church to preach the Gospel and establish fellowships of believers [in] all regions and people groups between China and Jerusalem."[340]

The Chinese have been so blessed and empowered by the Holy Spirit in their own nation that they are motivated now to reach out in mission to other nations.[341] Their goal is to raise up 100,000 Chinese missionaries to evangelize in the 10/40 Window.[342] This goal is certainly ambitious and dangerous, but as house church leader Zhang Rongliang has said, the Chinese people are already used to persecution.[343]

So, key leaders have been behind this missionary surge, providing vision and motivation. The large Chinese church has provided a large source for potential missionaries, as well as potential means for missionary support. Revival has helped provide an historical opportunity for a missionary surge. Yet, it appears that so far only a few hundred missionaries have been trained for the Back to Jerusalem movement. On the other hand, some Chinese have been doing missionary ministry among Chinese minority groups.[344] So, a small missionary surge has begun with the potential for much more in the future.

Short-Term Missionary Surge (Late Twentieth to Early Twenty-first Centuries)

Short-term missionary work has increased dramatically toward the end of the twentieth and the beginning of the twenty-first centuries. In 2005, about 1.5 million North Americans took short-term mission trips.[345] The short-term missionary surge has come about for several reasons. Similar to earlier surges, improvements in travel and communication in combination with increased wealth in the West have provided the means for more short-term missions.[346]

338. Lambert, *China's Christian Millions*, 19.
339. Cook, "The Great Commission in Asia," 159.
340. Pierson, *Dynamics of Christian Mission*, 276.
341. Pierson, *Dynamics of Christian Mission*, 276.
342. Aikman, *Jesus in Beijing*, 195.
343. Aikman, *Jesus in Beijing*, 202; Pierson, *Dynamics of Christian Mission*, 326.
344. Lambert, *China's Christian Millions*, 196–97, 199.
345. Robert, *Christian Mission*, 73.
346. Robert, *Christian Mission*, 73.

Some missionary organizations, like Operation Mobilization, specialize in doing short-term missions, using them as "opportunities for people to test whether they have the calling and the capacity for longer-term service."[347] They hope that short-term missionary work will provide vision for long-term missions. The one drawback is that missionary agencies that send short-term missionaries need to have a great many more home staff members to support them.[348]

So, the means for missionary organizations are significant, but the source for potential short-term missionaries is extremely large since, in most cases, any amateur can go. The historical circumstances have made it easy to travel long distances over short periods of time. Therefore, the only things needed are vision and motivation, which the leaders of many mission organizations, such as George Verwer, are happy to provide.

The CoMission Surge (Late Twentieth Century)

The leaders of the CoMission maintain that it was perhaps "the largest movement of missions in the shortest amount of time since the birth of Christ. Never had more people responded to a spiritual need so quickly and so effectively."[349] Although it was a short project of only five years from 1992 to 1997,[350] it was certainly a missionary surge. The idea behind the CoMission was to train school teachers across the former Soviet Union to teach Christian ethics to their students. However, since there was very little time to recruit, the CoMission accepted anyone who could serve for one year, without any theological or cultural training, or, in some cases, even educational training. These criteria made it much easier to recruit missionaries, tremendously broadening the source for potential missionaries, but this approach did not always yield the results desired on the mission field.[351]

The CoMission used professional marketing material in order to recruit quickly and networked with 82 mission organizations that gave "people pledges"[352] toward the cause. Famous Christian leaders such as Bruce Wilkinson and Joseph Stowell agreed to recruit missionaries themselves.[353] Overall, the CoMission raised up 1,500 missionaries and over sixty million

---

347. Maiden, "Life Well Lived," xi.
348. Johnstone, "Next Forty Years for Christian Missions," 189.
349. Wilkinson et al., *CoMission*, 17.
350. Wilkinson et al., *CoMission*, 26.
351. Penner, "Critical Evaluation," 128.
352. Wilkinson et al., *CoMission*, 78.
353. Wilkinson et al., *CoMission*, 36–37, 78.

APPENDIX A: THE HISTORY OF MISSIONARY SURGES   237

dollars for the project.³⁵⁴ The vision of reaching the former Soviet Union for Christ and teaching about Christianity in public schools was incredibly attractive, especially when it was heard from key Christian leaders. In addition, no one knew when the doors might shut again, so there was a feeling of urgency that motivated missionary recruits. Clearly, there were many powerful factors behind this large missionary surge.

Summary of Important Categories of Factors behind Missionary Surges

So, our six categories of factors, source, vision, motivation, means, key leaders, and historical opportunities, have proved to be very helpful. At this point we can list some of the more important factors in each category for consideration in the future.

The sources for potential missionaries that stood out the most in our historical survey of missionary surges were revival and awakening, monasteries in the Catholic and Orthodox churches, and student groups and missionary conferences in Protestant churches. We can agree with Pierson that young people throughout history have been a good source of potential missionaries.³⁵⁵ Certainly the amateurization of missionaries increased the number of potential missionaries, as did recruiting women for the first time. One other interesting source occurred in Korea, where there were more seminary trained graduates than available positions for ministry.

A great variety of kinds of vision for missionary work was brought out in this study. There were a number of spiritual visions, starting with a direct word from God in prayer, the desire to serve God and bring about His kingdom, and the desire to see sinners saved. New information also provided vision, such as from the Bible, education, missionary literature, and discovery and exploration of the world. A combination of these two could be seen in a vision about the needs of a certain group (e.g., inland China, poor women), the 10/40 Window, the need for Bible translation, and missionary conferences. Finally, different optimistic and pessimistic visions were seen, including the urgent need to preach before Christ's return, the obligation for every Christian to be a missionary, optimism from the Enlightenment that anything can be done, and the romance and adventure of missions. This is a wide variety of visions, indeed.

Motivations sometimes overlapped with vision, so repetition will be avoided here. Certainly some of the strongest motivations were a divine

354. Glanzer, *Quest for Russia's Soul*, 5–6; Wilkinson et al., *CoMission*, 33.
355. Pierson, *Dynamics of Christian Mission*, 246.

calling and a human challenge to go into missionary work, sometimes with that challenge coming directly from foreign missionaries. The testimonies of powerful Christians, especially in martyrdom, were very motivating. In certain cases, people were ordered to go into mission by their superiors or were drawn into mission through ceremonies and celebrations (e.g., in Africa). Public relations methods sometimes motivated people to go into missions as did an urgency based on the fear that the opportunity to share the Gospel would soon end. Of course, some of the best motivations came from simply following key leaders.

The means to go to the mission field varied considerably over the course of history. In the early years, the main source of means was from the state church, local governments, and monasteries, which provided both finances and logistical support. Later, missionary societies and parachurch organizations became the main logistical means for missionary work. In each of these cases, missionaries were better prepared for the mission field through education and training. Finances were obtained in various ways, including donations from wealthy individuals and self-support (tentmaking). Funds were sometimes given by foreigners and sometimes by the national church. In some cases, missionaries would simply migrate to a new area with their families to be self-supporting. Finally, some wouldn't strive to use any means but prayer, their spiritual means.

Key leaders played important roles throughout mission history. They were particularly important in starting a missionary surge, providing vision and motivation (e.g., Patrick, Gregory the Great, Francis Xavier, Constantine and Methodius, Count Zinzendorf, William Carey, and Hudson Taylor). Later, such key leaders could be powerful examples to those who followed. However, mission societies could sometimes become too dependent on them, so that if they left or died, the mission would come to an end for lack of vision, motivation, and means (e.g., in Korea). So, strong leaders are important, but they do not make up for weaknesses in other areas for long.

Finally, many historical opportunities were behind missionary surges. It is probably reasonable to agree with the earlier assertion that usually such surges come from the fringe of the church, although exceptions to this rule can be noted (e.g., Gregory the Great's missionary surge and Catholic control of mission through Propaganda Fide). Other historical opportunities for missionary surges came after revivals and awakenings, through the discovery of new places and peoples, through the Enlightenment and the philosophical changes associated with it, and through globalization. The Industrial Revolution led to the creation of wealth to support missionaries. The Reformation also brought new opportunities, but ironically, it was the Catholic Church that responded by sending far more missionaries than the Protestant

Church. Some very specific events, like the 1988 Seoul Olympics, brought unique opportunities for missionary surges as well.

Considering all of these factors together, generally speaking, all six categories of factors were present in each missionary surge. However, it will probably be more useful to reorganize our categories in the following matrix shown in Table A1.

The categories across the top are the same ones we used initially, removing the category of key leaders. These categories seem to form a complete group, answering the questions given in parentheses: who, what, why, how, and where. Although these categories are helpful, they may be a bit too abstract to use on their own when doing interviews. So, the categories in the left column form another way to look at missionary surges which might be more helpful. The categories spiritual, socio-political, ecclesial, leadership, and financial form another complete group, going from broad to specific, or, looking at it another way, from God to society to church to individuals to things. Connecting these two groups of categories produces a matrix in which we can capture many of the historical factors behind missionary surges and produces a list of possible factors to look for in the Ukrainian missionary surge of the 1990s.

Table A1. Examples of Missionary Surge Factors
Within a Category Matrix

Category of factors	Source (Who?)	Vision (What?)	Motivation (Why?)	Means (How?)	Opportunity (Where?)
Spiritual (God's work)	Revival or awakening	Theology of mission	Personal call	Open doors	Openness to hear the Gospel
Sociopolitical (big picture of broader society)	People available (young people, new believers)	New ideas, discoveries of new places	Needs of the poor, desire for exploration	Improved transportation, same language, new social networks, political access	Worldview changes
Ecclesial (within the church or Christian organizations)	People available (push/pull: wanting to leave or wanting to go)	Vision for missionary work	Encouragement to do missionary work, competition between churches	Structure for missionary work	Lack of churches; need for new church plants
Leadership (influential people)	Connections with people	Ideas; directing people to the mission field	Giving a call to missionary work	Enabling people to go to the mission field	Supporting and directing people on the mission field
Financial (economics in general and finances for missionary work)	Finances allow people to consider going	Finances allow people to consider sending	Enough money to serve as a missionary	Financial support of missionaries	Lack of finances can lead people to consider their need for the Gospel

Eastern and Central European Missionary Surges from 1989

Now considering our matrix of missionary surge factors, I would like to turn to a context close to Ukraine: Eastern and Central Europe. There has been very little written about missionaries from this entire area, but we can turn principally to two dissertations: Douglas Tiessen's[356] dissertation on the Evangelical Christian Missionary Union in Russia and Scott Klingsmith's dissertation on the missionary sending movements in Hungary, Romania, and Poland, which was published in 2012. Although Ukraine produced a much larger missionary surge than these examples,[357] it is still worthwhile to consider what factors played a role in these countries' missionary surges.

Missionary Surges from Hungary, Romania, and Poland

Spiritual factors were often reported as being behind the missionary sending movements in Hungary, Romania, and Poland. For example, the Aletheia Church in Romania reported "ubiquitous" accounts of God being at work.[358] In Poland, there were many cases of God being "specifically at work" in people's lives.[359] Klingsmith concluded that "almost all respondents in the three countries agree that missions activity has begun because God is doing something in their countries."[360]

The next significant factor seemed to be key people of influence and in leadership. Anne-Marie Kool was named as a key person in Hungary.[361] Pastors in Romania were the key to either supporting or undermining a vision for missions.[362] Key people included both nationals and foreigners in Poland and Romania.[363] Sometimes, just being exposed to foreign missionaries helped motivate nationals to consider missionary work.[364] Thus, key people or leadership factors were quite important.

---

356. Tiessen, "Invitational Partnership."

357. Klingsmith, *Missions Beyond the Wall*, 54; Tiessen, "Invitational Partnership," 146.

358. Klingsmith, *Missions Beyond the Wall*, 90.

359. Klingsmith, *Missions Beyond the Wall*, 110.

360. Klingsmith, *Missions Beyond the Wall*, 167.

361. Klingsmith, *Missions Beyond the Wall*, 85.

362. Klingsmith, *Missions Beyond the Wall*, 92.

363. Klingsmith, *Missions Beyond the Wall*, 113, 143.

364. Klingsmith, *Missions Beyond the Wall*, 158.

Furthermore, a "prepared context"[365] was as important as leadership. This idea included being exposed to a vision for missions, the freedom to travel to other countries, a source of people motivated to become missionaries (often young people who were less tied down), and having a supportive church, although not necessarily a financially giving church.[366] Thus, the source, vision, motivation, means, and socio-political (freedom to travel) and ecclesial factors are all tied together in the idea of a prepared context. Interestingly, the financial factor, although mentioned in all three countries as valid,[367] was downplayed by leaders as being less important than a vision for missions.[368] This fact is interesting in that, considering cultural similarities, I might expect a similar sentiment from Ukrainian mission leaders regarding finances.

Finally, the last factor that seemed to be very important was the fact that personal experience in some kind of ministry outside the local church (e.g., church planting) helped lead people to become missionaries.[369] People who get involved in a little ministry, such as short-term missions, are often interested in getting involved in long-term ministry, like missions. Essentially, the factor of personal experience provides a new source for missionaries from people who have been more exposed to ministry.

Further, considering our matrix of factors, it was clear that the socio-political changes that came with the Fall of Communism, and the new mission opportunities that accompanied them, were also important. For example, in Poland, "The experience of life under communism opened doors of ministry to others who had suffered similarly, and languages learned out of compulsion were able to be used to advantage."[370] Freedom to travel and even to imagine came with the Fall of Communism.[371] Thus, the changing socio-political context played a key role as well.

Missionary Surge from Southern Russia

In southern Russia, a new denomination called the Evangelical Christian Missionary Union (ECMU) was founded in the early 1990s out of a group of ten pastors, growing into forty-four churches and another ten church

---

365. Klingsmith, *Missions Beyond the Wall*, 184.
366. Klingsmith, *Missions Beyond the Wall*, 153, 184.
367. Klingsmith, *Missions Beyond the Wall*, 85, 93, 119, 149.
368. Klingsmith, *Missions Beyond the Wall*, 170.
369. Klingsmith, *Missions Beyond the Wall*, 161, 183.
370. Klingsmith, *Missions Beyond the Wall*, 136.
371. Klingsmith, *Missions Beyond the Wall*, 170.

APPENDIX A: THE HISTORY OF MISSIONARY SURGES

plants among unreached people groups by 2001.[372] The ECMU came out of a union of several Russian mission organizations. The Apocalypse Mission, founded in 1990, had a leader with the vision to plant evangelical churches across southern Russia.[373] The Apocalypse Mission grew to have sixteen missionaries and twelve office staff before beginning its partnership with the Good Seed Mission and Russian Navy Chaplain Ministry, legally forming the Evangelical Christian Missionary Union in 1994.[374] Later, other Russian mission organizations and Christian educational institutions decided to join the ECMU as well.[375]

Tiessen[376] focused on the partnership that the ECMU had with the foreign Christian and Missionary Alliance (C&MA), so he did not directly analyze what factors lay behind the missionary surge. Yet, a number of the factors that we have noted earlier were apparent, although Tiessen probably had a tendency to focus on categories of factors that more closely related to partnership, such as vision, means, and ecclesial and financial factors.

For example, Tiessen's research showed that the ECMU had a God-directed partnership with the C&MA.[377] Thus, the spiritual factor was evident. Connected with their spirituality, both the ECMU and the C&MA had a vision for mission work. The ECMU had the vision to start 200 churches by the year 2000. Yet, they lacked structure and direction, so the C&MA's partnership helped them, even though they obviously didn't meet their original goal.[378] Similarly, both the ECMU and C&MA had the vision to evangelize nearby unreached people groups.[379] So, their partnership, guided spiritually, was fruitful in setting vision and providing some structure or means for missionary work.

One way that the C&MA helped the ECMU improve its structure was by helping it form its missionary department, giving advice on how to plan mission work and church planting.[380] Leadership from the ECMU met regularly with the C&MA field leadership to receive advice.[381] The vast

372. Tiessen, "Invitational Partnership," 146; although Rybikov, director of the ECMU missionary department, gave slightly different figures in "Report from the Missionary Department" for 2001: 35 churches across 10 oblasts.
373. Tiessen, "Invitational Partnership," 84, 115.
374. Tiessen, "Invitational Partnership," 84–85, 89.
375. Tiessen, "Invitational Partnership," 90.
376. Tiessen, "Invitational Partnership."
377. Tiessen, "Invitational Partnership," 75.
378. Tiessen, "Invitational Partnership," 147.
379. Tiessen, "Invitational Partnership," 160.
380. Tiessen, "Invitational Partnership," 145.
381. Tiessen, "Invitational Partnership," 189.

majority of the ECMU leadership was young and needed mentoring since many of the "fathers of the church" had emigrated to the US.[382] It was a great blessing to have such a large source of young leaders, and C&MA missionaries considered it a privilege to help facilitate the ECMU's development.[383] Furthermore, the C&MA helped provide more formal leadership training as well by training key Russian leaders through a part-time degree program in Kyiv, Ukraine.[384] Thus, the C&MA helped provide and develop the leadership that the missionary surge needed.

The president of the ECMU said that gaining from the experience of the C&MA missionaries was far more valuable to their work than financial support. The key was to be able to learn from them—not just receive things from them.[385] Yet, many Russians really pushed to receive more funds from C&MA missionaries.[386] In any case, the C&MA leadership practically became the financial director of the ECMU, providing whatever financial means were necessary to promote the missionary surge.[387] Thus, much of the finances and means were, at least initially, given through foreign missionaries.

Yet, on the other hand, the C&MA used their position to teach ECMU churches about the importance of giving to missionary work. The vision of creating self-supporting churches that would also give to missions did start to take hold.[388] The ECMU also embraced the idea of a faith promise toward missions, and a national missionary fund was developed.[389] In addition, yearly local church conferences were started that both encouraged people to go into missionary work and raised financial support for missionaries.[390] Thus, a source for new missionaries was tapped as well as the financial means to send them through an ecclesial structure.

Summary of Findings

In summary, we can see that all the factors of our matrix played some kind of role in the missionary sending movements of Eastern and Central Europe in

382. Tiessen, "Invitational Partnership," 182.
383. Tiessen, "Invitational Partnership," 146.
384. Tiessen, "Invitational Partnership," 110–11.
385. Tiessen, "Invitational Partnership," 123.
386. Tiessen, "Invitational Partnership," 136–37.
387. Tiessen, "Invitational Partnership," 138.
388. Tiessen, "Invitational Partnership," 147.
389. Tiessen, "Invitational Partnership," 148.
390. Tiessen, "Invitational Partnership," 114–15.

the 1990s. My test cases from contexts that are similar to Ukraine have given me some idea of what to expect when I conduct interviews among those involved in the Ukrainian missionary surge of the 1990s. It was especially interesting to note how in both our cases there was a downplaying of finances by the national leadership. This fact does not necessarily mean that financial factors were not important in the missionary surge, but it does indicate a tendency of mission leadership to avoid discussing it. So, I can now turn to the socio-political context of the former Soviet Union and look for factors that might have played a role in the Ukrainian missionary surge.

Appendix B

Participant Information

Table B1. Participant Information

Pseudonym	Gender	Origin	Sending or Mission Field	Affiliation
Fyodor	M	Belarus	Western Ukraine	Light of the Gospel
Oksana	F	Western Ukraine	Western Ukraine	Light of the Gospel
Stepan	M	Western Ukraine	Western Ukraine	Light of the Gospel
Bogdan	M	Western Ukraine	Eastern Ukraine	Light of the Gospel
Mikhail	M	Eastern Ukraine	Eastern Ukraine	Light of the Gospel
Nancy	F	United States	Eastern Ukraine	Light of the Gospel
Samuel	M	United States	Eastern Ukraine	Light of the Gospel
Filipp	M	Eastern Ukraine	Volga Russia	Light of the Gospel
Gennady	M	Central Ukraine	Volga Russia	Light of the Gospel
Radislav	M	Central Ukraine	Volga Russia	Light of the Gospel
Yaroslav	M	Eastern Ukraine	Ural Russia	Light of the Gospel
Philemon	M	Eastern Ukraine	Yakutia or Russian Far North	Light of the Gospel
Milana	F	Eastern Ukraine	Russian Far East	Light of the Gospel
Sophia	F	Eastern Ukraine	Russian Far East	Light of the Gospel
Gerhard	M	Germany	Central Ukraine	Baptist
Grigory	M	Central Ukraine	Central Ukraine	Baptist
Scott	M	United States	Central Ukraine	Baptist

APPENDIX B: PARTICIPANT INFORMATION

Pseudonym	Gender	Origin	Sending or Mission Field	Affiliation
Oleg	M	Russia	Eastern Ukraine	Baptist
Kevin	M	United States	Moscow or St. Petersburg	Baptist
Shawn	M	United States	Moscow or St. Petersburg	Baptist
Vincent	M	United States	Moscow or St. Petersburg	Baptist
Georgi	M	Eastern Ukraine	Central Russia	Baptist
Tristan	M	Russia	Southern Russia	Baptist
Yulian	M	Russia	Southern Russia	Baptist
Gleb	M	Western Ukraine	Western or Central Siberia	Baptist
Stanislav	M	Moldova	Western or Central Siberia	Baptist
Timofey	M	Western Ukraine	Western or Central Siberia	Baptist
Denis	M	Western Ukraine	Western Ukraine	Pentecostal
Dmitro	M	Western Ukraine	Western Ukraine	Pentecostal
Oles	M	Western Ukraine	Western Ukraine	Pentecostal
Rodion	M	Southern Ukraine	Southern Ukraine	Pentecostal
Damian	M	Western Ukraine	Eastern Ukraine	Pentecostal
Daniel	M	Western Ukraine	Volga Russia	Pentecostal
Ruslan	M	Western Ukraine	Volga Russia	Pentecostal
Yevgeny	M	Western Ukraine	Volga Russia	Pentecostal
Miroslav	M	Western Ukraine	Ural Russia	Pentecostal
Rostislav	M	Western Ukraine	Ural Russia	Pentecostal
Tamara	F	United States	Ural Russia	Pentecostal
David	M	Western Ukraine	Western or Central Siberia	Pentecostal
Roman	M	Western Ukraine	Russian Far East	Pentecostal

Note: The categories Baptist and Pentecostals include some variety within them, but in order to ensure anonymity, I thought it was best to use these broad categories instead of referring to more specific denominations. The category Light of the Gospel is also considered Baptist, but since I had so many participants from this category, I wanted to differentiate it.

Appendix C
Comparison of Change Models with the Missionary Surge

TABLES C1–C4 COMPARE THE Ukrainian evangelical missionary surge of the 1990s with several different models of culture change, most notably the models of Rogers, Rochon, Gladwell, and Heath and Heath.[1] These tables were helpful in the Chapter 6 development of the five-point model for the Ukrainian evangelical missionary surge of the nineties. The first two points, centers of missionary development and change (the rational side), are explained in table C1. Next, the third point of change (the emotional side) is detailed in table C2 and communication and facilitation agents are considered in table C3. Finally, context is analyzed in table C4. Thus, these tables are helpful for seeing the big picture of how the five-point model for the Ukrainian evangelical missionary surge was developed.

---

1. Rogers, *Diffusion of Innovations*; Rochon, *Culture Moves*; Gladwell, *Tipping Point*; Heath and Heath, *Switch*.

250 APPENDIX C: COMPARISON OF CHANGE MODELS

Table C1. Comparison of Change Models With the Missionary Surge: Centers and Change (Rational Side)[2]

Source	Center	Change (Rational Side)			
		Innovation	Relative advantage	Compatibility	Complexity
Rogers	Response to a need	Innovation	Relative advantage	Compatibility	Complexity
Naylor	Innovator	Plan	Directed change	—	—
Rochon	Critical communities	—	—	Value creation, conversion, or connection	—
Gladwell	Context: Magic #150	Sticky message	—	—	—
Heath and Heath, *Made to Stick*	—	—	Credible	—	Simple
Collins and Porras	—	—	—	—	—
Crouch	Alternative culture	—	—	Make new culture	—
Hunter	Elites outside power center	—	—	Influence worldview	—
Heath and Heath, *Switch*	Path: Gather reformers together	—	Rider: Bright spots	—	Rider: Script critical moves
Ukrainian Evangelical Missionary Surge	Centers for Missionary Development	Vision, Motivation	Vision 1: Enthusiasm, idea of missions	Vision 1 and 2: Connect Missions to Bible, Call	Vision 2: God's call, answer to prayer

Note. — = No comparable idea.

2. Rogers, *Diffusion of Innovations*; Naylor, *Culture and Change*; Rochon, *Culture Moves*; Gladwell, *Tipping Point*; Heath and Heath, *Made to Stick*; Collins and Porras, *Built to Last*; Crouch, *Culture Making*; Hunter, *To Change the World*; Heath and Heath, *Switch*.

Table C2. Comparison of Change Models With the Missionary Surge: Change (Emotional Side)[3]

	Change (Emotional Side)		
Source	Triability	Observability	Inspiration
Rogers	Triability	Observability	—
Naylor	—	—	—
Rochon	—	—	—
Gladwell	—	—	—
Heath and Heath, *Made to Stick*	—	Concrete	Emotional, stories, unexpected
Collins and Porras	—	—	—
Crouch	—	—	—
Hunter	—	—	—
Heath and Heath, *Switch*	Elephant: Grow your people; identity	Elephant: Shrink the change	Elephant: Feeling
Ukrainian Evangelical Missionary Surge	Motivation 1: Short-term missions; Vision 2: Prayer for missions	Motivation 1: Go where is greatest need; Motivation 2: Example of missionaries	Motivation 2: Inspiration from missionaries; Vision 1: Idea of missions romantic, interesting

Note: — = No comparable idea.

3. Rogers, *Diffusion of Innovations*; Naylor, *Culture and Change*; Rochon, *Culture Moves*; Gladwell, *Tipping Point*; Heath and Heath, *Made to Stick*; Collins and Porras, *Built to Last*; Crouch, *Culture Making*; Hunter, *To Change the World*; Heath and Heath, *Switch*.

Table C3. Comparison of Change Models With the Missionary Surge: Communication and Facilitation Agents[4]

	Communication and Facilitation Agents				
Source	Communication Channels	Innovators	Change Agents	Opinion Leaders	Organizers
Rogers	Communication Channels	Innovators	Change Agents	Opinion Leaders	Social structure
Naylor	Participants	Innovators	Change Agents	—	—
Rochon	Movements	—	—	—	—
Gladwell	Law of the Few	—	Salesmen	Mavens and Connectors	—
Heath and Heath, *Made to Stick*	—	—	—	—	—
Collins and Porras	—	—	—	—	Organizers
Crouch	—	—	—	—	—
Hunter	—	—	—	Faithful presence: True, good, beautiful	—
Heath and Heath, *Switch*	—	—	—	—	Elephant: Shrink the change
Ukrainian Evangelical Missionary Surge	Inspiration, Means	Initiators and Examples	Inviters	Initiators	Organizers; Missionary Structures

Note: — = No comparable idea.

4. Rogers, *Diffusion of Innovations*; Naylor, *Culture and Change*; Rochon, *Culture Moves*; Gladwell, *Tipping Point*; Heath and Heath, *Made to Stick*; Collins and Porras, *Built to Last*; Crouch, *Culture Making*; Hunter, *To Change the World*; Heath and Heath, *Switch*.

Table C4. Comparison of Change Models With the Missionary Surge: Context[5]

Source	Context	
	Environmental Change	Connections
Rogers	Social System	Influence of peers
Naylor	Setting barriers vs. stimulants	Interactional setting
Rochon	Societal niches open to change	—
Gladwell	Context: Environmental tipping point	Context: Peer pressure
Heath and Heath, *Made to Stick*	—	—
Collins and Porras	—	—
Crouch	World is broken and complex; hard to change	—
Hunter	—	Will and power more important than other kinds of context
Heath and Heath, *Switch*	Path: Tweak the environment	Path: Peer perception
Ukrainian Evangelical Missionary Surge	Freedom for ministry	Motivation 1: Connections; Motivation 2: Examples

Note: — = No comparable idea.

5. Rogers, *Diffusion of Innovations*; Naylor, *Culture and Change*; Rochon, *Culture Moves*; Gladwell, *Tipping Point*; Heath and Heath, *Made to Stick*; Collins and Porras, *Built to Last*; Crouch, *Culture Making*; Hunter, *To Change the World*; Heath and Heath, *Switch*.

Bibliography

Adams, Richard Newbold. *Energy and Structure: A Theory of Social Power*. Austin: University of Texas Press, 1975.
Addison, Steve. *Movements that Change the World: Five Keys to Spreading the Gospel*. Downers Grove, IL: InterVarsity, 2011.
Aikman, David. *Jesus in Beijing*. Washington, DC: Regnery, 2003.
Ambert, Anne-Marie, et al. "Understanding and Evaluating Qualitative Research." *Journal of Marriage and Family* 57/4 (November 1995) 879–93.
Barrett, David B., et al. "Missiometrics 2007." *International Bulletin of Missionary Research* 31/1 (January 2007) 25–32.
Bebbington, David W. *Evangelicalism in Modern Britain: A History from the 1730s to the 1980s*. London: Routledge, 1989.
Beuttler, Fred W. "Evangelical Missions in Modern America." In *The Great Commission: Evangelicals and the History of World Missions*, edited by Martin I. Klauber and Scott M. Manetsch, 108–32. Nashville: B&H Academic, 2008.
"Bibleyskiy kolledzh" [Bible college]. *Informatsionnyy byulleten': Missionerskoe obshchestvo "Svet Yevangeliya"* [Information bulletin: Missionary society "Light of the Gospel"] 1 (1993) 29–31.
Biola University. "PHRRC Part II Application Form." Updated October 10, 2011. http://www.biola.edu/offices/clear/phrrc.
Bolman, Lee G., and Terrence E. Deal. *Reframing Organizations: Artistry, Choice, and Leadership*. San Francisco: Jossey-Bass, 2003.
Bondarenko, Joseph. *The KGB's Most Wanted*. Grand Rapids: Credo, 2014.
Bosch, David J. *Transforming Mission*. Maryknoll, NY: Orbis, 1991.
Bourdeaux, Lorna, and Michael Bourdeaux. *Ten Growing Soviet Churches*. Bromley, Kent, UK: MARC Europe, 1987.
Bourdeaux, Michael. "Glasnost and the Gospel: The Emergence of Religious Pluralism." In *The Politics of Religion in Russia and the New States of Eurasia*, edited by Michael Bourdeaux, 113–27. Armonk, NY: M.E. Sharpe, 1995.
———. "Introduction." In *The Politics of Religion in Russia and the New States of Eurasia*, edited by Michael Bourdeaux, 3–12. Armonk, NY: M.E. Sharpe, 1995.
Boyechko, Vasyl. *Neskorena tserkva* [The unconquered church]. Lviv, Ukraine: Mission of Mercy "Good Samaritan," 2010.
Brumbelow, Gary. "The Other Side of Russia: Evangelical Ministries in Siberia." *East-West Church Ministry Report* 3/2 (Spring 1995) 1–3. http://www.eastwestreport.org/articles/ewo3201.htm.
Cahill, Thomas. *How the Irish Saved Civilization*. New York: Anchor, 1995.

Case, Jay R. "And Ever the Twain Shall Meet: The Holiness Missionary Movement and the Birth of World Pentecostalism, 1870–1920." *Religion and American Culture: A Journal of Interpretation* 16/2 (Summer 2006) 125–60.
Casier, Tom. "The Shattered Horizon How Ideology Mattered to Soviet Politics." *Studies in East European Thought* 51/1 (March 1999) 35–59.
Chaplin, Vsevolod. "The Church and Politics in Contemporary Russia." In *The Politics of Religion in Russia and the New States of Eurasia*, edited by Michael Bourdeaux, 95–112. Armonk, NY: M.E. Sharpe, 1995.
Charmaz, Kathy. *Constructing Grounded Theory: A Practical Guide through Qualitative Analysis*. Thousand Oaks, CA: Sage, 2006.
Cherevko, Olexandr. "Constructing a Theology of Mission for Evangelical Christian and Baptist Churches in the Contemporary Post-Communist Context of Ukraine." Master's thesis, University of Wales, Prague, Czech Republic, 2005.
Christensen, Paul T. "Perestroika and the Problem of Socialist Renewal." *Social Text* 27 (1990) 123–46.
Coleman, Heather J. "Conversion Narratives and Social Experience." *Russian Review* 61/1 (January 2002) 94–112.
Collins, Jim, and Jerry I. Portas. *Built to Last: Successful Habits of Visionary Companies*. New York: HarperBusiness Essentials, 2002.
Conforti, Joseph. "David Brainerd and the Nineteenth Century Missionary Movement." *Journal of the Early Republic* 5/3 (Autumn 1985) 309–29.
Cook, Richard R. "The Great Commission in Asia." In *The Great Commission: Evangelicals and the History of World Missions*, edited by Martin J. Klauber and Scott M. Manetsch, 149–63. Nashville: B&H Academic, 2008.
Corrado, Sharyl. "Serving by Faith on Sakhalin Island." *East-West Church & Ministry Report* 13/3 (Summer 2005) 1–2.
Creswell, John W. *Qualitative Inquiry and Research Design: Choosing among Five Approaches*. 2nd ed. Thousand Oaks, CA: Sage, 2007.
———. *Research Design: Qualitative, Quantitative, and Mixed Methods Approaches*. 3rd ed. Thousand Oaks, CA: Sage, 2009.
Crouch, Andy. *Culture Making: Recovering Our Creative Calling*. Downers Grove, IL: InterVarsity, 2008.
Daneel, Marthinus L. "African Initiated Churches in Southern Africa: Protest Movements or Mission Churches?" In *Christianity Reborn: The Global Expansion of Evangelicalism in the Twentieth Century*, edited by Donald M. Lewis, 181–218. Grand Rapids: Eerdmans, 2004.
Davey, Gerry. "Literature in Missions and Church Development." In *Global Passion: Marking George Verwer's Contribution to World Mission*, edited by David Greenlee, 144–51. Carlisle, UK: Authentic Lifestyle, 2003.
Davidson, Allan K. "The Pacific is No Longer a Mission Field?" In *Christianity Reborn: The Global Expansion of Evangelicalism in the Twentieth Century*, edited by Donald M. Lewis, 133–53. Grand Rapids: Eerdmans, 2004.
Davie, Grace. "Europe: The Exception that Proves the Rule?" In *The Desecularization of the World: Resurgent Religion and World Politics*, edited by Peter L. Berger, 65–84. Grand Rapids: Eerdmans, 1999.
"Delayte uchenikami" [Make disciples]. *Informatsionnyy byulleten': Missionerskoe obshchestvo "Svet Yevangeliya"* [Information bulletin: Missionary society "Light of the Gospel"] 3 (1990) 11–13.

Deyneka, Anita, and Peter Deyneka Jr. *Christians in the Shadow of the Kremlin.* Elgin, IL: David C. Cook, 1974.

———. "Evangelical Foreign Missionaries in Russia." *International Bulletin of Missionary Research* 22/2 (April 1998) 56–61.

D'Souza, Joseph. "Global Missions and the Role of the Two-Thirds World Church." In *Global Passion: Marking George Verwer's Contribution to World Mission*, edited by David Greenlee, 95–105. Carlisle, UK: Authentic Lifestyle, 2003.

Dunn, Ethel, and Stephen P. Dunn. "Religion as an Instrument of Culture Change: The Problem of the Sects in the Soviet Union." *Slavic Review* 23/3 (September 1964) 459–78.

Durasoff, Steve. *The Russian Protestants: Evangelicals in the Soviet Union: 1944–1964.* Rutherford, NJ: Fairleigh Dickinson University Press, 1969.

Dyck, Johannes. "Missiya yevangel'skikh tserkvey v SSSR. Mezhdu tyur'moy i svobodoy (1929–1987)" [The mission of evangelical churches in the USSR. Between prison and freedom (1929–1987)]. In *Novye gorizonty missii* [New horizons of mission], edited by P. Penner et al., 206–12. Cherkasy, Ukraine: Colloquium, 2015.

———. "Revival as Church Restoration: Patterns of a Revival among Ethnic Germans in Central Asia after World War II." In *Mission in the Former Soviet Union*, edited by Walter W. Sawatsky and Peter F. Penner, 74–93. Schwarzenfeld, Germany: Neufeld, 2005.

Elliott, Mark, and Sharyl Corrado. "The Protestant Missionary Presence in the Former Soviet Union." *Religion, State and Society* 25/4 (1997) 333–51.

Elliott, Mark, and Robert Richardson. "Growing Protestant Diversity in the Former Soviet Union." In *Russian Pluralism: Now Irreversible?*, edited by Uri Ra'anan et al., 189–214. New York: St. Martin's, 1992.

Ennis, Ralph, et al. *An Introduction to the Russian Soul.* Raleigh, NC: The Navigators, 1995.

Fiedler, Klaus. *The Story of Faith Missions: From Hudson Taylor to Present Day Africa.* Oxford: Regnum, 1994.

Field, Mark G. "Soviet Society and Communist Party Controls: A Case of Constricted Development." In Understanding Soviet Society, edited by Michael Paul Sacks and Jerry G. Pankhurst, 119–46. Boston: Unwin Hyman, 1988.

"Finansovyy otchet" [Financial statement]. *Informatsionnyy byulleten': Missionerskoe obshchestvo "Svet Yevangeliya"* [Information bulletin: Missionary society "Light of the Gospel"] 1–2 (1990) 22.

"Finansovyy otchet" [Financial statement]. *Informatsionnyy byulleten': Missionerskoe obshchestvo "Svet Yevangeliya"* [Information bulletin: Missionary society "Light of the Gospel"] 1 (1991) 35.

Fitzpatrick, Sheila. "Social Parasites: How Tramps, Idle Youth, and Busy Entrepreneurs Impeded the Soviet March to Communism." *Cahiers du Monde Russe* 47/1–2 (January–June 2006) 377–408.

Fletcher, Richard. *The Barbarian Conversion: From Paganism to Christianity.* New York: Henry Holt, 1997.

Fletcher, William C. *Soviet Believers: The Religious Sector of the Population.* Lawrence, KS: Regents, 1981.

"Fond teologicheskogo obrazovaniya" [Foundation for theological education]. *Informatsionnyy byulleten': Mezhdunarodnaya assotsiatsiya "Svet Yevangeliya"* [Information bulletin: International association "Light of the Gospel"] 1 (1994) 14.

Forest, Jim. *Religion in the New Russia: The Impact of Perestroika on the Varieties of Religious Life in the Soviet Union.* New York: Crossroad, 1990.

Franchuk, Vladimir. *Probuzhdenie ot tsentra Odessy do okrain Rossii* [Revival: From the center of Odessa to the outskirts of Russia]. Odessa, Ukraine: Simeks-Print, 2011.

———. *Prosila Rossiya dozhdya u Gospoda* (Tom tretiy) [Russia asked the Lord for rain (Volume III)]. Kyiv, Ukraine: Christian Mission Possibility, 2003.

Freeman, Melissa, et al. "Standards of Evidence in Qualitative Research: An Incitement to Discourse." *Educational Researcher* 36/1 (January–February 2007) 25–32.

Garrison, David. *Church Planting Movements.* Richmond, VA: International Mission Board, 2000.

George, Timothy. "Evangelical Revival and the Missionary Awakening." In *The Great Commission: Evangelicals and the History of World Missions,* edited by Martin I. Klauber and Scott M. Manetsch, 44–63. Nashville: B&H Academic, 2008.

Gibson, James R. "Russian Expansion in Siberia and America." *Geographical Review* 70/2 (April 1980) 127–36.

Gladwell, Malcolm. *The Tipping Point: How Little Things Can Make a Big Difference.* New York: Back Bay, 2002.

Glanzer, Perry L. *The Quest for Russia's Soul.* Waco, TX: Baylor University Press, 2002.

Glick, Daniel. *Chto govoryat novoobrashchennye khristiane Ukrainy* [What do new Christian converts of Ukraine say]. Zaporozhye, Ukraine: Pilgrim, 2008.

Glukhovskiy, Vladimir S. *Kratkaya istoriya Khristian Yevangel'skoy Very* [A short history of the Christians of Evangelical Faith]. Kyiv, Ukraine: Foundation, 2006.

Goldman, Marshall I. "Perestroika." In *The Concise Encyclopedia of Economics.* Library of Economics and Liberty. 1992; http://www.econlib.org/library/Enc1/Perestroika.html.

Golovin, Sergei. *Bibleyskaya strategiya blagovestiya* [A biblical strategy of evangelism]. Simferopol, Ukraine: Christian Scientific-Apologetic Center, 2003.

———. *Mirovozzrenie* [Worldview]. Simferopol, Ukraine: DIP, 2008.

———. "Worldview: The Missing Dimension of Evangelism in Postcommunist Society." DMin diss., Asbury Theological Seminary, 2009. ProQuest (UMI 3385083).

Gruenwald, Oskar. "The Icon in Russian Art, Society and Culture." In *Christianity and Russian Culture in Soviet Society,* edited by Nicolai N. Petro, 161–82. Boulder, CO: Westview, 1990.

Gundlach, Bradley J. "Early American Missions from the Revolution to the Civil War." In *The Great Commission: Evangelicals and the History of World Missions,* edited by Martin I. Klauber and Scott M. Manetsch, 66–88. Nashville: B&H Academic, 2008.

Hattaway, Paul, et al. *Back to Jerusalem.* Waynesboro, GA: Authentic Media, 2003.

Heath, Chip, and Dan Heath. *Made to Stick: Why Some Ideas Survive and Others Die.* New York: Random House, 2008.

———. *Switch: How to Change Things When Change is Hard.* New York: Broadway, 2010.

Henige, David P. *Historical Evidence and Argument.* Madison: University of Wisconsin Press, 2005.

Hesselgrave, David J. *Paradigms in Conflict: 10 Key Questions in Christian Missions Today.* Grand Rapids: Kregel, 2005.

Heydt, Barbara von der. *Candles Behind the Wall.* Grand Rapids: Eerdmans, 1993.

Heyns, Barbara. "Emerging Inequalities in Central and Eastern Europe." *Annual Review of Sociology* 31 (2005) 163–97.
Hiebert, Paul G. *Missiological Implications of Epistemological Shifts: Affirming Truth in a Modern World*. Harrisburg, PA: Trinity, 1999.
———. *Transforming Worldviews: An Anthropological Understanding of How People Change*. Grand Rapids: Baker Academic, 2008.
Hill, Kent R. *The Soviet Union on the Brink*. Portland, OR: Multnomah, 1991.
Hinkson, Jon. "Missions among Puritans and Pietists." In *The Great Commission: Evangelicals and the History of World Missions*, edited by Martin I. Klauber and Scott M. Manetsch, 23–43. Nashville: B&H Academic, 2008.
Hogan, Edmund M. "The Congregation of the Holy Ghost and the Evolution of the Modern Irish Missionary." *The Catholic Historical Review* 70/1 (January 1984) 1–13.
———. "The Motivation of the Modern Irish Missionary Movement 1912–1939." *Journal of Religion in Africa* 10/3 (1979) 157–73.
Hollingworth, Harry L. *The Psychology of the Audience*. New York: American Book, 1935.
Hopkins, C. Howard. "The Kansas-Sudan Missionary Movement in the Y.M.C.A., 1889–1891." *Church History* 21/4 (December 1952) 314–22.
Hunter, George G., III. *The Celtic Way of Evangelism*. Nashville: Abingdon, 2000.
Hunter, James Davison. *To Change the World: The Irony, Tragedy, and Possibility of Christianity in the Late Modern World*. Oxford: Oxford University Press, 2010.
Informatsionnyy byulleten': Missionerskoe obshchestvo "Svet Yevangeliya" [Information bulletin: Missionary society "Light of the Gospel"] 4 (1990) 1.
Iosifides, Theodoros. *Qualitative Methods in Migration Studies: A Critical Realist Perspective*. Farnham, Surrey, UK: Ashgate, 2011.
Iraola, Antton Egiguren. *True Confucians, Bold Christians: Korean Missionary Experience: A Model for the Third Millennium*. Amsterdam: Rodolpi, 2007.
Irvin, Dale T., and Scott W. Sunquist. *History of the World Christian Movement*. Vol. 2, *Modern Christianity from 1454–1800*. Maryknoll, NY: Orbis, 2012.
Ivanilov, S. A. "'Khristianskiy lager'" [Christian camp]. *Informatsionnyy byulleten': Mezhdunarodnaya assotsiatsiya "Svet Yevangeliya"* [Information bulletin: International association "Light of the Gospel"] 3 (1998) 8–9.
James, R. Alton. "Turbulent and Transitional: The Story of Missions in the Twentieth Century." In *Missiology: An Introduction to the Foundations, History, and Strategies of World Missions*, edited by John Mark Terry et al., 245–59. Nashville: Broadman & Holdman, 1998.
Jenkins, Philip. *The Lost History of Christianity: The Thousand-Year Golden Age of the Church in the Middle East, Africa, and Asia—and How it Died*. New York: HarperOne, 2008.
"The Jesuit Missions in 1773." *The Catholic Historical Review* 2/3 (October 1916) 316–20.
Johnstone, Patrick. *The Future of the Global Church*. Downers Grove, IL: InterVarsity, 2011.
———. "The Next Forty Years for Christian Missions." In *Global Passion: Marking George Verwer's Contribution to World Mission*, edited by David Greenlee, 180–90. Carlisle, UK: Authentic Lifestyle, 2003.
———. *Operation World*. 5th ed. Grand Rapids: Zondervan, 1993.

Johnstone, Patrick, and Jason Mandryk. *Operation World*. 6th ed. Waynesboro, GA: Authentic Media, 2001.

———. *Operation World on CD ROM*. 6th ed. [CD ROM.] Waynesboro, GA: Authentic Media, 2001.

Karetnikova, Marina S. "The Missionary Movement in Russia: The 19th and 20th Centuries." In *Mission in the Former Soviet Union*, edited by W. W. Sawatsky and P. F. Penner, 64–73. Schwarzenfeld, Germany: Neufeld, 2005.

Kartavenko, Leonid. ". . . Budete mne svidetelyami . . . dazhe do kraya zemli" [". . . Be my witnesses . . . even to the end of the earth"]. *Informatsionnyy byulleten'*: *Mezhdunarodnaya assotsiatsiya "Svet Yevangeliya"* [Information bulletin: International association "Light of the Gospel"] 3 (1998) 2–3.

———. "Sluzhite Gospodu" [Serve the Lord]. *Informatsionnyy byulleten'*: *Mezhdunarodnaya assotsiatsiya "Svet Yevangeliya"* [Information bulletin: International association "Light of the Gospel"] 3–4 (1997) 4–5.

———. "Zavtrashniy den' Assotsiatsii" [Tomorrow in the Association]. *Informatsionnyy byulleten'*: *Mezhdunarodnaya assotsiatsiya "Svet Yevangeliya"* [Information bulletin: International association "Light of the Gospel"] 2 (1997) 6–7.

Kearney, Michael. *World View*. Novato, CA: Chandler & Sharp, 1984.

Kelley, Robert. *The Power of Followership*. New York: Doubleday Currency, 1992.

Kerr, Ron, and Sarah Robinson. "The Hysteresis Effect as Creative Adaptation of the Habitus: Dissent and Transition to the 'Corporate' in Post-Soviet Ukraine." *Organization* 16/6 (2009) 829–53.

Keyes, Lawrence E. *The Last Age of Missions: A Study of Third World Mission Societies*. Pasadena, CA: William Carey Library, 1983.

———. "Third World Missionaries: More and Better." *Evangelical Missions Quarterly* 18 (October 1982) 217–24.

"Khristianskaya missiya 'Evangelie – Vostoku'" [Christian mission "Gospel to the East"]. *Informatsionnyy byulleten'*: *Mezhdunarodnaya assotsiatsiya "Svet Yevangeliya"* [Information bulletin: International association "Light of the Gospel"] 1 (1994) 15.

"Khristianskiy blagotvoritel'nyy fond 'Dobrota'" [Christian charitable foundation "Kindness"]. *Informatsionnyy byulleten'*: *Mezhdunarodnaya assotsiatsiya "Svet Yevangeliya"* [Information bulletin: International association "Light of the Gospel"] 3–4 (1996) 50–51.

"Khristianskiy blagotvoritel'nyy izdatel'skiy fond" [Christian charitable publishing foundation]. *Informatsionnyy byulleten'*: *Mezhdunarodnaya assotsiatsiya "Svet Yevangeliya"* [Information bulletin: International association "Light of the Gospel"] 1 (1994) 12–13.

"Khristianskoe obshchestvo 'Dobraya Vest'"" [Christian society "Good News"]. *Informatsionnyy byulleten'*: *Mezhdunarodnaya assotsiatsiya "Svet Yevangeliya"* [Information bulletin: International association "Light of the Gospel."] 1 (1994) 6–7.

"Khristianskoe obshchestvo 'Dobraya Vest'"" [Christian society "Good News"]. *Informatsionnyy byulleten'*: *Mezhdunarodnaya assotsiatsiya "Svet Yevangeliya"* [Information bulletin: International association "Light of the Gospel."] 4 (1995) 8–11.

"Khristianskoe obshchestvo 'Dobraya Vest'"" [Christian society "Good News"]. *Informatsionnyy byulleten'*: *Mezhdunarodnaya assotsiatsiya "Svet Yevangeliya"*

[Information bulletin: International association "Light of the Gospel."] 3-4 (1996) 10-11.

"Khristianskoe obshchestvo 'Evangel'skoe sluzhenie'" [Christian society "Evangelical ministry"]. *Informatsionnyy byulleten': Mezhdunarodnaya assotsiatsiya "Svet Yevangeliya"* [Information bulletin: International association "Light of the Gospel"] 1 (1994) 4-5.

"Khristianskoe obshchestvo 'Missionerskoe Bratstvo'" [Christian society "Missionary Brotherhood"]. *Informatsionnyy byulleten': Mezhdunarodnaya assotsiatsiya "Svet Yevangeliya"* [Information bulletin: International association "Light of the Gospel"] 1 (1994) 2-3.

"Khristianskoe obshchestvo 'Svet Voskreseniya'" [Christian society "Light of the Resurrection"]. *Informatsionnyy byulleten': Mezhdunarodnaya assotsiatsiya "Svet Yevangeliya"* [Information bulletin: International association "Light of the Gospel"] 1 (1994) 8-10.

"Khristianskoe obshchestvo 'Svet Voskreseniya'" [Christian society "Light of the Resurrection"]. *Informatsionnyy byulleten': Mezhdunarodnaya assotsiatsiya "Svet Yevangeliya"* [Information bulletin: International association "Light of the Gospel"] 1 (1998) 6-12.

Killingray, David. "The Black Atlantic Missionary Movement and Africa, 1780s-1920s." *Journal of Religion in Africa* 33/1 (February 2003) 3-31.

Klingsmith, Scott. "Factors in the Rise of Missionary Sending Movements in East-Central Europe." PhD diss., Trinity International University, 2002. ProQuest (UMI 3087178).

———. *Missions Beyond the Wall: Factors in the Rise of Missionary Sending Movements in East-Central Europe*. Nürnberg, Germany: VTR, 2012.

Koehler, Paul F. *Telling God's Stories with Power: Biblical Storytelling in Oral Cultures*. Pasadena, CA: William Carey Library, 2010.

Kolarz, Walter. *Religion in the Soviet Union*. London: Macmillan, 1961.

Kolodny, Anatoly M., et al. *Religion and the Churches in Modern Ukraine: A Collection of Scientific Reports*. Kyiv, Ukraine: Svit znan', 2001.

Kotter, John P., and Dan S. Cohen. *The Heart of Change*. Boston: Harvard Business School, 2002.

Kraeuter, Tom. *The Great Soviet Awakening: The True Story the West was Never Told*. Hillsboro, MO: Training Resources, 2012.

Lambert, Tony. *China's Christian Millions*. Oxford: Monarch, 2006.

Lambert, Yves. "Trends in Religious Feeling in Europe and Russia." *Supplement: An Annual English Section, Revue Française de Sociologie* 47 (2006) 99-129.

Latourette, Kenneth Scott. "The Christian Missionary Movement of the Nineteenth and Twentieth Centuries: Some Peculiar and General Characteristics." *The Catholic Historical Review* 23/2 (July 1937) 153-59.

———. *A History of the Expansion of Christianity*. 7 vols. New York: Harper, 1937-1941.

Lawrence, John. "Observations on Religion and Atheism in Soviet Society." *Canadian Slavonic Papers/Revue Canadienne des Slavistes* 14/4 (Winter 1972) 577-85.

Lewis, Donald M., ed. *Christianity Reborn: The Global Expansion of Evangelicalism in the Twentieth Century*. Grand Rapids: Eerdmans, 2004.

Lingenfelter, Sherwood G. *Leading Cross-Culturally: Covenant Relationships for Effective Christian Leadership*. Grand Rapids: Baker Academic, 2008.

———. *Transforming Culture: A Challenge for Christian Mission*. Grand Rapids: Baker, 1998.
Lőfstedt, Torsten. "Pentecostal and Charismatic Denominations in Russia." *East-West Church & Ministry Report* 19/1 (Winter 2011) 9–11.
Lovelace, Richard. *Dynamics of Spiritual Life: An Evangelical Theology of Renewal*. Downers Grove, IL: InterVarsity, 1979.
Lyubashchenko, Viktoriya. "Protestantism in Ukraine: Achievements and Losses." *Religion, State and Society* 38/3 (2010) 265–89.
Maiden, Peter. "Gratitude for a Life Well Lived." In *Global Passion: Marking George Verwer's Contribution to World Mission*, edited by David Greenlee, xi–xix. Carlisle, UK: Authentic Lifestyle, 2003.
Malov, Aleksandr. "Chto znachit byt' docher'yu missionera?!" [What does it mean to be the daughter of a missionary?!]. *Informatsionnyy byulleten': Mezhdunarodnaya assotsiatsiya "Svet Yevangeliya"* [Information bulletin: International association "Light of the Gospel"] 1 (1998) 4–5.
———. "Zhenshchina—propovednik, missioner?!" [Woman—preacher, missionary?!]. *Informatsionnyy byulleten': Mezhdunarodnaya assotsiatsiya "Svet Yevangeliya"* [Information bulletin: International association "Light of the Gospel"] 2 (1998) 4–7.
———. "Zhenshchina—propovednik, missioner?!" [Woman—preacher, missionary?!]. *Informatsionnyy byulleten': Mezhdunarodnaya assotsiatsiya "Svet Yevangeliya"* [Information bulletin: International association "Light of the Gospel"] 3 (1998) 4–7.
Marsh, Christopher. *Religion and the State in Russia and China: Suppression, Survival, and Revival*. New York: Continuum, 2011.
Martin, David. *Tongues of Fire: The Explosion of Protestantism in Latin America*. Oxford: Blackwell, 1990.
Matthews, Mervyn. *Class and Society in Soviet Russia*. New York: Walker, 1972.
Mayer, Tom. "The Collapse of Soviet Communism: A Class Dynamics Interpretation." *Social Forces* 80/3 (March 2002) 759–811.
McDowell, E. W. "The Ancient Nestorian Church and Its Present Influence in Kurdistan." *The Journal of Race Development* 2/1 (July 1911) 67–88.
Melnychuk, Aleksei. "Istoriya i uroki pervoy vostochnoslavyanskoy missii 'Svet Yevangeliya'" [The history of and lessons from the first Eastern Slavic mission "Light of the Gospel"]. *Vitchiznyaniy yevangel'skiy protestantizm: Istoriya, dosvid, problemi* [National evangelical Protestantism: History, experience, and problems] 58 (2011) 218–25.
———. "Missionerskaya shkola missii 'Svet Yevangeliya'" [Missionary school of the mission "Light of the Gospel"]. *Informatsionnyy byulleten': Missionerskoe obshchestvo "Svet Yevangeliya"* [Information bulletin: Missionary society "Light of the Gospel"] 2 (1991) 13.
———. "Poydi i skazhi . . ." [Go and tell . . .]. *Informatsionnyy byulleten': Missionerskoe obshchestvo "Svet Yevangeliya"* [Information bulletin: Missionary society "Light of the Gospel"] 3 (1990) 4–5.
———. "Tret'ya konferentsiya" [Third conference]. *Informatsionnyy byulleten': Mezhdunarodnaya assotsiatsiya "Svet Yevangeliya"* [Information bulletin: International association "Light of the Gospel"] 3 (1994) 4–5.

Menshov, A. "My propoveduem Khrista tem, kto Yego ne znaet: Neskol'ko voprosov rukovoditelyu missionerskogo otdela Tarasu Pristupe" [We preach Christ to those who don't know Him: A few questions for the director of missionary work, Taras Pristupa]. *Informatsionnyy byulleten': Missionerskoe obshchestvo "Svet Yevangeliya"* [Information bulletin: Missionary society "Light of the Gospel"] 1 (1991) 4–10.

"Mezhdunarodnaya assotsiatsiya 'Svet Yevangeliya'" [International association "Light of the Gospel"]. *Informatsionnyy byulleten': Mezhdunarodnaya assotsiatsiya "Svet Yevangeliya"* [Information bulletin: International association "Light of the Gospel"] 2 (1994) 2–3.

"Mezhdunarodnaya obshchestvennaya blagotvoritel'naya khristianskaya organizatsiya 'Nadezhda—Lyudyam'" [International social charitable Christian organization "Hope to people"]. *Informatsionnyy byulleten': Mezhdunarodnaya assotsiatsiya "Svet Yevangeliya"* [Information bulletin: International association "Light of the Gospel"] 3-4 (1996) 34–41.

"Mezhdunarodnaya obshchestvennaya blagotvoritel'naya khristianskaya organizatsiya 'Nadezhda—Lyudyam'" [International social charitable Christian organization "Hope to people"]. *Informatsionnyy byulleten': Mezhdunarodnaya assotsiatsiya "Svet Yevangeliya"* [Information bulletin: International association "Light of the Gospel"] 3 (1998) 27–31.

Moffett, Samuel Hugh. *A History of Christianity in Asia.* Vol. 2, 1500–1900. Maryknoll, NY: Orbis, 2005.

Mokienko, Michael. "Summary—Modern Protestants in Ukraine: Evangelistic and Missionary Activities (1988–2004)." In *Forum 20*, edited by Mikhail Cherenkov, 295–317. Kyiv, Ukraine: Spirit/Letter, 2011.

"Molitva" [Prayer]. *Informatsionnyy byulleten': Missionerskoe obshchestvo "Svet Yevangeliya"* [Information bulletin: Missionary society "Light of the Gospel"] 3 (1990) 16–17.

Moon, Steve Sang-Cheol. "The Protestant Missionary Movement in Korea: Current Growth and Development." *International Bulletin of Missionary Research* 32/2 (April 2008) 59–64.

———. "The Recent Korean Missionary Movement: A Record of Growth, and More Growth Needed." *International Bulletin of Missionary Research* 27/1 (January 2003) 11–17.

Motyl, Alexander J. "Structural Constraints and Starting Points: The Logic of Systemic Change in Ukraine and Russia." *Comparative Politics* 29/4 (July 1997) 433–47.

Murarka, Dev. "Religion in Russia Today: Renewal and Conflict." *Economic and Political Weekly* 28/51 (December 18, 1993) 2841–43, 2845–47, 2849–52.

Nalitov, N. "Yubiley Tashkenskoy tserkvi—100 let" [Jubilee of the Tashkent church—100 years]. Unpublished manuscript, 2002. History of Euro-Asian Evangelical Movement, Primary sources 2.0. Euro-Asian Accrediting Association, Odessa, Ukraine.

Naylor, Larry L. *Culture and Change: An Introduction.* Westport, CT: Bergin & Garvey, 1996.

Neill, Stephen. *A History of Christian Missions.* Middlesex, UK: Penguin, 1964.

Nikolskaya, Tatyana. *Russkiy protestantizm i gosudarstvennaya vlast' v 1905–1991 godakh* [Russian Protestantism and government power from 1905–1991]. Saint Petersburg, Russia: European University in Saint Petersburg, 2009.

Noll, Mark A. *The New Shape of World Christianity: How American Experience Reflects Global Faith*. Downers Grove, IL: InterVarsity Academic, 2009.

"Otdel blagotvoritel'nosti" [Department of humanitarian aid]. *Informatsionnyy byulleten': Missionerskoe obshchestvo "Svet Yevangeliya"* [Information bulletin: Missionary society "Light of the Gospel"] 1 (1992) 18–19.

"Otdel pisem" [Correspondence department]. *Informatsionnyy byulleten': Missionerskoe obshchestvo "Svet Yevangeliya"* [Information bulletin: Missionary society "Light of the Gospel"] 1 (1991) 16–17.

Pankhurst, Jerry G. "The Sacred and the Secular in the USSR." In *Understanding Soviet Society*, edited by Michael Paul Sacks and Jerry G. Pankhurst, 167–92. Boston: Unwin Hyman, 1988.

Parker, Michael. *The Kingdom of Character: The Student Volunteer Movement for Foreign Missions, 1886–1926*. Pasadena, CA: William Carey Library, 2008.

Parker, Richard. "Assessing Perestroika." *World Policy Journal* 6/2 (Spring 1989) 265–96.

Parsons, Howard L. *Christianity Today in the USSR*. New York: International, 1987.

Pate, Larry D. "The Changing Balance in Global Mission." *International Bulletin of Missionary Research* 15/2 (April 1991) 56–61.

Pedersen, Paul B. *Batak Blood and Protestant Soul: The Development of National Batak Churches in North Sumatra*. Grand Rapids: Eerdmans, 1970.

Pelkmans, Mathijs. "Introduction: Post-Soviet Space and the Unexpected Turns of Religious Life." In *Conversion After Socialism: Disruptions, Modernisms and Technologies of Faith in the Former Soviet Union*, edited by Mathijs Pelkmans, 1–16. New York: Berghahn, 2009.

Penner, Peter F. "Critical Evaluation of Recent Developments in the CIS." In *Mission in the Former Soviet Union*, edited by Walter W. Sawatsky and Peter F. Penner, 120–62. Schwarzenfeld, Germany: Neufeld, 2005.

Petrov, Kristian. "Construction, Reconstruction, Deconstruction: The Fall of the Soviet Union from the Point of View of Conceptual History." *Studies in East European Thought* 60/3 (September 2008) 179–205.

Pierson, Paul E. *The Dynamics of Christian Mission: History through a Missiological Perspective*. Pasadena, CA: William Carey International University Press, 2009.

Piirainen, Timo. "Survival Strategies in a Transition Economy: Everyday Life, Subsistence and New Inequalities in Russia." In *Change and Continuity in Eastern Europe*, edited by Timo Piirainen, 89–113. Aldershot, UK: Dartmouth, 1994.

Pocock, Michael, et al. *The Changing Face of World Missions*. Grand Rapids: Baker Academic, 2005.

Poysti, Pirkko. "Soul Winning and Soul Searching." *East-West Church & Ministry Report* 1/4 (Fall 1993) 6. http://www.eastwestreport.org/articles/ew01406.htm.

Pristupa, Taras. "Kto mozhet byt' missionerom?" [Who can be a missionary?]. *Informatsionnyy byulleten': Missionerskoe obshchestvo "Svet Yevangeliya"* [Information bulletin: Missionary society "Light of the Gospel"] 4 (1991) 2–4.

———. "Prepyatstviya stoyashchie na puti razvitiya missionerskogo sluzheniya v Rossii" [Obstacles that are preventing the growth of the missionary work in Russia]. Paper presented at the Rus'-Mission in the 21st Century Conference, Moscow, Russia, March 2000. http://baptist.org.ru/go/46.

Prokhanoff, Ivan S. *In the Cauldron of Russia 1869–1933: Autobiography of I.S. Prokhanoff*. New York: All-Russian Evangelical Christian Union, 1933.

"Propoved' v narode" [Preaching among the people]. *Informatsionnyy byulleten': Missionerskoe obshchestvo "Svet Yevangeliya"* [Information bulletin: Missionary society "Light of the Gospel"] 4 (1990) 14–15.

Puzynin, Andrey P. *The Tradition of the Gospel Christians: A Study of Their Identity and Theology during the Russian, Soviet, and Post-Soviet Periods.* Eugene, OR: Pickwick, 2011.

"Raspredelenie sredstv v missionerskom obshchestve 'Svet Yevangeliya'" [Allocation of funds for the missionary organization "Light of the Gospel"]. *Informatsionnyy byulleten': Missionerskoe obshchestvo "Svet Yevangeliya"* [Information bulletin: Missionary society "Light of the Gospel"] 1 (1992) 22.

"Raspredelenie sredstv v missionerskom obshchestve 'Svet Yevangeliya'" [Allocation of funds for the missionary organization "Light of the Gospel"]. *Informatsionnyy byulleten': Missionerskoe obshchestvo "Svet Yevangeliya"* [Information bulletin: Missionary society "Light of the Gospel"] 1 (1993) 34.

Reimer, Johannes. "Mission in Post-Perestroika Russia." *Missionalia* 24/1 (April 1996) 16–39. http://www.oocities.org/missionalia/reimer96.htm.

———. *Operation Soviet Union: How to Pray for the 160 People Groups in the USSR.* Fresno, CA: Logos, 1990.

Remington, Thomas F. "Words and Deeds: CPSU Ideological Work." In *Understanding Soviet Society*, edited by Michael Paul Sacks and Jerry G. Pankhurst, 147–63. Boston: Unwin Hyman, 1988.

Richardson, James T. "The Active vs. Passive Convert: Paradigm Conflict in Conversion/Recruitment Research." *Journal for the Scientific Study of Religion* 24/2 (June 1985) 163–79.

Richmond, Yale. *From Nyet to Da: Understanding the Russians.* Yarmouth, ME: Intercultural, 1996.

Robert, Dana L. *Christian Mission: How Christianity Became a World Religion.* Malden, MA: Wiley-Blackwell, 2009.

———. "The First Globalization: The Internationalization of the Protestant Missionary Movement between the World Wars." *International Bulletin of Missionary Research* 26/2 (April 2002) 50–66.

Rochon, Thomas R. *Culture Moves: Ideas, Activism, and Changing Values.* Princeton, NJ: Princeton University Press, 1998.

Rogers, Everett M. *Diffusion of Innovations.* New York: Free Press, 2003.

Rowe, Michael. *Russian Resurrection.* London: Marshall Pickering, 1994.

Rybikov, Sergei F. "Missionerskoe sluzhenie sredi narodov ispoveduyushchikh razlichnye religii" [Missionary ministry among peoples that follow different religions]. Paper presented at the Rus'-Mission in the 21st Century Conference, Moscow, Russia, March 2000. http://baptist.org.ru/go/46.

———. "Report from the Missionary Department." Paper presented at the General Conference of the Evangelical Christian Missionary Union, Novorossiysk, Russia, May 30–June 2, 2001.

Satsyuk, T. "Seminar: Prepodavateli obuchayutsya" [Seminar: Teachers are taught]. *Informatsionnyy byulleten': Missionerskoe obshchestvo "Svet Yevangeliya"* [Information bulletin: Missionary society "Light of the Gospel"] 2 (1991) 11–12.

Savinskii, S. N., et al. "Istoriya YeKhB v SSSR" [History of the ECB in the USSR]. Unpublished manuscript, Moscow, Russia: AUCECB, 1989. History of Euro-Asian Evangelical Movement, Primary sources 2.0. Euro-Asian Accrediting Association, Odessa, Ukraine.

Sawatsky, Walter. "After the Glasnost Revolution: Soviet Evangelicals and Western Missions." *International Bulletin for Missionary Research* 16/2 (April 1992) 54–59.

———. "Protestantism in the USSR." In *Protestantism and Politics in Eastern Europe and Russia: The Communist and Post-Communist Eras*, edited by Sabrina Petra Ramet, 237–75. Durham, NC: Duke University Press, 1992.

———. "Protestantism in the USSR." In *Religious Policy in the Soviet Union*, edited by Sabrina Petra Ramet, 319–49. Cambridge: Cambridge University Press, 1993.

———. "Return of Mission and Evangelization in the CIS (1980's–Present): An Assessment." In *Mission in the Former Soviet Union*, edited by Walter W. Sawatsky and Peter F. Penner, 94–119. Schwarzenfeld, Germany: Neufeld, 2005.

———. *Soviet Evangelicals since World War II*. Scottdale, PA: Herald, 1981.

Schattschneider, David A. "William Carey, Modern Missions, and the Moravian Influence." *International Bulletin of Missionary Research* 22/1 (January 1998) 8–12.

Shaw, Mark. *Global Awakening: How 20th-Century Revivals Triggered a Christian Revolution*. Downers Grove, IL: InterVarsity Academic, 2010.

Shaw, Ryan. "A Haystack that Changed the World." *Evangelical Missions Quarterly* 42/4 (October 2006) 480–85.

Shenk, Wilbert R. *Changing Frontiers of Mission*. Maryknoll, NY: Orbis, 1999.

Sinichkin, Alexei. *Vsyo radi missii* [All for the sake of mission]. Irpin, Ukraine: Association for Spiritual Renewal, 2011.

Sipko, Yuriy K. "Sotsial'nyy portret rossiyanina. Regiony, okhvachennye missiey, i 'belye pyatna' Rossii" [Social portrait of a Russian. Regions reached by mission and the "unreached spot" of Russia]. Paper presented at the Rus'-Mission in the 21st Century Conference, Moscow, Russia, March 2000. http://baptist.org.ru/go/46.

Smirnov, Alexei. "Missionerskaya strategiya na postsovetskom prostranstve" [Missionary strategy for the post-Soviet world]. Paper presented at the Rus'-Mission in the 21st Century Conference, Moscow, Russia, March 2000. http://baptist.org.ru/go/46.

Smith, Donald K. *Creating Understanding*. Grand Rapids: Zondervan, 1992.

Solodnikov, Svetlana, and Nikita Sokolov. "What are They Teaching Our Kids?" *East-West Church Ministry Report* 13/1 (Winter 2005) 6–7. http://eastwestreport.org/articles/ew13103.html.

"Soobshcheniya" [Reports]. *Informatsionnyy byulleten': Mezhdunarodnaya assotsiatsiya "Svet Yevangeliya"* [Information bulletin: International association "Light of the Gospel"] 1 (1995) 1.

"Soobshcheniya" [Reports]. *Informatsionnyy byulleten': Mezhdunarodnaya assotsiatsiya "Svet Yevangeliya"* [Information bulletin: International association "Light of the Gospel"] 3–4 (1996) 6–7.

"Soobshcheniya" [Reports]. *Informatsionnyy byulleten': Missionerskoe obshchestvo "Svet Yevangeliya"* [Information bulletin: Missionary society "Light of the Gospel"] 2 (1992) 6–9.

Stanley, Brian. "'Commerce and Christianity': Providence Theory, the Missionary Movement, and the Imperialism of Free Trade, 1842–1860." *The Historical Journal* 26/1 (March 1983) 71–94.

———. "Twentieth-Century World Christianity: A Perspective from the History of Missions." In *Christianity Reborn: The Global Expansion of Evangelicalism in the Twentieth Century*, edited by Donald M. Lewis, 52–83. Grand Rapids: Eerdmans, 2004.

Starcher, Richard L. "Qualitative Research in Missiological Studies and Practice." *Dharma Deepika* (July–December 2011) 54–63.
Stark, Rodney. *The Triumph of Christianity: How the Jesus Movement Became the World's Largest Religion*. New York: Harper Collins, 2011.
Steffen, Tom. *Reconnecting God's Story to Ministry: Cross-Cultural Storytelling at Home and Abroad*. Waynesboro, GA: Authentic Media, 2005.
Strauss, Anselm, and Juliet Corbin. *Basics of Qualitative Research: Techniques and Procedures for Developing Grounded Theory*. 2nd ed. Thousand Oaks, CA: Sage, 1998.
Sweeney, Douglas A. "Introduction." In *The Great Commission: Evangelicals and the History of World Missions*, edited by Martin I. Klauber and Scott M. Manetsch, 1–11. Nashville: B&H Academic, 2008.
Syed, Matthew. *Black Box Thinking: Why Most People Never Learn from Their Mistakes—But Some Do*. New York: Penguin, 2015.
Tarantal, Peter. "The Place of Networks in World Evangelization." In *Global Passion: Marking George Verwer's Contribution to World Mission*, edited by David Greenlee, 116–23. Carlisle, UK: Authentic Lifestyle, 2003.
Taylor, Howard, and Mrs. Howard Taylor. *Hudson Taylor's Spiritual Secret*. Chicago: The Moody Bible Institute, 1989.
Teckenberg, Wolfgang. "The Social Structure of the Soviet Working Class: 'Toward an Estatist Society?'" *International Journal of Sociology* 11/4 (Winter 1981–1982) 1–163.
Thubron, Colin. *In Siberia*. New York: HarperCollins, 1999.
Tiessen, Douglas P. "A Historic Ethnographic Document Analysis of an Invitational Partnership: A Case Study of the Evangelical Christian Missionary Union and the Christian and Missionary Alliance." PhD diss., Reformed Theological Seminary, 2004.
"Tret'ya konferentsiya mezhdunarodnoy assotsiatsii 'Svet Yevangeliya'" [Third conference of the international association "Light of the Gospel"]. *Informatsionnyy byulleten': Mezhdunarodnaya assotsiatsiya "Svet Yevangeliya"* [Information bulletin: International association "Light of the Gospel"] 3 (1994) 2–3.
Tucker, Ruth A. *From Jerusalem to Irian Jaya*. Grand Rapids: Zondervan, 2004.
Tupchik, Sergei. *Informatsionnyy byulleten': Missionerskoe obshchestvo "Svet Yevangeliya"* [Information bulletin: Missionary society "Light of the Gospel"] 1–2 (1990) 2–3.
———. "Mir vam, dorogie druz'ya Assotsiatsii 'Svet Yevangeliya!'" [Peace to you, dear friends of the "Light of the Gospel" Association!]. *Informatsionnyy byulleten': Mezhdunarodnaya assotsiatsiya "Svet Yevangeliya"* [Information bulletin: International association "Light of the Gospel"] 2 (1997) 3.
———. "Poseshchenie Yakutii" [Visiting Yakutia]. *Informatsionnyy byulleten': Mezhdunarodnaya assotsiatsiya "Svet Yevangeliya"* [Information bulletin: International association "Light of the Gospel"] 3–4 (1996) 12–29.
———. "Spaseny, chtoby spasat'" [Saved in order to save]. *Informatsionnyy byulleten': Missionerskoe obshchestvo "Svet Yevangeliya"* [Information bulletin: Missionary society "Light of the Gospel"] 1 (1992) 3–5.
———. "Staroe novoe" [Old new]. Informatsionnyy byulleten': Missionerskoe obshchestvo "Svet Yevangeliya" [Information bulletin: Missionary society "Light of the Gospel"] 3 (1991) 2–3.

———. "Tret'ya konferentsiya" [Third conference]. *Informatsionnyy byulleten': Mezhdunarodnaya assotsiatsiya "Svet Yevangeliya"* [Information bulletin: International association "Light of the Gospel"] 3 (1994) 46–54.

———. "O vashey pomoshchi" [About your help]. *Informatsionnyy byulleten': Missionerskoe obshchestvo "Svet Yevangeliya"* [Information bulletin: Missionary society "Light of the Gospel"] 1 (1991) 30–31.

Uspensky, Michail V. "An Orthodox Icon by Yamashita Rin—The Japanese Painter of the Meiji Period." *Japan Review* 6 (1995) 37–50.

Vallikivi, Laur. "Christianization of Words and Selves: Nenets Reindeer Herders Joining the State through Conversion." In *Conversion After Socialism: Disruptions, Modernisms and Technologies of Faith in the Former Soviet Union*, edited by Mathijs Pelkmans, 59–83. New York: Berghahn, 2009.

Varg, Paul A. "Motives in Protestant Missions, 1890–1917." *Church History* 23/1 (March 1954) 68–82.

"Vifezda—dom miloserdiya" [Pool of Bethesda—House of mercy]. *Informatsionnyy byulleten': Mezhdunarodnaya assotsiatsiya "Svet Yevangeliya"* [Information bulletin: International association "Light of the Gospel"] 1 (1994) 15.

Vihavainen, Timo. "The Cultural and Moral Upheaval in Russia." In *Change and Continuity in Eastern Europe*, edited by Timo Piirainen, 76–88. Aldershot, UK: Dartmouth, 1994.

Vishnyakova, Lyudmila. "Priyut Dobrogo Pastyra" [Good Shepherd Orphanage]. *Informatsionnyy byulleten': Mezhdunarodnaya assotsiatsiya "Svet Yevangeliya"* [Information bulletin: International association "Light of the Gospel"] 3 (1998) 9–10.

Voloshin, Ruvim. "Analiz razvitiya missionerskogo sluzheniya v period 1990–2000 godov" [An analysis of the missionary work over the period of 1990–2000]. Paper presented at the Rus'-Mission in the 21st Century Conference, Moscow, Russia, March 2000. http://baptist.org.ru/go/46.

———. "Sviditel'stvo Ruvima Voloshina" [Testimony of Ruvim Voloshin]. Unpublished manuscript, 2002.

———. "20 let spustya . . ." [20 years later . . .]. December 3, 2008. http://baptist.org.ru/articles/missions/279.

"Vostochnoe otdelenie" [Eastern branch]. *Informatsionnyy byulleten': Missionerskoe obshchestvo "Svet Yevangeliya"* [Information bulletin: Missionary society "Light of the Gospel"] 1 (1993) 12–18.

"Vsemirnyy molitvennyy plan" [Worldwide prayer plan]. *Informatsionnyy byulleten': Missionerskoe obshchestvo "Svet Yevangeliya"* [Information bulletin: Missionary society "Light of the Gospel"] 1–2 (1990) 4–6.

"Vystavka" [Art exhibition]. *Informatsionnyy byulleten': Missionerskoe obshchestvo "Svet Yevangeliya"* [Information bulletin: Missionary society "Light of the Gospel"] 2 (1992) 19.

"Vystavka 'Zhizn' Iisusa Khrista i Apokalipsis'" [Art exhibition "The life of Jesus Christ and the Revelation"]. *Informatsionnyy byulleten': Mezhdunarodnaya assotsiatsiya "Svet Yevangeliya"* [Information bulletin: International association "Light of the Gospel"] 1 (1994) 11.

Walls, Andrew F. *The Cross-Cultural Process in Christian History*. Maryknoll, NY: Orbis, 2002.

———. *The Missionary Movement in Christian History*. Maryknoll, NY: Orbis, 1996.

Wallstrom, Timothy C. *The Creation of a Student Movement to Evangelize the World.* Pasadena, CA: William Carey International University Press, 1980.
Walters, Philip. "Religion in the Soviet Union: Survival and Revival." In *Christianity and Russian Culture in Soviet Society,* edited by Nicolai N. Petro, 3–15. Boulder, CO: Westview, 1990.
———. "The Russian Orthodox Church and the Soviet State." *Annals of the American Academy of Political and Social Science* 483 (January 1986) 135–45.
Wanner, Catherine. "Advocating New Moralities: Conversion to Evangelicalism in Ukraine." *Religion, State and Society* 31/3 (2003) 273–87.
———. *Communities of the Converted: Ukrainians and Global Evangelism.* Ithaca, NY: Cornell University Press, 2007.
———. "Explaining the Appeal of Evangelicalism in Ukraine." In *Rebounding Identities: The Politics of Identity in Russia and Ukraine,* edited by Dominique Arel and Blair A. Ruble, 243–72. Washington, DC: Woodrow Wilson Center, 2006.
———. "Missionaries of Faith and Culture: Evangelical Encounters in Ukraine." *Slavic Review* 63/4 (Winter 2004) 732–55.
Weiss, Robert S. *Learning from Strangers: The Art and Method of Qualitative Interview Studies.* New York: Free Press, 1994.
White, John E. "Growth Amidst Persecution: A Comparison of the Evangelical Church in Communist China and the Soviet Union." *International Journal of Frontier Missiology* 29/3 (Fall 2012) 139–47.
White, Stephen. *Russia Goes Dry: Alcohol, State and Society.* Cambridge: Cambridge University Press, 1996.
Wildavsky, Aaron. *Moses as Political Leader.* Jerusalem: Shalem, 2005.
Wilkinson, Bruce, et al. *The CoMission: The Amazing Story of Eighty Ministry Groups Working Together to Take the Message of Christ's Love to the Russian People.* Chicago: Moody, 2004.
Wright, N. T. *The New Testament and the People of God.* Minneapolis: Fortress, 1992.
Wu, Chao-Kwang. *The International Aspect of the Missionary Movement in China.* Baltimore: The Johns Hopkins University Press, 1930.
Yelensky, Viktor. "Religiosity in Ukraine According to Sociological Surveys." *Religion, State and Society* 38/3 (2010) 213–27.
Yohannan, K. P. *Revolution in World Missions.* Carrollton, TX: GFA, 2003.
Yurchak, Alexei. *Everything Was Forever, Until It Was No More.* Princeton, NJ: Princeton University Press, 2005.
"Zhizn' Iisusa Khrista" [The life of Jesus Christ]. *Informatsionnyy byulleten': Missionerskoe obshchestvo "Svet Yevangeliya"* [Information bulletin: Missionary society "Light of the Gospel"] 1 (1991) 18–25.
Znakevich, Valery. "Evangelism and Church Planting in Russia." DMin diss., Haggard School of Theology, 2004. ProQuest (UMI 3171376).
Zuckerman, Phil. *Society without God.* New York: New York University Press, 2008.

Index

1 Corinthians 4:10, 50

Acts 1:8, 50, 111
AD 2000 and Beyond Movement, 224, 228
Africa, 214–15, 232–33; Central, 232; missionaries from, 232–33, 238; missionaries in, 199, 202–3, 204, 214–15, 226; North, 199; South, 215. *See also Missionary Travels and Researches in South Africa*; Missions Africaines de Lyons
Aidan, 197
Alaska, 204
alcoholism, 12, 14–15, 23
Aletheia Church, 241
Algiers, 202
Almaty (or Alma-Ata), 143
America, 94, 122, 135, 144, 145, 149, 151, 200, 211, 217, 222, 223; Latin, 233; North, 216, 221, 223; South, 226. *See also* United States
American, 41, 55, 85, 95, 98, 131, 134, 135–36, 146, 162, 213, 222–24, 225; African, 214–15; Latin, 233; Native, 210; North, 221, 235
Anderson, Rufus, 210
Andover, 214
Anglo-Saxons, 198–99

Apocalypse Mission, 243. *See also* Evangelical Christian Missionary Union
Arabia, 205
Argentina, 228
army, 217; of the church, 201; Soviet, 82, 83, 97, 114, 123
art exhibition ministry, *The Life of Jesus Christ and the Revelation*, 46, 47, 49, 50, 53, 118, 126–27
Asia, 5, 204, 206, 216, 217, 226. *See also* Central Asia
Assemblies of God (of America), 40, 135
atheism, ix, 15, 16, 23, 25, 28, 35, 109, 115
Auca Indians, 122. *See also* Operation Auca
audit trail, 78, 79
Augustine, 198
autonomous Baptist churches. *See under* Baptist
awakening, 86–87, 99, 116, 122, 188, 194, 195, 237, 238, 240; among the Batak, 229; first Evangelical, 211; in Ireland, 197; missionary, 193; no, 31, 86–87, 156; at Oleviste Church, 86; second Evangelical, 216–17. *See also* revival
Azusa Street Revival, 226

INDEX

Back to Jerusalem vision, 235
Bak, Pavel, 123, 141, 160
baptism, 18, 31, 46, 104, 122; of Kievan Rus', 159, 185
Baptist, 21, 28–29, 38, 84–85, 154, 172, 188; autonomous churches, 29n59, 41, 45, 87, 91, 92, 93, 128, 137; centers of missionary development, 81–82, 86, 91–95, 163, 166, 167; church support of missionaries, 128–30, 132, 139, 146; comparing with Pentecostals, 23, 82, 110, 137, 144, 148, 158–63, 171; desire to do missions at the end of the earth, 112, 113; desire to plant churches where none existed, 111; Donetsk oblast, 92–93, 97, 161, 168, 169; emigration of, 34; financial support of missionaries, 144–48, 149, 162; foreign missions' support of, 134–35, 148, 149, 162, 181; independent missions, 132; interview participants, 65, 67, 79, 84, 85, 165, 246–48; leaders, 17, 40, 41, 58, 84–85, 92, 118, 129, 137–38, 159, 169, 171, 172, 181; missionaries with Light of the Gospel, 137–40, 144, 158, 159–60, 161, 162; Missionary Society, 212; mission work, x, 23, 29, 41, 45, 58, 81–82, 84–85, 86, 87, 91–95, 118, 132, 137–40, 158–63, 171; recruiting missionaries, 120–21, 130; underground (or unregistered) churches, 26, 29–30, 38, 41, 45, 51, 87, 90, 93, 137; vision for missions, 23, 85, 106, 107, 108, 110–14, 161; Western Ukrainian churches, 91–92, 96–97, 161. *See also* Union of Evangelical Christians-Baptists
Baptist Missionary Society. *See* Baptist
Baptist Union. *See* Baptist; Union of Evangelical Christians-Baptists
Bashkirs, 115

Bass, Joe, 25
Bataks, 229
Beecher, Catharine, 218
Belarus, 40, 84, 92, 119, 123, 246
Belarusian, 40, 83, 89, 91
Benedictine, 198, 199
Berlin, 232
Bible (or Scriptures, Word of God), 4, 5, 25–26, 28, 30, 38, 90, 91, 99, 126, 127, 135, 197, 206, 223, 237; inspiration for missions, 89, 171, 187, 232, 250; interest in, 19, 25, 109, 155; limited access to, 19, 25–26, 109; publishing and/or importing, 18, 26, 32, 40, 125, 187; as tools for missionaries, 25, 57, 91, 110, 125, 157; translation of, 204–5, 224–25, 237
Bible League, 134
Bible schools, 22, 39, 140, 141. *See also* Jelgava Bible School; seminaries
Birobidzhan, 84
Bitterman, Chet, 223
Bondarenko, Andrei, 55, 123
Bondarenko, Joseph, 40, 123
Boniface, 199
Borodin, Simon, 123
Botsyan, Vasily, 149
Boyechko, Vasily, 82–83, 112, 119, 121, 130, 159, 181
Bradcovich, Steve, 98, 135, 160
Brainerd, David, 210
Bratskii Vestnik (Fraternal Herald), 26
Brazil, 233
Brest, 119
Bring Them the News about Christ, 26
Britain, 135, 197, 209, 213, 215, 216. *See also* England
Brother Andrew, 25
Buddhist, 141
Bulletin of Prisoners' Relatives, 116
Buryatia, 43
Bush, Luis, 228

call to missions, x, 49, 105, 106–8, 115, 124, 152, 156, 158, 161, 162, 163, 166, 171, 173, 188,

INDEX   273

189, 190, 195, 218, 236, 250; invitation from someone to go into missions, 121, 130, 152, 195, 198, 218–19, 220, 230, 237–38, 240; inward call from God, 50, 89, 103, 106–7, 122, 132, 146, 187, 198, 213, 217, 226–27, 232, 234, 237–38, 240; outward sign from God, 107–8
Calvary International, 98, 135–36, 151, 160, 162. *See also* Jelgava Bible School
Cambridge Seven, 219
Campus Crusade for Christ, 44
Canada, 220
Canadian immigrants, 214
Carey, William, 209, 210, 212–13, 218, 238
Caribbean, 208
Caspian Sea, 205
Catholic, 200, 201, 205, 237; Greco-Catholic, 92; Irish Church, 203; missionaries, 199, 200, 201–4, 207, 238; monasteries, 187
Caucasus, 14, 43, 44, 46, 83
Celtic missions, 196–98
centers of missionary development, 85–100, 135, 163, 165, 166, 167–69, 180, 187, 189, 190, 249–50; Baptist, 91–95, 166, 167; Donetsk Christian University, 94–95, 167; Donetsk Oblast Baptist Union, 92–93, 167; Donetsk Oblast Pentecostal churches, 97, 167; families as, 88–89; Jelgava Bible School, 98–100, 167; Light of the Gospel mission organization, 93–94, 167; Odessa Missionary School, 97–98, 167; Pentecostal, 96–100, 166, 167; Ukraine as, 89–91; Western Ukrainian Baptist churches, 91–92, 167; Western Ukrainian Pentecostal churches, 96–97, 167
Central Asia, 43, 46, 83, 140, 199, 205, 206
Central Europe. *See* Europe

Central Russia, 41, 46, 112, 130, 142, 247
change agents, 169, 179, 180–81, 182, 183; of mission, 179, 180–81, 182, 188
change (emotional side), 165, 166, 174–78, 189, 249, 251
change (rational side), 165, 166, 169–73, 174, 176, 177, 189, 190, 249–50
Chernivtsi, 92, 129
children: atheist and communist influence on, 16, 25; in the evangelical church, 23, 27, 99, 100; ministry to, 27, 56–57, 150, 218 on the mission field, 37, 115. *See also* youth
China, 5, 14, 39, 195, 201, 206, 216, 218–19, 235, 237
China Inland Mission, 216, 218–19
Chita, 84, 118, 159
Christ for All Nations. *See* Jelgava Bible School
Christ is the Answer Crusades, 44
Christian Charitable Foundation Kindness, 47. *See also* Light of the Gospel
Christian Charitable Publishing Foundation, 47. *See also* Light of the Gospel
Christian literature, 16, 25–26, 30, 32, 45, 157, 187, 204, 223; inspiration for missions, 171, 187, 223, 237; interest in, 1, 109; limited access to, 25–26, 125; publishing and/or importing, 26, 83, 125, 223; as tools for missionaries, 2, 47, 56, 57, 84, 93, 125, 126, 133, 134, 135, 140, 149, 150, 162, 225–26
Christian and Missionary Alliance (C&MA), 243–44
Christian reading libraries, 16, 126
Christ for the Nations of Siberia, 127
Chukotka, x, 49, 123
Church of the East (Nestorian), 205–6
church growth (evangelical), 22–23, 30–32, 37–38, 86, 92, 139, 195, 211, 226, 231; lack of, 33–36, 37

Church Missionary Society, 212, 215
church planting, 2, 89, 106, 126, 151, 154, 193, 225, 229, 232, 233, 240; Evangelical Christian Missionary Union doing, 242–43; foreign support for, 41, 146; Good Samaritan doing, 44, 140, 150; importance of, 84; in large cities, 98; Light of the Gospel doing, 46, 51, 118, 181; Possibility doing, 43, 141; underground Pentecostals doing, 29; in Western Europe, 129; where none exist, 88, 103, 111, 161
church subculture. *See* subculture (evangelical church)
city (cities): call to missionary work in, 89, 98, 99, 108, 114; former Soviet Union, 43 fig. 3; New York, 225; Russian, 64, 85, 89, 98, 99, 113–14, 115, 127; Soviet, 11, 28, 37, 53, 87, 110, 111; Ukrainian, 42, 42 fig. 2, 63–64, 84, 92. *See also* urban areas; urbanization
Clapham Sect, 214
coding, 65, 73, 74–76, 77, 79; focused, 74, 75–76; initial, 65, 74–75, 77; theoretical 74, 76
Colombia, 223
Columba, 197
Columbanus, 197
COMIBAM mission conference. *See* missionary conferences
CoMission, ix, 236
Commonwealth of Independent States (CIS), ix, 98
communication and facilitation agents, 165, 178–84, 187, 188, 189, 190, 249, 252; change agents as, 180–81; innovators as, 179–80; inspiration from missionaries as, 166; Light of the Gospel as, 166; opinion leaders, 181–82; organizers and missionary structures, 182–84; Pentecostal churches as, 166

communism, 1, 5, 10, 14, 15, 19, 20, 22, 23, 24, 25, 37, 53, 54, 58, 87, 100, 109, 143, 148, 153, 154, 155, 186, 242; Fall of, 1, 5, 8, 12, 19, 30, 36, 50, 53, 54, 122, 143–45, 148, 150, 153, 157, 158, 242
communist, 1, 14, 16, 17, 22, 25, 35, 89, 189, 232; ideology, 15, 17, 19, 34; Party, 10, 17, 18, 19
Communist Youth League, 16
concerts of prayer for missions, 211
conferences. *See* missionary conferences
Congregation du Saint Esprit (Congregation of the Holy Ghost), 203–4
connections, 13, 64, 139, 240, 253; with family and friends, 115–16, 161, 176, 186; with foreigners, 12, 13, 83, 133, 148; with mission organizations, 83, 186; to people on the mission field, 166, 176, 183, 184, 186, 187, 189, 190; to places, 109, 114–17, 166, 183; to prisons, 116–17; through short-term missions, 114–15, 161, 176, 186
connectors, 182, 183, 194–95, 252. *See also* opinion leaders
Constantine, 204–5, 238
context, 7, 61, 63, 72, 165, 189, 190, 195, 204, 229, 233, 241, 242, 245, 249, 250, 253; change, 168, 169, 188, 242; of freedom, 155–56, 190; for missions, 165, 166, 171, 184–87, 188, 189, 190; socio-political, 8–20, 242, 245
Cook, Captain James, 209
Copenhagen, 208
Crimea, 140
Crimean War, 215
critical realism, 59–60
Crouch's model for change from *Culture Making*. *See* model
Crowther, Samuel, 215
crystallization, 78
Czechoslovakia, 82–83, 159

Danish: Halle mission, 207; territory, 207

INDEX

Davidyuk, Vasily, 118
Denmark, 207
Denver Seminary, 94, 134, 160, 162
diaspora, 229; African, 232
disciple, 111, 157, 204
discipleship, 35
discovery of America, 200
Dominic, 199
Dominicans, 199, 200
Donetsk, 42, 46, 47, 64, 92–93, 94, 97, 140, 160
Donetsk Bible College. *See* Donetsk Christian University
Donetsk Christian University (DCU), ix, xi, 45, 47, 93, 94–95, 108, 161, 167, 183; financial support from, 144; founding of, 56, 94–95, 138, 160; leadership of, 118, 160; partnership with Denver Seminary, 94, 134; preparing missionaries, 46, 54, 95, 114, 120–21, 123, 124; recruiting students, 120
Donetsk Oblast, 42, 91, 92–93, 96, 97, 118, 126, 130, 141, 161, 162, 167, 168, 169
drug addicts, 12, 23
Duff, Alexander, 216
Duke, Charles, 123

Eastern Europe. *See* Europe
Eastern Ukraine, 92, 94, 141, 246, 247
East India Trading Company, 213
Ecuador, 122, 223
Edinburgh World Missionary Conference, 222
education, 6, 16, 19, 28, 50, 57, 97, 157, 162, 170, 187, 195, 203, 221, 222, 232, 237, 238, 243; foreign help in, 32, 123, 133, 134, 135–36, 162; legal restrictions on, 53; limited, x, 28, 52, 107, 218, 236; theological, 32, 47, 54, 56, 57, 123, 134, 206, 222. *See also* training
Edwards, Jonathan, 210, 211, 212
Elista, 127
Elliot, Jim, 122

emigration of evangelicals, 24, 31, 33, 34, 38, 57, 140, 145, 157, 244; mission work through, 129
Emmanuel mission, 125, 135
Emmanuel singing group, 119, 125n7, 136
"end of the earth," 50, 111–12, 113, 114, 161, 169
England, 196, 198, 212. *See also* Britain
Enlightenment, 200, 213, 237, 238
enthusiasm for missions, ix, 100, 101–2, 103, 166, 170, 220, 250
entrepreneurial spirit, 90, 91, 105, 161, 168, 225
Estonia, 86
ethics, ix, 5, 36, 59, 70–71, 156, 236
Ethiopia, 232
Ethiopian church, 232
Europe, 196, 198–99, 216, 222, 232; Central, 39, 44, 58, 188–89, 194, 197, 241–45; Eastern, ix, 39, 188–189, 194, 241–45; Western, 15, 21, 83, 129, 197
European governments, 200
European Russia, 49
Evangelical Christian Missionary Union (ECMU), 189, 241, 242–44
Evangelical Christians, 21–22, 28
evangelical church subculture. *See* subculture (evangelical church)
Evangelical Ministry mission, 47. *See also* Light of the Gospel
evangelism, 24, 29, 40, 87, 94, 97, 216, 217; difficulties in, 1, 24, 35; foreign missionaries and, 32, 133; by Light of the Gospel, 56, 57; opportunities for, 29, 39, 50, 109, 154, 155; by Pentecostals, 119–20, 130, 140
evangelist(s), 16, 27, 28, 33, 86, 87, 119, 140, 233; foreign, 18, 29, 55, 100, 122, 123
example of missions (or missionaries), 121–24, 163, 175, 178, 179, 180, 186, 189, 190, 197, 199, 201, 206, 212, 218, 228, 238, 251, 252, 253; foreign, 85, 122–23; national 48, 117, 118, 119, 123–24, 141, 189; negative, 133

expedition across Siberia, 49, 111, 118, 127

faith missions, 216, 218
Fall of Communism. *See under* communism
family, 13, 23, 26, 37, 83, 87, 90, 97, 103, 104, 120, 138, 141, 142, 146, 147, 186, 217, 223, 227, 229, 238; connections, 115–16, 132; large Christian, 1, 23; role in preparing missionaries, 28, 88–89, 161, 166, 167
Far East, 199; Russian, x, 24, 49, 51, 82, 83, 84, 112, 116, 123–24, 138, 140, 143, 152, 159, 169, 246, 247
Far North (Russian), x, 43, 49, 111, 127, 152, 169, 246
financial support, 11, 27, 41, 45, 47, 48, 49, 65, 98, 100, 102, 129, 136, 142–52, 158, 162, 183, 187, 188, 196, 207, 216, 217, 218, 221, 222, 238, 240; foreign, 27, 40, 41, 133, 135, 136, 145–46, 147, 148, 149, 151, 162, 187, 189, 234, 244; lack of, 100, 102, 129, 132, 136, 148, 218, 227, 228. *See also* self-supporting missionaries
Finland, 83
Forman, John, 220
Franchuk, Vladimir, 42–43, 44, 58, 119, 140, 159
Francis of Assisi, 199
Franciscans, 199, 200
Francke, A.H., 207
freedom, 23, 33, 38, 98, 100, 101, 117, 153–56, 162, 163; church's lack of readiness for, 30, 34, 38; connected with Millennium of Christianity celebration, 9, 18, 20, 82, 159, 185; fear it was a trap, 87, 88, 155; laws and policies increasing, 9, 16, 18, 21–22, 30, 50, 152, 153–56, 157, 185, 242; laws restricting, x, 16; leading to interest in Christianity, 1, 20, 30, 33, 155, 171; leading to missionary work, 4, 50, 88, 96, 100, 101, 106, 117, 153–56, 166, 185, 188, 189, 190, 213, 231, 242, 253; for speaking in interviews, 66, 71; for writing memos, 77
Friends Missionary Prayer Band, 234
foreign mission (missionaries), ix, 1–2, 3, 6, 25, 27, 30, 32–33, 38, 40, 128, 133–36, 140, 211, 213–14, 230, 232, 233; inspiration from, 117, 122–23, 177, 238, 241; laws restricting, 33; leaders, 3, 6, 213; providing Bibles and Christian literature, 26, 32, 40, 41, 125, 133–35; providing leadership training, 32; providing theological education, 32, 40, 41, 133–35; supporting national missionaries, 40, 41, 85, 126, 133, 135–36, 147–48, 189, 243–44. *See also* Western missionaries
Foundation for Theological Education, 47. *See also* Donetsk Christian University
France, 200, 201, 203
Frederick IV, 207
French, 203; missionary societies, 203–4; Revolution, 201

Garland, John, 212
Georgia, ix
Germans, 26, 34, 41, 55, 96, 125, 126, 134–135, 136, 145, 149, 162, 229
Germany, 25, 39, 135, 149, 207, 246
Gladwell's model for change from *Tipping Point*. *See* model
glasnost (openness), 1, 9, 45, 53, 54, 154
globalization, 195, 209, 223, 231, 238
Global Outreach Mission, 44
Good News mission, 47, 140. *See also* Light of the Gospel
Good Samaritan, 42, 44, 96, 137, 140, 162, 182–83; branches of, 44, 140, 159; financial support of, 149–50; founding of, 43, 44, 83, 119, 140, 159; leadership of, 44, 58, 83, 119, 140, 159;

places of mission work, 43, 140;
recruiting missionaries, 119;
relationship with Pentecostal
churches, 43–44, 96, 119, 130,
140, 159; training missionaries,
44, 119
Good Seed Mission, 243. *See also*
Evangelical Christian
Missionary Union
Gorbachev, Mikhail, 9, 18
Gospel for Asia, 146, 234
Gospel to the East, 47, 140. *See also*
Light of the Gospel
Grabovenko, Eduard, 99
grace of God, 156, 162, 163, 166, 189, 226
Graham, Billy, 18, 122, 123, 225
Great Britain. *See* Britain
Great Century of Missions, 209–22
Great Commission, 199, 232
Great Depression, 221
greatest need for missions, 109, 110–14, 166, 175, 251
Greco-Catholic. *See* Catholic
Greece, 204
Gregory the Great, 198, 238
grounded theory, 3, 4, 61–63, 65, 67, 73, 74
"Growth Decade" of the evangelical church, 22
Guts, Sergei, 118, 140

Heath and Heath's model for change from *Switch*. *See* model
Herrnhut, 208
Hope to People (or Missionary Brotherhood), 3, 47–48
Hungary, 241–42
Hunter's model for change from *To Change the World*. *See* model

idea of missions, the, 49, 95, 100–5, 106, 108, 109, 111, 124, 154, 155, 161, 168, 169–73, 177, 178, 180, 182, 188, 195, 222, 250, 251; against, 143, 168; developed in multiple places, 162, 167–68; foreigners inspired, 122, 133; importance of, 152, 163, 166, 170, 176, 189–90; as a new idea, 101, 105, 167, 172, 187; younger generation embraced, 90, 96. *See also* enthusiasm for missions
Ignatius Loyola, 201
Illinois, 224
independent spirit (of missionaries), 53, 84, 90, 91, 118, 128, 131–33, 136, 137, 139, 162, 187
India, 201, 207, 215–16, 233–34
Indian Mutiny, 215
Indonesia, 201, 229
Industrial Revolution, 188, 209, 238
innovators, 168, 195, 250, 252; of mission, 117, 118, 179–80, 182, 188
inspiration, 174, 176, 251, 252; from conferences, 94; from missionaries, 117–24, 161, 163, 166, 178, 189, 212, 251; from training school, 134; stories, 177
InterAct Ministries, 55, 146
interest in Christianity, 1, 2, 30, 31, 33, 34, 35, 109, 110, 127, 155, 157, 171, 196, 198; changes in class and social networks effect on, 10; evangelical vs. Orthodox, 19; minority nationalities,' 14; no, 153; writing letters because of, 50; youth's, 27–28. *See also* spiritual thirst
International Fellowship of Evangelical Students (IFES), 44
Inter-Varsity Christian Fellowship, 223–24
Iona, 197
Ireland, 196–97, 203–4
Irish, 197; missionary surge, 203–4
Irkutsk Oblast, 43, 136
Islam, 14, 39, 97, 115, 199, 205. *See also* Muslim
Ivano-Frankivsk, 44, 140, 159

Japan, 201, 204
Jelgava, 98, 114, 160
Jelgava Bible School (Christ for All Nations), 96, 98–100, 114, 121, 135, 161, 167; closing of, 160; controversy about teaching, 131; financial support from, 100, 135, 151; founding of, 98, 160; leadership of, 98, 160; missionary teams sent from, 99, 135; recruiting students, 98; relationship with Pentecostal churches, 98, 100, 131. *See also* Calvary International
Jerusalem, 235
Jesuits, 200, 201, 202
Jesus Christ to the Communist World. *See* Voice of the Martyrs
Jesus Film, 85, 114, 126, 136
Jewish Autonomous Oblast, 84
Judson, Adoniram, 214

Kalmykia, 43, 127, 141
Kamchatka, x, 125
Karelia, 44
Kartavenko, Leonid, 48, 49, 58, 118
Kasprov, Stanislav, 47, 48
Kazakhstan, 23, 143
Kazan, 46, 47, 146
KGB, 1, 16, 93, 104
Khakassia, 112
Kharkiv, 46, 47, 91
Khrushchev, Nikita, 17, 26, 27, 87
Kievan Rus', 18, 21, 122, 159, 185
Kislyak, Pyotr, 49, 53, 118, 127
Komendant, Grigorii, 40
Komi Republic, 44, 116
Kopuria, Ini, 230
Korea: churches, 55; missionary organization leaders, 231, 238; missions 230–31; revival in, 231; surplus of seminary graduates, 231, 237
Kurdistan, 205
Kyiv, 2, 25, 48, 63, 91, 92, 94, 118, 125, 126, 138, 160, 197, 232, 244
Kyiv Oblast, 92
Kyrgyz, 14

Kyzyl, 43

Latvia, 96, 98, 123, 160, 167
Latvian Christian Mission (Latvian Tent Mission), 40, 42, 55, 138
Lausanne conferences, 228; in Lausanne, 224; in Manila, 84–85, 126, 159, 228; in Moscow, 40–41, 84–85, 160
Lavigirie, Cardinal of Algiers, 202
Law on Freedom of Conscience, 18
Law on Religious Associations (Law on Cults), 16, 18, 25
leadership. *See* Donetsk Christian University, Good Samaritan, Jelgava Bible School, Light of the Gospel, Possibility, Voice of Hope
Lehtinen, Kalevi, 123
Light in the East, 25, 44, 55, 125, 134–35, 146, 162
Light of the Gospel, ix, 2, 3, 5, 42, 44, 45–57, 58, 67, 81, 93–94, 118, 126–27, 137–140, 141, 161, 162, 166, 181, 183, 246, 248; branches of, 46–48, 139–40; change to international association, 46–48, 139, 160, 183; closing of, 5, 48; Donetsk Baptist Union youth joining, 92–93; financial support of, 45, 47, 54, 55–57, 138, 139, 145–48, 149; founding of, 45–46, 84, 85, 137, 154, 159; leadership of, 46–48, 49, 51–55, 58, 67, 91, 92, 118, 123, 137, 139, 159, 160; letters to, 50; missionary conferences, 54, 94, 160; partnerships, 51, 55, 94, 123, 125, 134–35, 145–48, 181; places of mission work, 46–47, 49–50, 51, 127; practicing missionaries joining, 47, 84, 93, 118, 123, 132; recruiting missionaries, 93–94, 100, 118, 120, 123, 181, 183; relationship with Baptist churches, 51, 91, 92, 96, 129, 137, 139, 158; structure of, 52–

53, 138; training missionaries, 54, 94–95, 134, 138, 160; vision of, 49–50, 111, 114; women and children in, 37. *See also* art exhibition ministry; Donetsk Christian University
Light of the Gospel Bible College. *See* Donetsk Christian University
Light of the Gospel's *Information Bulletin*, 37, 45, 48, 49. 51, 55, 56, 57
Light for the Peoples, 83, 135. *See also* Slaviska Missionen
Light of the Resurrection, 47. *See also* Light of the Gospel
Linnik, Sergei, 141, 160
Livingstone, David, 215
London, 153, 232
London Missionary Society, 212, 215
Los Angeles, 226
Lugansk, 91, 97
Lutsk, 42, 160
Lviv, 44, 63, 92, 140, 159

majority world missions, 194, 227–35
Makiivka, 46, 47, 118, 126
Manila, Philippines, 84, 159
Mariupol, 42, 140–41, 159
married (missionaries), 67, 90, 168, 217
Martyn, Henry, 210
martyrdom, 238; white, 197
martyred missionaries, 223, 230
martyrs, 116
Massachusetts, 219
Matthew 7:6, 1; 24:14, 112; 28:19–20, 232
mavens, 182, 183, 194–95, 252. *See also* opinion leaders
Melanesian Brotherhood, 230
Meeting of the Ten Nations, The, 219
Melnychuk, Oleksii, 46, 48–49, 53, 54, 58, 84, 118, 160
member checking, 78–79
memo writing, 62, 73, 76, 77, 79
Mennonites, 34
Mesopotamia, 206; Upper, 205
Methodius, 204–5, 238

Mexico, 224, 233
Middle Ages, 199, 205
Middle East, 199, 226
Millennium celebration of Christianity, 5, 9, 12, 18, 20, 39, 40, 82, 83, 119, 122, 159
Mills, Samuel, 210, 213–14
Minsk, 43, 119
miracle, 154, 156
missionary bands (at colleges), 220
Missionary Brotherhood. *See* Hope to People
missionary conferences, 120, 124, 129, 134, 187, 195, 216, 222, 223, 224, 237; COMIBAM, 233; Edinburgh World, 222; Lausanne, 40–41, 84–85, 126, 159, 160, 224, 228; Light of the Gospel, 54, 94, 160; Moscow Congress on Evangelization, 40–41, 84–85, 160; Pentecostal, 135; Rus'-Mission, 3, 72–73; student, 217, 219–20, 222, 224; Urbana, 224; Voice of Hope, 150; "Youth of Czechoslovakia for Christ," 82–83, 159
missionary structure, 82, 128–142, 163, 176, 179, 182–84, 185, 187, 189, 190, 194, 240, 252; Baptist church as a, 128–30; Calvary International as a, 135–36; church as a, 128–31; Denver Seminary as a, 134; foreign mission organization as a, 133–36; Good Samaritan as a, 140; Light in the East as a, 134–35; Light of the Gospel as a, 45, 46, 137–40, 166, 183; national mission organization as a, 137–42; Nehemiah mission as a, 136; no (independent missionary), 131–33; Pentecostal church as a, 130–31, 166; Possibility as a, 140–41; Voice of Hope as a, 141–42
Missionary Travels and Researches in South Africa, 215

Mission Eurasia. *See* Russian Ministries
Missions Africaines de Lyons, 203
model, 163; for change, 163, 164, 165, 170, 173, 176, 249–53; for coding data, 74; from Crouch's *Culture Making,* 164, 250–53; George Müller's, 55–56; from Gladwell's *Tipping Point,* 164, 165, 249–53; from Heath and Heath's *Switch,* 164, 165, 170, 173, 176, 249–53; from Hunter's *To Change the World,* 164, 250–53; for interviewing 66; from Naylor's *Culture and Change,* 164, 250–53; for partnership, 135; from Rochon's *Culture Moves,* 164, 165, 249–53; from Rogers's *Diffusion of Innovations,* 164, 165, 249–53; for the Ukrainian evangelical missionary surge, 60, 81, 164, 165, 166, 185, 189–90, 191, 249–53; for Ukrainian missionaries, 123
Moldova, 129, 247
Moldovans, 84, 118, 159
monasteries, 197; source for missionaries, 187, 196, 205, 238
monastic missions, 196–99, 200, 201–4, 205–6, 211
Mongolia, 5, 82, 147
Mongols, 206
Moody Bible Institute, 222
Moody, Dwight L., 216–17, 218, 220, 221–22
Moravia, 208
Moravian Brethren, 207–8, 211, 212, 217
Morokhovets, Yuri, 123, 140
Moscow, 3, 40, 46, 47, 49, 64, 84–85, 89, 98, 130, 136, 154, 160, 247; Congress on Evangelization, 40–41, 84–85, 160
Mott, John, 221–22, 223
Mount Hermon student missionary conference, 219–20, 222
Müller, George, 55, 122, 145
Murza, Vladimir, 131

Muslims, 97, 104, 115, 201, 203, 229. *See also* Islam

Napoleon, 202
Naylor's model for change from *Culture and Change. See* model
Nehemiah mission, 119, 126, 136, 149, 162
Nenets, 14
Nestorians. *See* Church of the East
New World, 200
New York City, 225, 232
Nicholas II, Tsar, 21
Niger, 215
Nigeria, 215, 232
Nikonenko, Valentin, 123
Nommenson, Ludwig, 229
Nsiblis, 206
NVivo, 69, 74, 79

Ob River, 127
Oceania, 230
Odessa, 44, 91, 97, 119, 125n7, 140, 159
Odessa Missionary School, 96, 97–98, 120, 160, 161, 167
Oleviste Church, 86
Olomouc, 83
Olympic Games in Seoul, 231, 239
Open Doors, 25
Operation Auca, 223. *See also* Auca Indians
Operation Mobilization (OM), 44, 224, 225–26, 236
Operation Soviet Union, 100
Operation World, 31, 44
opinion leaders, 181–82, 252; of evangelical churches, 179, 181; of mission, 179, 181–82, 188, 252
Opium War: First, 215; Second, 215
Order of the Mustard Seed, 207
organizers of mission, 119, 141, 182–84, 188, 252
orphanage, 11, 23, 154, 207
Orthodox Church, 18, 24, 36, 112, 115; Communists' negative influence against, 14, 22, 23, 35; conflict with evangelicals, 22, 32–33,

104; historical, 15, 18, 19, 21, 39, 56, 92; missionary work, 187, 204–5, 205–6, 237; modern resurgence of, 35–36, 38

Palau, Luis, 18, 122

pastor(s), 28, 53, 90, 151; against missions, 50, 141, 241; persecution and government control of, 16–17, 22, 28, 104–5, 143; supportive of missions, 16, 83, 92, 98, 119, 131, 133, 140, 168, 233, 241, 242–43; Western Ukrainian, 92, 119

Patrick, 196–97, 238

peer, 186, 221, 253; perception, 186, 253; pressure, 186, 253

Pentecostal, 30, 38, 84–85, 86, 89, 226–27, 233; centers of missionary development, 81–82, 86, 91, 96–100, 163, 166, 167; church support of missionaries, 96, 128, 130–31, 137, 149–50, 159, 166, 167, 168, 169, 171, 174, 179, 182; comparing with Baptists, 23, 82, 110, 128, 137, 144, 148, 158–63, 171; desire to go to the unreached, 112–13; Donetsk oblast (or Eastern Ukrainian), 42, 96, 97, 140–41, 161, 162, 167; financial support of missionaries, 144–45, 148–52, 227; foreign missions working with, 125, 134, 135–36, 149, 151, 181; independent missions, 132–33, 137, 144–45, 227; interview participants, 65, 67, 79, 165, 247–48; leaders, 44, 58, 119–20, 130–31, 136, 140–42, 159, 160, 169, 181, 182, 226; missionaries with Good Samaritan, 43, 44, 83, 96, 140, 149–50, 159, 161; missionaries with Possibility, 97, 140–41, 159, 162; missionaries with Voice of Hope, 44, 96, 141–42, 149–51, 160, 162; mission work, x, 23, 24, 29, 40, 41, 42–45, 81–83, 85, 87, 96–100, 119–20, 123, 130, 137, 140–42, 158–63, 169, 171, 226–27, 233; recruiting missionaries, 121; underground (or unregistered) churches, 26, 29–30, 38, 41, 87, 90, 137; vision for missions, 106, 107, 108, 110–14, 226–27; Western Ukrainian churches, 43, 96–97, 141, 161, 162, 167, 179, 181. *See also* Russian Church of Christians of Evangelical Faith

Pentecostal Union of Churches of Christians of Evangelical Faith, 30, 43–44, 96, 119, 130, 131, 140, 159

perestroika (restructuring), 9, 10, 21, 122; economic and structural turmoil from, 12, 13, 173; ideology changes from, 15, 17; opportunities and freedom for mission during, 9, 19, 29, 30, 35, 50, 84, 87, 88, 109, 126, 132, 152, 153, 154–55, 157, 184

persecution: of Catholic missionaries, 202; of the Chinese church, 235; of the Ethiopian church, 232; of the evangelical church in the Soviet Union, 1, 11, 16–17, 23, 26, 27, 29, 33, 53, 86, 156, 181

Persia, 205

Philadelphian Society, 214

Pietism, 206–7

Poland, 39, 241–242

Pool of Bethesda—House of Mercy, 47. *See also* Light of the Gospel

pope, 198, 199, 200, 202, 203

Pope Pius VII, 202

Popov, Sergei, 84

Portugal, 200, 202

Portuguese government, 200

Possibility (mission organization), 42, 97, 137, 141, 162, 183; founding of, 43, 140–41, 159; leadership of, 58, 119, 140, 159; places of mission work, 43, 141; recruiting missionaries, 97, 119; relationship with Pentecostal churches, 97, 130, 141

Poysti, Earl, 55, 94, 100, 123, 181

Prague, 83

INDEX

prayer, 36, 45, 46, 51, 133, 135, 158, 174, 208, 210, 211, 213, 219, 234, 237, 238, 251; answered, 106–9, 123, 156, 161, 166, 173, 187, 188, 250; fasting and, 49, 108
preparation for missionary surge, 14, 82–85, 86–87, 123
Prigodich, Ray, 94, 134
Primorsky Krai, 51, 89. *See also under* Far East
Princeton: College, 214, 219; Pledge, 220, 221
printing presses, 83, 125
prisoners of faith, 18, 83, 116–17
Pristupa, Taras, 3, 33, 50, 53, 55, 58, 72, 84, 118, 120–21, 137, 159
Prokhanov, Ivan, 22
Propaganda Fide, 200, 238
publishing Christian literature, 38, 40, 41, 47, 57, 209
Puritans, 206

qualitative research, 59, 60–61, 62, 63, 66, 71, 78, 80, 190

Radchuk, Pavel, 123
Radchuk, Slavik, 44, 58, 83, 86, 112, 119, 121, 123, 130, 140, 159, 181
radio ministry, 23, 25, 47, 55, 84, 121, 122
Redeemed Christian Church of God, 232
Reformation, 188, 200
refugees, 208
rehabilitation, 12
Reimer, Johannes, 11, 94, 100, 123
religious freedom. *See* freedom
reverse mission, 232
revival, 31, 33, 51, 65, 86–87, 101, 188, 194, 195, 211, 216, 218, 223, 231, 237, 238, 240; Azusa Street, 226–27; in China, 234–35; in Korea, 231; among the Moravians, 208; no, 86–87. *See also* awakening
Revival That We Need, 26
rich, thick description, 78, 79

Rivne, 42–44, 47–48, 63, 83, 84, 92, 93, 94, 119, 121, 140, 154, 159, 160
Rogers's model for change from *Diffusion of Innovations*. *See* model
Roman Empire, 14, 196–97, 198
Romania, 241–42
Romanian pastors, 83, 241
Rus'-Mission (or Eastern Slavic Mission) in the 21st Century conference, 3, 72–73
Russian Christian Radio, 55
Russian Church of Christians of Evangelical Faith (Pentecostal), 40, 99
Russian Far East. *See under* Far East
Russian language (speaking), 14, 32, 38, 64, 68, 73, 83, 94, 96, 97, 123, 134, 152, 162, 240
Russian Ministries (or Mission Eurasia), 134
Russian Navy Chaplain Ministry, 243. *See also* Evangelical Christian Missionary Union
Russian Orthodox Church. *See* Orthodox Church

Sakhalin, 43, 125
salesmen, 180, 183, 194–95, 252. *See also* change agents
São Paulo, 233
Sardachuk, Waldemar, 119, 136, 149
Schmidt, Gustav, 96
Scotland, 197
Scottish missionary, 216
Scriptures. *See* Bible
self-supporting missionaries, 132, 143, 144, 146, 150, 187, 208, 229, 238, 244
seminaries, 40, 41, 64, 94, 134, 160, 162, 203, 214, 220, 231, 237. *See also* Bible schools
Seoul Olympic Games. *See* Olympic Games in Seoul
Serdichenko, Pyotr, 97, 119–20, 130, 160, 181
Seymour, William, 226, 227
Shalenko, Yakov, 122

Sharapa, Sergei, 43, 83, 112
short-term missions, 40, 129, 135, 171, 174, 186, 188, 225, 235–36; leading to long-term missions, 106, 107, 108, 114–15, 116, 120, 161, 174, 176, 186, 236, 242, 251
Shumeiko, Franz, 84, 94, 181
Siberia, x, 2, 5, 16–17, 23, 41, 43, 44, 46, 49, 67, 82, 83, 84, 87, 89, 103, 104, 111, 112, 113, 118, 123, 126, 127, 130, 136, 138, 140, 141, 144, 147, 152, 159, 161, 169, 177, 204, 247
Sierra Leone, 214–15
single (missionaries), 67, 88, 90, 104, 152, 167, 168, 217
Sinyuk, Nikolai, 44, 58, 119, 141–42, 160
Slavic Gospel Association, 25, 125, 134
Slaviska Missionen (or Slavic Christian Mission, Light for the Peoples), 25, 83
Slavonic language, 204–5
Smith, Oswald, 26, 101
Smolensk, 136
Societies of Inquiry on the Subject of Missions, 214
Society of Brethren, 214
Soghdians, 206
Southern Russia, 123, 242–44, 247
South Korea. *See* Korea
Spain, 200, 202
Spanish government, 200
Spener, Philip Jacob, 206, 207
spiritual thirst, 25, 98, 102, 109, 110, 115, 127, 155. *See also* interest in Christianity
spiritual vacuum, 17, 109, 166, 175
Spurgeon, Charles, 218
Stalin, Joseph, 26, 27
Star of Bethlehem mission, 44
Stowell, Joseph, 236
St. Petersburg, 247
Student Volunteer Movement (SVM), 219–22, 223
subculture (evangelical church), 11, 33–34, 38, 41, 57, 157
Sumatra, 229
Sweden, 25, 83

Syria, 205
Syriac, 206

Tajikistan, 47
Talinn, 86
Tashkent, 34
Tatars, 115, 146, 206
Tatarstan, 44, 98
Taylor, Hudson, 218–19, 238
Tbilisi, ix
Television and Radio Company Resurrection, 47. *See also* Light of the Gospel
10/40 Window, 224, 228, 235, 237
Ternopil Oblast, 47
theological education. *See under* education
Tientsin treaty, 216
Timchenko, Pavel, 84
Timothy (patriarch), 205, 206
Toronto, 224
Townsend, William Cameron, 224–25
training, 84, 90, 183, 236, 237; at Donetsk Christian University, 54, 94, 118, 134, 138, 183; through Good Samaritan, 44; at Jelgava Bible School, 98; lack of, 100, 102, 170; leadership, 32, 53–54, 244; through Light of the Gospel, 54, 94; missionary, 6, 54, 162, 197, 200, 203, 204, 206, 207, 215, 222, 228, 232, 235, 238; at Odessa Missionary School, 120; pastoral, 28; through Voice of Hope, 142. *See also* education
Tranquebar, 207
Transbaikal, 82
Transcaucasia, 43, 83
Trubchik, Mikhail, 84, 123
Tupchik, Sergei, 46–47, 48, 49, 51, 58, 84, 94, 118, 137, 141, 159
Turkey, 39
Turks, 206
Tyva Republic, 43, 83, 112, 159

Udmurtia, 43, 44, 141
Ukrainian language, 64

Ukrainian mission organizations. *See* Good Samaritan; Light of the Gospel; Possibility (mission organization); Voice of Hope
underground (or unregistered) Baptist churches. *See under* Baptist
Underground Evangelism, 25
underground mission, 43, 83, 119, 159. *See also* Good Samaritan
underground (or unregistered) Pentecostal churches. *See under* Pentecostal
Uniate Church. *See* Catholic
Union of Churches of Christians of Evangelical Faith. *See* Pentecostal Union of Churches of Christians of Evangelical Faith
Union of Evangelical Christians-Baptists (or Baptist Union), 21n4, 23, 26, 27, 29, 30, 40, 41, 45, 51, 89; Donetsk Oblast, 92–93; Russian, 2, 31, 58, 118, 120, 129–30, 146; split with Pentecostals, 30; Ukrainian, 31, 58, 93, 129; underground, 29. *See also* Baptist
United Bible Societies, 26, 32, 125
United States, 25, 202, 209, 213, 214, 216, 220, 222, 223, 224, 226, 232, 246–47. *See also* America
University of Halle, 207
unreached (peoples or people groups), 4, 83, 112–13, 114, 119, 141, 159, 161, 174, 220, 224, 234, 243
Ural Mountains, 5, 82, 115, 116, 123, 130, 246, 247
Urbana, 224
Urbana Missionary Conference, 224
urban areas, 23. *See also* city
urbanization, 28. *See also* city
Uygurs, 206
Uyuk, 43, 83, 159
Uzbekistan, 34, 94

Verwer, George, 225–26, 236
Vinnytsia, 92
Vladivostok, 82, 89

Voice of Hope, 42, 137, 141–42, 162, 183; financial support of, 142, 149–151; founding of, 44, 115, 123, 141–42, 160; leadership of, 44, 58, 119, 123, 141–42, 160; places of mission work, 44, 113, 142; practicing missionaries joining, 44, 142; relationship with Pentecostal churches, 44, 96, 130, 149–50; structure of, 142; training missionaries, 142
Voice of the Martyrs (or Jesus Christ to the Communist World), 25, 83
Volga, 43, 83, 89, 112, 118, 127, 130, 140, 246, 247
Voloshin, Ruvim, 2, 27, 118, 120
volunteer missionary societies, 211, 212, 213, 216; women's, 217
volunteers, 100, 151, 170, 209; Light of the Gospel, 46; short-term missionary, ix
Volyn Oblast, 44, 101, 130, 142
Vorzel, 94

Wesley, John, 210
Western Europe. *See* Europe
Western missionaries, ix–x, 32–33, 40, 133, 137, 145, 228. *See also* foreign missionaries
Western Ukraine, 39, 47, 89, 91–92, 93, 96–97, 111, 119, 141, 162, 167, 181, 246, 247
West Indies, 208
White Fathers and White Sisters, 202–3
Wilberforce, William, 213, 214
Wilder, Robert, 219–20
Wilfrid, 199
Wilkinson, Bruce, 236
Williams College, 213
Williams, John, 230
Willibrod, 199
women: doing ministry on the mission field, 37, 38, 51, 88, 100, 104, 120, 124, 217–218, 237; interest in evangelical churches, 11; as interview participants, 67; inviting missionaries, 138;

ministry to, 217–18, 237; supporting missionaries, 145
Women's Missionary Movement, 217–18
Word of God. *See* Bible
World Student Christian Federation, 221
World War I, 221
World War II, 17, 92, 223, 230
Wurmbrand, Richard, 25, 83
Wycliffe Bible Translators, 224–25

Xavier, Francis, 201, 238

Yakutia, x, 2, 44, 49, 51, 89, 112, 116, 120, 123, 246
Yakutsk, 46, 84, 115, 127, 144
Yarmolyuk, Pyotr, 123–24
Yohannan, K.P., 234
Young Men's Christian Association (YMCA), 214
youth: growing number and activity in evangelical churches, 23, 27–28, 30, 34, 38, 45, 84, 86–87, 157, 188; interest in missions, 38, 51, 57, 93, 96–97, 101, 103, 115, 124, 157; limited in church ministry, 38, 57, 92–93, 101, 188; ministry to, 28, 29, 96, 124, 181; pressure against bringing to church, 17. *See also* children
"Youth of Czechoslovakia for Christ" conference, 82–83, 159
YWAM (Youth with a Mission), 44
Yugoslavia, 39

Zaporozhye, 154
Zdolbuniv, 84
Zhang Rongliang, 235
Zimbabwe, 232
Zinzendorf, Count Ludwig von, 207, 208, 238

www.ingramcontent.com/pod-product-compliance
Lightning Source LLC
Chambersburg PA
CBHW061433300426
44114CB00014B/1664